The Lord Shiva Narrative

Copyright © 2021 by Shiv Mahalingham. All rights reserved including moral rights of the author.

Cover image of Lord Shiva by Vectomart[i] ©.

Published by Kindle Direct Publishing.

ISBN: 9798705435210

March 2021

Om Namah Shivaya

- adoration to Lord Shiva...

...and adoration to my parents (Maha and Siva Mahalingham) who weaned me on tales of the Hindu gods and introduced me to Advaita philosophy.

ASHRAMA – THE FOUR LIFE STAGES

& the four parts of *THE LORD SHIVA NARRATIVE*

A. Brahmacharya
Student devoted to the acquisition of knowledge and obedience to one's teacher and parents.

B. Grihastha
Householder providing for and carrying out one's duty to others.

C. Vanaprastha
Retired and withdrawing from material attachments.

D. Sannyasa
Aesthetic renouncing possessions

MAYA (ILLUSION)

PARABRAHMAN - THE SUPREME STAGE

PURUSHARTHAS – THE FOUR ASPECTS

Values for a Balanced Life

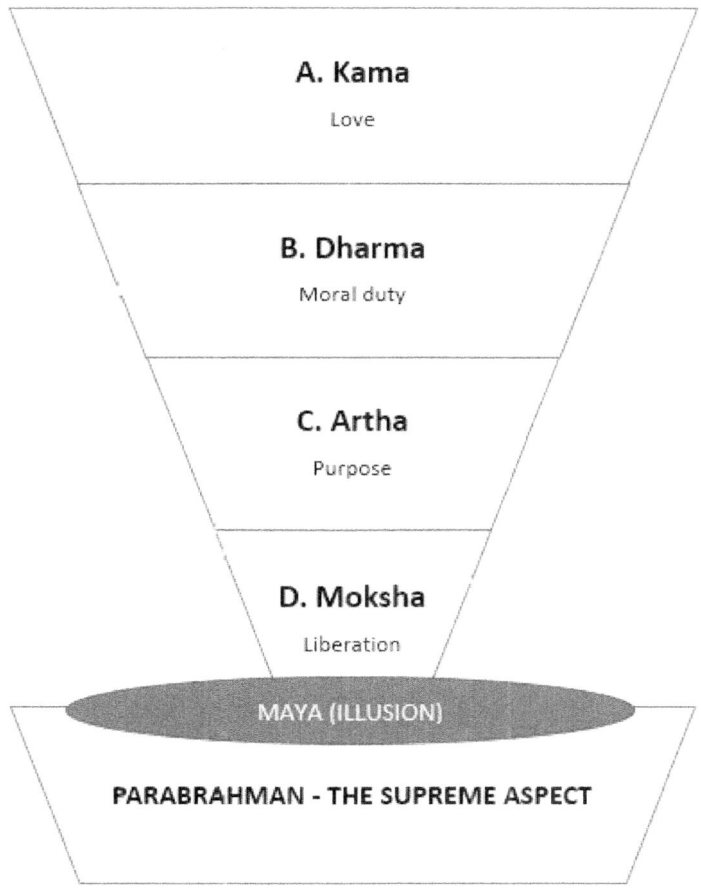

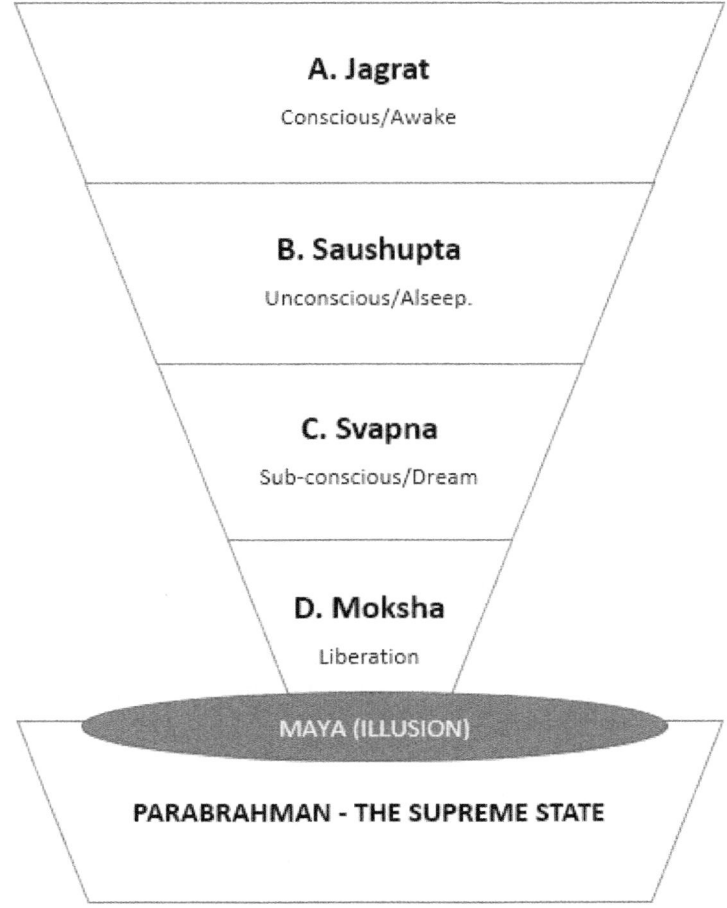

ATMAN - THE SELF

PARABRAHMAN is equivalent to the PARAMATMAN

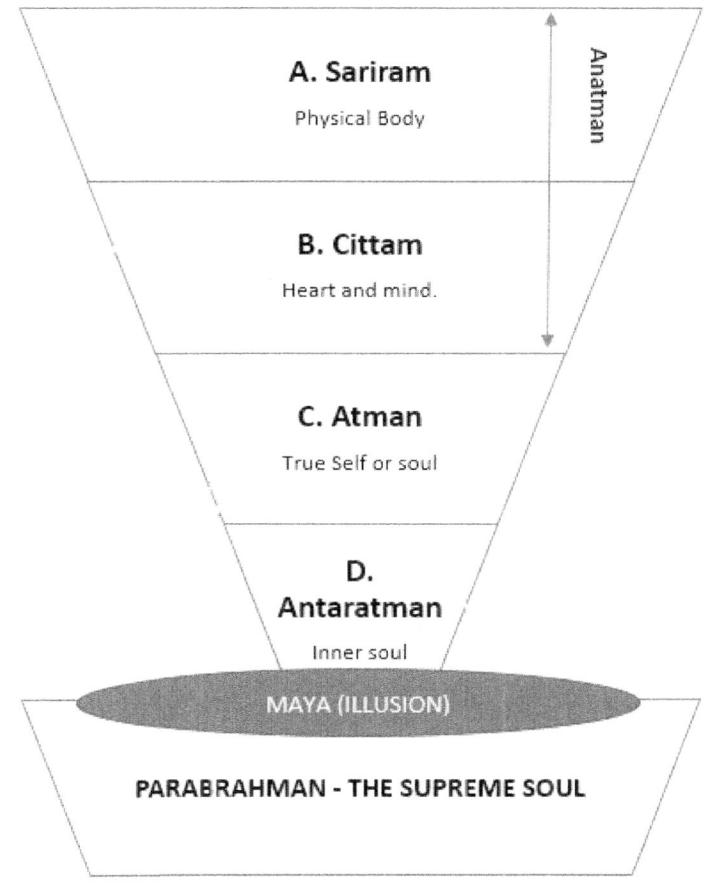

Contents

Preface 11

Foreword 23

Introduction – a "Primer" on Lord Shiva 29

PART A: BRAMACHARYA - The Tales of Lord Shiva

Chapter A1 – Victory over the God of Death 46

Chapter A2 – Eternal Love and Goddess Parvati 51

Chapter A3 – The Divine Progeny of Lord Shiva 59

Chapter A4 – Lord Shiva fights Arjuna 68

Chapter A5 – The Bow of Lord Shiva 75

Chapter A6 – Lord Shiva imprisons Ravana 80

Chapter A7 – Nataraja "King of the Dance" 84

Chapter A8 – The Three Demon Brothers 89

Chapter A9 – The Decapitation of Shankachuda 94

Chapter A10 – Lord Shiva The Merciful 97

Chapter A11 – Scourge of the Three Worlds 101

Chapter A12 – Collaboration of the Trinity 106

Chapter A13 -The Great Chariot of Lord Shiva 110

Chapter A14 – The Creation of the Universe 113

Chapter A15 – Fifty-Two Morals 117

PART B: GRIHASTHA - The Core Scriptures

Introduction to Part B 122

Chapter B1 - Lord Shiva in the Mahabharata 123

Chapter B2 - Lord Shiva in the Ramayana 129

Chapter B3 - Lord Shiva in the Vedas 136

Chapter B4 - Lord Shiva in the Upanishads 146

PARTC: VANAPRASTHA - Lord Shiva Temples

Introduction to PART C 171

Chapter C1 - Amarnath, Kashmir 175

Chapter C2 - Chidambaram, Tamil Nadu 178

Chapter C3 - The Elephanta Caves, Maharashtra 182

Chapter C4 - Kailasnath, Maharashtra 186

Chapter C5 - Kedarnath, Uttarakhand 190

Chapter C6 – Koneswaram, Sri Lanka 193

Chapter C7 - Mohenjo-Daro, Pakistan 195

Chapter C8 - Murudeshawara, Karnataka 197

Chapter C9 - Pashupatinath, Nepal 199

Chapter C10 – Prambanan Temple, Indonesia 201

Chapter C11 - Rameswaram, Tamil Nadu 204

Chapter C12 - Somnath, Gujarat 205

Chapter C13 – Unakoti, Tripura 209

Chapter C14 - Vadakunnathan, Kerala 211

Chapter C15 - Viswanath, Uttar Pradesh 213

PART D: SANNYASA - The Shiva Sutras

Introduction to Part D 217

Chapter D1 – *Sambhavopaya*. The Way of Shiva 219

Chapter D2 – *Saktopaya*. The Way of the Competent One . 230

Chapter D3 – *Anavopaya*. The Fine Way 236

Epilogue – In Search of Lord Shiva 253

Glossary of Key Characters and Key Concepts 255

Bibliography and Suggested Further reading 261

Picture and Photo Credits 262

Acknowledgements..264
Author Biography..265
Excerpt from the Novella "Glory to Hanuman" 266
End Notes..267

Preface

This book contains a collection of stories, lessons and philosophy relating to Lord Shiva. It is an apologue of adventures, endeavors, exploits, and existentialism that I hope will enthrall and inspire readers of all ages. The book is structured into four main parts, each of which corresponds to one of four stages of the readers' life journey from student to householder to retiree to renunciate. Philosophical themes are explored alongside references from Hindu scriptures scribed thousands of years ago. Like the hundreds of millions of children originating from the Indian Sub-continent, I grew up listening to the fantastic adventures of Lord Shiva. The folklore surrounding this Hindu deity was relayed to me by my parents, uncles, and aunts. I was captivated by his humble appearance as an aesthetic, the finality with which he passes judgment, and the ferocity of his martial skill equaled[i] only by Lord Vishnu (see the Introduction chapter to this book for a discussion of the Hindu Trinity of Gods). One adventure of Lord Shiva that I will never forget being told as a child is that of his challenge and defeat of Lord Yama, the unsurpassable God of Death.

Most religions and mythologies have a version of Death as the final arbiter for all who instills supreme fear into devotees. By way of example: Mictlantecuhtli, the colourful Aztec Lord of Death; Anubis, the Egyptian God of Death who weighs hearts against the Feather of Truth; Thanatos, who in Greek mythology wields a scythe to cut down mortals; Hel, who in Norse Mythology possesses a rake to collect up a multitude of souls during times of disaster, war, or plague; and Death himself who was visualized most famously in Milton's Paradise Lost[iii] as a terrifying figure with insatiable hunger, produced from the unholy union of Satan and Sin, and causing all life to succumb to him. Hinduism is no exception; in the Vedas[iv] (discussed in chapter B3 of this book) Lord Yama is the first mortal who died and so was appointed god of departed souls past and present.

Figure 1: Lord Shiva in Meditation

The Puranas[v] and the Upanishads[vi] also describe Lord Yama in detail as having four arms, protruding fangs, adorned with a garland of flames, and holding a hangman's noose with which to seize the necks of those who are about to die and drag them to his Kingdom. He also has the "Rod of Chastisement" and a sword, most likely to make sure that anyone who attempts to put up a futile fight against his noose is vanquished with a swift and devastating stroke. Lord Yama is a truly terrifying and inescapable god that all Hindus will meet at some point (hopefully a long time from now...), yet he is also accredited as the Hindu Lord of Dharma. Dharma is an important concept referred to throughout this book as the spiritual law underscoring the moral, correct, and righteous way to conduct one's life.

In the Hindu scriptures, dharma (moral duty), kama (love), and artha (purpose) are key aspects or values of understanding as one journeys through life before hoping to realize moksha (liberation or enlightenment). The title of Lord of Dharma conveys that there is divine purpose and destiny to the actions of Lord Yama. Lord Shiva's victory over Lord Yama to protect the life of his devotee is therefore a symbolic act that provides hope when there is none. The defeat of the God of Death is not the end of this parable for Lord Shiva is oft depicted in Hindu art/sculpture dancing upon a fallen Lord Yama. This image provides us with some much-needed levity to the subject of death and further explores Lord Shiva's character in celebrating the victory by dancing on his subdued opponent[vii]. I became a lifetime devotee of Lord Shiva from the very instant that I heard about this extraordinary intervention on behalf of one individual. Was the person in question exceptional or is such divine favour to change one's fate possible for anyone? The saga of Lord Shiva versus Lord Yama is covered in more detail in chapter A1 of this book and one moral is clear - living a devoted and ethical life will be more likely to win divine favour than not.

Preface

Stories such as the conquer of the Lord of Death can be found in the Introduction chapter and in Parts A of this book. They are bequeathed from generation to generation and contain important lessons about love, family, friendship, devotion, honesty, integrity, honour, bravery, compassion, temperance, and forgiveness. They help children to understand the importance of ethical behaviour and they help to strengthen one's faith when overcoming obstacles as an adult.

Background to this book

There are two reasons for writing this book:

1. To provide readers with a comprehensive account of Lord Shiva's ethos in a single reference location,
2. To highlight where the information about Lord Shiva originates from and to identify the many credible and consistent elements between these different sources.

A special and deserving mention should be made to the Amar Chitra Katha[viii] graphic comics that introduce young children to the icons of Hinduism. I still have my copies of these comics although the covers have worn down over the years. Long before researching this book, and long after my Amar Chitra Katha days, I read English translations of The Hindu Epics of The Ramayana and The Mahabharata. As a young adult I found that these were lucid imaginings of the interactions between gods, demons, and mankind. I also skimmed through the English translations of the Vedas and the Upanishads; however, I had never read the rich philosophy enshrined in the Shiva Sutras[ix] (explored in Part D of this book) nor had I read the Puranas which contain an ocean of knowledge with many thousands of pages about Lord Shiva and the Hindu deities. It was comforting to find source material written over a millennia ago for the stories that had been told to me as a child. I also discovered whilst researching this book that I had been told stories that were absent from the core Hindu texts. I was keen to explore this further and look at the other Vedic and Puranic writings. This is not to dispute or discredit anything relayed by word of mouth[x]. In fact, anything recounted verbally that survives through generations deserves the utmost respect. However, the academic within often searches for a source of authority. Therefore, this book identifies the main source(s) for each of the aspects of Lord Shiva.

Structure, content, and sources of this book

The Lord Shiva Narrative is structured into four main parts, each of which represents one of the Hindu Ashrama[xi] stages of life that readers will find themselves at:

1. *Branmacharya* (student acquiring knowledge),
2. *Grihastha* (householder building a family),
3. *Vanaprastha* (retired and free of material desires),
4. *Sannyasa* (aesthetic renouncing possessions).

Note that this does not mean that a Brahmacharyan[xii] seeking rectitude should not read the Sannyasan section and vice-versa. In fact, the aesthetic, retiree, or householder may find Part A instructional in helping to guide the younger Brahmacharyan. In the same way, the young student may find the philosophy of Part D of this book to be appealing as the Shiva Sutras[xiii] include three different routes to enlightenment depending on one's level of experience. However, in setting out the book into these four stages, readers of all ages, experiences, backgrounds, and levels will be able to take something away. The Parts of the book are therefore as follows:

Firstly, there is an opening Introduction "Primer" into Lord Shiva and his traits. It is an understatement to say that Lord Shiva possesses a distinctive appearance. The Introduction chapter discusses the origin of his many colourful characteristics including the cobra around his neck, the crescent moon and the River Ganges in his hair, and his blue neck. The different forms of

Preface

Lord Shiva are also introduced in this section including "Destroyer", "Primeval Sage", and "Lord of the Animals".

Part A of the book is *Brahmacharya* (for the student and the parent/teacher of the student who are devoted to the accumulation of knowledge). Part A comprises the moral tales of Lord Shiva. It is a novella of fourteen chapters followed by a fifteenth chapter summarizing the aforementioned fables into fifty-two moral lessons so that the student (and indeed all of us) can absorb one of these teachings per week. The stories should provide a helpful reference point for readers, in particular when they are instructing their own students, children, nephews, and nieces and may wish to draw upon a Lord Shiva anecdote each week to help consolidate an important lesson on kama, dharma, or artha, and the manner in which to conduct oneself. The morals also serve as a reminder for those who have moved beyond the Brhamacharya phase on their life's journey. Each of the main chapters in Part A is dedicated to an adventure of Lord Shiva including his many triumphs on the cosmic battlefield and his family interactions as a devoted husband and father. This is a novella of heroism, love, and destruction (mainly the destruction of arrogance, demons, or arrogant demons...). There are also strong themes in relation to forgiveness before the possibility of redemption. Much of the content for Part A is drawn from the Shiva Purana which is one of the eighteen main or "Mukhya[xiv]" puranas that exist today and is an important source for the Shaivism[xv] religion and for Vedanta[xvi] philosophy. The other Mukhya Puranas[xvii] are also referred to where relevant. These writings contain a significant number of stories relating to the Hindu gods and their encounters with each other and with mankind. The Shiva Purana, the Padma Purana, the Linga Purana, and many of the other Mukhya Puranas are the root of many of the familiar stories about Lord Shiva that are told to Hindu children across the world; a selection of such stories can be found in Part A.

Part B of this book is *Grihastha* (for the householder). It catalogues the main appearances of Lord Shiva in the following Hindu Scriptures:

- The Vedas,
- The Upanishads,
- The Hindu Epics of The Ramayana and The Mahabharata (including The Bhagavad Gita[xviii]).

Most scholars would agree that the above writings make up the core of Hindu scripture and one begins to see the importance in these texts of taking care of others, and charity alongside the principles of dharma. Part B of this book considers each of the sacred texts in turn and itemizes the key mentions of Lord Shiva that are contained within them. The scriptures reviewed here were written down over the course of many centuries and survive today. They contain an abundance of knowledge and I have attempted to draw out and summarize some of this information pertaining to Lord Shiva in one single repository for the convenience of readers. As discussed above, the purpose of utilizing these different source documents is to demonstrate that there is consistency in the information in existence relating to Lord Shiva despite these texts being recorded at different times, in different parts of India, by different sages and scholars. The Shiva Agamas[xix] are not covered here in depth as the focus of *The Lord Shiva Narrative* is on the chronicles and metaphysics that surround the Mahadeva[xx] (a.k.a. Lord Shiva). In Part B, the anthropomorphic image of Lord Shiva in the Hindu Epics, begins to give way to the philosophical, formless force of Lord Shiva in the Upanishads as the Destroyer of ignorance and arrogance (emotional demons as opposed to physical demons). I invite suggestions from readers in relation to the other sacred texts that should be considered in future editions.

Part C of this book is *Vanaprastha* (for the retiree who is freeing themselves from material desires and attachments). It explores the depiction of Lord Shiva in Temple artwork, idols, statues, and carvings as these patient works of devotion provide additional visual commentaries on the stories relating to this popular Hindu deity. I have visited some of these sacred locations in person and these Temple renderings have been applied in supplementing the Lord Shiva stories in the Introduction and Parts A and B of this book. Once again, I would welcome comments from readers on other places of worship for Lord Shiva that I should consider for future editions. *The Lord Shiva Narrative* should strive to be as complete as possible. Part C sets out the dates on which these Temples were constructed (or re-constructed after being demolished by marauders). These dates can be contrasted with the dates on which the Hindu scriptures were written. The earliest recorded (potential) carving of Lord Shiva may be as early as ten thousand years ago in the Bhimbetka rock caves.

Part D of this book is *Sannyasa* (for the aesthetic moving closer to enlightenment...). It sets out the thought-provoking extracts of the Shiva Sutras (or sivasutra) in Sanskrit and in English. These are seventy-seven short verses that relate to Advaita (non-dualist[xxi]) philosophy, meditation practices, and the concept of the soul (self) as scripted in c.900 C.E. by Vasgupta[xxii]. In Part D, Lord Shiva is no longer the trident wielding deity who destroys demons on the battlefield. In Part D, Lord Shiva is the destroyer of ignorance of the mind. I have included alternative translations for each of the Sutras after each verse to assist readers with their journey through the text; however, I will not pretend to comprehend the sivasutra. I invite comments from readers in relation to my analysis and I look forward to hearing about their own interpretations of the more vexing verses.

A Note on Sanskrit-English Translations

I will concede to readers that English translations from the original Sanskrit cannot do justice to the true meaning within the language. This is less of an issue in Part A of the book in which the morality tales can be assembled with inference if there are subjective areas[xxiii]. However, this is a potential issue for interpretation of the Sutras in Part D where the intricacies of translated prose may lead us to a different conclusion when compared to the original intent behind the Sanskrit words chosen. However, let us all acknowledge this point, stand on the shoulders of giants who have made these translations (see Bibliography), and then proceed with the observance and comprehension of that which is possible. To quote the sivasutra in this regard (and hopefully not mis-quote it through translation inaccuracy...):

"One should enter with one's own mind immerged."

For the convenience of readers, Sanskrit words have been presented in English characters without accents for tone/pitch. By way of example "s vasutra" is used instead of "śivasutra".

A Chronology of Hindu Texts

The Vedas are believed, by historians, to have been recorded in the period from 1800 - 1000 B.C.; the Upanishads in 900 - 300 B.C.; the Hindu Epics of The Ramayana and The Mahabharata in 600 - 300 B.C.[xxiv]; the Shiva Sutras in 900 C.E.; and the Puranas in 200 -1000 C.E.[xxv] Note that these chronologies are based on forensic evidence relating to the physical manuscripts and by a study of the language used; however, as with many faiths, the content has been passed down through generations in verbal form and the date of inception of the stories will predate the point in time at which they were actually written down. The dates are listed here for readers' academic interest and should not detract from the content within the texts. In this book, there is no regard to hierarchy of the Hindu scriptures as they all provide beautiful symbology when addressing Lord Shiva. However, it is interesting to track the etymology and development of Lord Shiva worship through these different sections of scripture.

Preface

Who should read this book?

Readers do not require any prior knowledge of Hindu scriptures to be able to enjoy *The Lord Shiva Narrative*. In addition to anyone of the Hindu faith, this book will be of interest to:

- Anyone at any of the four stages[xxvi] of life who is a student, intermediary, expert, or master of ethics, religion, religious art, spirituality, and philosophy,
- Those who enjoy vivid stories with strong ethical foundations and would appreciate fifty-two moral lessons that can be absorbed each week,
- The second, and third generation of Hindus brought up and educated outside of the Indian-Subcontinent,
- Parents/grandparents/uncles/aunts who are in search of stories with moral lessons that they can read to their younger family members,
- Children who enjoy fantasy/adventure stories. The book is suitable for a younger audience and the stories in Part A are succinct enough to hold the attention; however, young readers should be prepared for the occasional demon (or even family member…) to have their head cut off by Lord Shiva's terrible Trident throwing accuracy – do not worry it all works out in the end…

I have added my own commentary in the text, and I have highlighted some of the lessons that can be gleaned from Lord Shiva prajna (wisdom). As a final note, 100% of the profits from sales of *The Lord Shiva Narrative* will be granted each year through The MAHA Foundation to charitable projects in support of children and young adults in need around the world. This first edition has been published on the auspicious occasion of Mahashivaratri (The Great Night of Shiva).

Shiv Mahalingham, March 2021.

Figure 2: Lord Yama

Lord Yama, the Hindu God of Death depicted in the above picture riding on his black bullock who is roaring to the souls of the departed. Lord Yama is carrying his trademark noose, sword, and Rod of Chastisement that none shall escape. The story of Lord Shiva's defeat of Lord Yama is set out in chapter A1 of this book.

Preface

Figure 3: Chronology of Hindu Texts

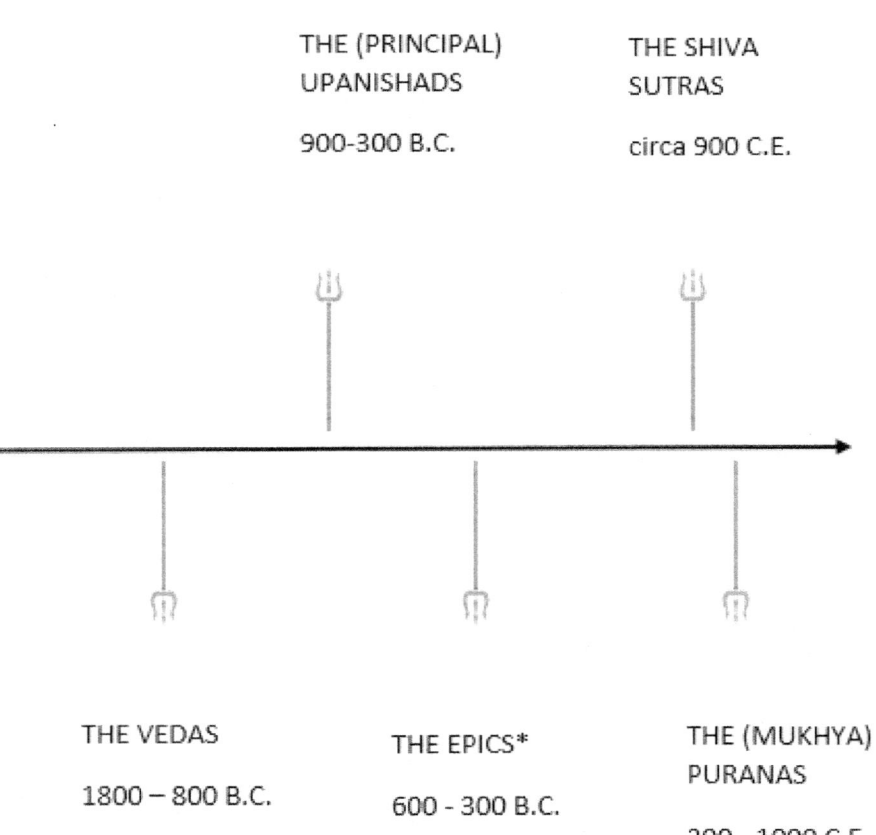

The above dates are based on the most reliable estimates historians can make with forensic techniques available to them.

*The Epics comprise The Ramayana and The Mahabharata (containing The Bhagavad Gita verses).

Foreword

The author has accomplished a mammoth task in publishing this compendium of *The Lord Shiva Narrative* relevant to all ages. It is well structured for a younger audience in part A whilst also serving as a comprehensive source of reference to others for the philosophy of Shaivism. This philosophy is one of the oldest active in the world today with Lord Shiva at the centre, pervading its manifold manifestations. The theology ranges from Lord Shiva's role in creation to his identity within oneself and every life within the Universe.

Liberation (moksha) can be achieved through Yoga, or methods of reunion with the Supreme. There are four pathways:

- Bhakti Yoga (devotional love),
- Raja Yoga (meditation),
- Jnana Yoga (pursuit of knowledge),
- Karma Yoga (service to humanity).

Though these pathways are not exclusive from each other, the predominant pathway applied by many is Bhakti Yoga, which is intense selfless love focused on one of the manifold forms. *The Lord Shiva Narrative* provides background within this context in relation to the forms of Lord Shiva and their origin. The ethical principles Shiv Mahalingam has extracted in this book will facilitate personal development and aid in the practice of the above four forms of Yoga. Meditative techniques of Raja Yoga developed and spread throughout the world becoming an integral part to many major religions such as Hinduism, Buddhism, and Jainism. In the West, these techniques were formalized as Mindfulness. The sacred Hindu texts of the Vedas, the Upanishads, and the Agamas formed the basis for Jnana Yoga and work, as service, was based on ethical principles underlying Karma Yoga.

In the field of literature, the Hindu Epics such as The Ramayana, The Mahabharata, Periya Puranam[xxvii], and the Bhakti hymns (Tevaram)[xxviii], influenced developments in the fine arts of sculpture, architecture, music, and dance including Bharatanatyam dance and Carnatic music. In Elephanta[xxix], Ellora[xxx], and Mahabalipuram[xxxi], different scenes from Part A of *The Lord Shiva Narrative* are seen in all their glory. The statues of Nataraja (Lord Shiva as King of the Dance) symbolize the cosmic dance of what the Agamas proclaim as "the birth of the world, its maintenance, its destruction, the soul's obscuration and liberation". Lord Shiva in Nataraja form is renowned worldwide and, as it also reflects the quantum field theory at a subatomic level, a gifted statue of Nataraja is on display outside the CERN scientific facility in Switzerand.

In the field of architecture, towering gopurams[xxxii] adorn religious sites with inscriptions that pay tribute to Lord Shiva and other deities. With Shaivism principles and philosophy spreading to the East as far as China, Cambodia, Indonesia, Sri Lanka, and other countries, the remains of temples which have survived willful destruction from invaders can still be seen. In China, Quanzhou, Tenavari Nayanar (Lord Shiva) had been worshipped at the Kai Yuan Temple. In Cambodia, the vast temple complex of Angkor Wat, built in 1200 C.E. was a Hindu Temple dedicated to Lord Vishnu. The Bayon, which is a mountain temple, was built to represent Mount Meru[xxxiii] as the center of the universe for many major religions. The galleries and works of art include bas reliefs carved into the walls and hills based on Lord Shiva stories such as Ravana shaking Mount Kailas (see chapter A6), and the churning of the oceans of milk (see Introduction "Primer" on Lord Shiva). The Bayon Temple has a number of serene faces decorating many towers, believed to be that of Lord Brahma. In Indonesia, many of the islanders of Bali practice Shaivism rites and they honour the characters from The Mahabharata (see chapter B1 of this book). In Java, Prambanan Temple is a vast complex build in 900 C.E. with Lord Shiva as the main deity (see chapter C10). In Sri Lanka, five Lord Shiva temples known as the Pancha Ishwarams with pre-Vedic origins were established along the coast with the Shiva linga as the main shrines. These temples are (1) Naguleswaram in the North, (2) Koneswaram in the East, (3) Tondeswaram in the South, (4) Thiruketheeshwaram, and (5) Muneshwaram. The deity is referred to as Tenavarai Nayanar and there is a stone tablet inscribed with three languages (Mandarin, Tamil, and Persian) with offerings to three different religions. The inscription invoked blessings for a peaceful world built on trade relationships. The temples have been partially destroyed by invaders; however, the remaining structures and the sentiment of the stone tablet are a testament to a tolerant and inclusive philosophy.

The relevance of this book to the understanding of Shaivism culture and philosophy cannot be underestimated. These were central to the lives of the author's parents and this book is an appropriate homage from a loving son.

-

Dr. Rajaratnam Thavasothy, 26 February 2021.

Figure 4: Lord Shiva Temple at Mahabalipuram

The UNESCO World Heritage Site at Mahabalipuram includes thousands of sculptures in honour of Lord Shiva. Part C of this book explores a number of other sites dedicated to Lord Shiva.

INTRODUCTION
A "PRIMER" ON LORD SHIVA

Introduction – a "Primer" on Lord Shiva

Figure 5: Lord Shiva Genealogy

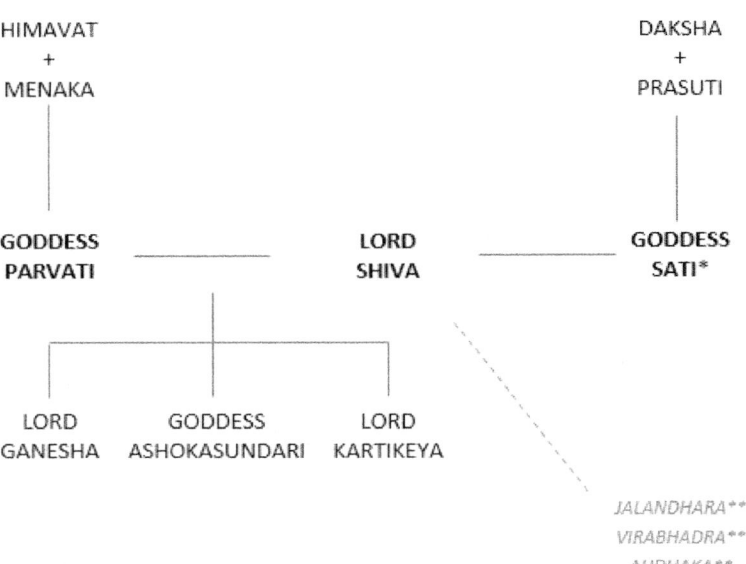

*Goddess Sati was reincarnated as Goddess Parvati (or Uma as she sometimes referred to).

**Andhaka, Virabhadra, and Jalandhara were demons created from Lord Shiva's sweat, hair, and third eye, respectively.

The above stories and the creation of Lord Ganesha, Goddess Ashokasundari, and Lord Kartikeya are in Part A of this book. Goddess Ashokasundari is not renowned despite being praised in the Main Puranas as a daughter of Lord Shiva and Goddess Parvati.

Introduction – a "Primer" on Lord Shiva

Lord Shiva is one of the Hindu Trimurti (Trinity) of Supreme gods: (i) Lord Brahma, (ii) Lord Vishnu and (iii) Lord Shiva who are The Creator, The Preserver/Protector and The Destroyer, respectively. With respect to this fearsome title, and as readers will discover in this book, Lord Shiva does engage in a good deal of destruction when required for which he is celebrated. However, there are other facets to Lord Shiva's character that will be explored throughout the book. These characteristics are always specific to a purpose fulfilled for his devotees. In the Shiva Purana, Lord Shiva has one hundred and eight names; whilst this book does not cover all of these, it does consider the more common and popular depictions of Lord Shiva which include:

- The Destroyer (Rudra[xxxiv]),
- The First Teacher (Adiyogi),
- The Dancer (Nataraja),
- The combined androgynous form for Shiva and Parvati (Ardhanarishwar),
- The Primeval Sage (Dhakshinamurti), and
- The Lord of Animals (Pasupathi).

Like Lord Vishnu, Lord Shiva is worshipped throughout the Indian Sub-continent. Mahashivaratri (the Great Night of Shiva) is his most celebrated festival occurring in February or March each year[xxxv]. On this night, hundreds of millions of devotees come together to praise Lord Shiva's name and seek his blessings. Many remain awake all night, others fast and others undertake long journeys/pilgrimages in honour of Lord Shiva. The Great Night of Shiva is believed by many to represent the night when Lord Shiva performed his dance that stopped the universe (see chapter A7 of this book for a recital of the tale of Lord Shiva as

Introduction – a "Primer" on Lord Shiva

"Nataraja" or King of the Dance). Here is the extract from the Shiva Purana in which Lord Shiva sets out the importance of Mahashivaratri:

"Among all the austerities and fastings, Mahashivaratri holds a supreme place. It falls on the fourteenth day of the dark lunar month of Phalgun[xxxvi]. On this day, the devotee should take a vow to observe a fast after awakening in the morning and finishing daily choirs. A fast must be observed for the whole day and night. In the night, worship me either in the temple or in your own home according to convenience...The devotee should engage in my devotion for the whole day. At the end of the day, feed the brahmins[xxxvii] and make donations to them. A fast observed in this way gives infinite virtues to the devotee."

Lord Shiva's celestial abode is Mount Kailas[xxxviii] and he is oft pictured there in meditation with two or four arms and one head (this may sound like a strange comment to some readers but often Hindu gods are depicted with a multitude of heads and limbs). Lord Shiva is portrayed frequently with the distinctive matted black hair/dreadlocks of an aesthetic. He dons no ornaments, no jewelry, no armour, and no helmet. He wears sacred rudraksha[xxxix] beads and a serpent around his neck and only the hide of a leopard (or tiger[xl]) adorns his frame with no other garb. Readers will note that these traits describe an anthropomorphic image of Lord Shiva. This Hindu deity is also represented in aniconic image through a linga (meaning symbol or sign). This Shivalinga, which represents Lord Shiva's energy force, could be constructed out of sand or earth by a devotee, or a more permanent form could be made from materials such as black stone and placed in a Temple.

There are many representations of Lord Shiva with Nandi, his trusted guardian and vahana (animal chariot). Nandi is normally visualized as a magnificent white bull; he is mentioned in several of the Mukhya Puranas and the Shiva Agamas also. In addition,

Part C sets out the particulars of the fabled "Pasupathi Seal" which is a stamp dated 2500 B.C. which many historians believe to be a carving of Lord Shiva and Nandi (the carving is named after Pasupathi, Lord of Animals).

Lord Shiva's preferred weapons in warfare are the trident[xli] and the bow and arrow. On rare occasions, he is called upon to use the devastating Pasupatastra[xlii] weapon which could destroy all Creation if not deployed correctly... Note that a battle axe is also mentioned in the Upanishads as discussed in Part B of this book. A deity with the title of "Destroyer" would of course have such instruments at their disposal and Lord Shiva has multiple arms with which to wield them if required. Lord Shiva also carries a drum confirming the importance of music and dance to his otherworldly persona. There is an extract from the Padma Purana that confirms the many characteristics of Lord Shiva (referred to in the text as "Sankara" in this instance). The extract confirms his third eye, his trident, and the River Ganges flowing from his hair (see below), plus his white bull chariot.

The name Sankara for Lord Shiva was popularized in the movie Indiana Jones and the Temple of Doom[xliii] The plot of this Hollywood production involves the search for the five "Sankara stones" that glow with a brilliant light. The film also refers to the main antagonists as the "betrayers of Shiva". There is no mention of these specific artefacts in the Puranas; however, the Shiva Purana does detail the appearance of Lord Shiva as columns of fire at various locations on Earth (which are the Jyotirlinga as described in more detail in Part C to this book). The Sankara stones may have been symbols of these columns of fire. To this day, the twelve Jyotirlinga Temples across the Indian Sub-Continent, can be visited by devotees and many of these are explored in part C of this book.

Set out below are a few additional stories as to how Lord Shiva obtained his striking appearance.

Introduction – a "Primer" on Lord Shiva

Lord Shiva's Blue Neck

The Shiva Purana, The Shiva Agama, The Ramayana, and the Bhagavat Purana all discuss how Lord Shiva acquired a blue neck. The Shiva Purana dictates that during the time when the ocean was being churned, first poison appeared (one is not sure why this poison appeared, but it was clear that something needed to be done...). The deities were terrified to see the tremendous heat generated by this poison and they petitioned Lord Shiva and requested for him to protect them. Lord Shiva duly took up the poison in his cupped hands and drank it all, but he did not let it pass down his throat. As a result of this display of supreme power, Lord Shiva has become known as Neelkanth: the blue-throated one. The Bhagavat Purana confirms that on witnessing the pernicious predicament of all living beings, Lord Shiva, the friend of all creatures, out of his compassion for their distress spoke to his beloved Goddess Sati. Lord Shiva said:

"Dear Bhavani,[xliv] just see how pitiable this situation is of all the living beings under the threat of the poison produced by churning the ocean. Feeling responsible for all their lives, I must do something for their safety...Devotees at the cost of their own lives protect other living beings who, time bound and bewildered by the external energy, are of enmity with one another....
May there be the well-being of all creatures with me drinking this poison."

After Lord Shiva, the well-wisher of the universe, had addressed his celestial bride she gave her permission (it always a good idea to confer with one's spouse in advance of such an undertaking...). Goddess Sati was fully aware of the capabilities of her husband and so Lord Shiva proceeded to drink the poison with her blessing. He took the widespread poison in his hand and drank it. The poison exhibited its potency by turning the neck of Lord Shiva dark blue, a feature considered an ornament of benevolence by the virtuous souls, the saints, and the sages.

The Shiva Agama refers to the incident also by calling Lord Shiva "the remover of the force of the terrible poison". This scripture mentions that the terrible toxin, resembling the brilliance of the fire of deluge, was consumed by Lord Shiva with sympathy. The poison made a dark mark on his throat and he became forever Neelkanth, the blue-throated one. There are frequent mentions to the blue neck of Lord Shiva in the Vedas and Upanishads also as set out in Part B of this book.

Author's note: Lord Shiva's benevolent act to swallow the poison and save all living creatures teaches us a prime lesson in putting the needs of others above one's own self-absorbed desires. Lord Shiva mentions this in the extract of the Bhagavat Purana citing the selfless acts of his devotees who protect each other, sometimes with their own lives. In other versions told in folklore, Lord Shiva is assisted by the Goddess Parvati (the reincarnation of Goddess Sati above) who was alarmed by the fast spreading of the poison and grasped Lord Shiva's throat thus controlling the spread of the poison and keeping it in his neck for eternity. Many of us rely upon the unwavering support of a spouse and can relate to such welcome assistance from a loved one. Further, it is hard to imagine that anyone other than his beloved Goddess Parvati would be able to grasp Lord Shiva's throat without being reduced to a pile of ash (reference the tragedy of poor Kamadeva[xlv] below...).

There is more to this tale for the Shiva Purana also tells us that after the poison, soma (nectar[xlvi]) appeared next from the churning of the ocean. This nectar was summarily drunk by the deities. The demons on observing this also wanted to drink their share of the nectar and this resulted in a tremendous encounter between the demons and the deities (presumably the nectar was the drink of the righteous and not fit for demons who were practiced in wicked acts of adharma[xlvii]...or maybe there was just not enough divine nectar to go around...). Unfortunately for the demons, the deities became victorious in this tumultuous struggle because the nectar had made them immortal.

Introduction – a "Primer" on Lord Shiva

However, this resounding victory made the deities arrogant, and Lord Shiva became duly concerned about their hubris. He took it upon himself to teach them a lesson and appeared before them in the guise of a yaksha[xlviii] (spirit of the forest). The spirit asked the deities what had made them so arrogant. The deities (seemingly unperturbed by this impertinent question and in full admission of their arrogance...) replied that it stemmed from a legendary victory over the lowly demons. The spirit countered that their pride was based on a false notion because they would not have achieved victory except though someone else's grace and blessing. The deities disagreed with the spirit (one can picture them laughing and jeering at anyone questioning their superiority in the wake of triumph). The spirit asked the deities to cut the grass in front of them if they considered themselves so powerful (he placed a blade of grass on the ground).

Each of the deities set out to cut that blade of grass with their respective divine weapons but they all remained unsuccessful in their attempts. They were stunned with amazement at their inability to complete this most simple of tasks and suddenly a heavenly voice was heard which revealed to them that the spirit was none other than Lord Shiva himself who had been less than impressed with their arrogant behaviour. The deities realized their mistake and they apologized to Lord Shiva. After vanquishing the false pride of the deities, Lord Shiva was satisfied and returned to his home on Mount Kailas.

Author's note: Aside from warning against the dangers of arrogance, the above anecdote also underscores the importance of assessing the situation at hand. If one is challenged to do something that appears to be a remarkably simple task, then perhaps think again to assess if there are hidden risks or factors (i.e., the proverbial "too good to be true").

The Kena Upanishad (see chapter B4 of this book) sets out this story as an interaction with "Brahman"[xlix] (who was said to have won the war between the "Good Gods" and the "Wicked

Demons"). In this extract from Hindu scripture, the gods were said to have "foolishly claimed victory for themselves" and Brahman set about testing them. He set a straw in front of Agni, God of Sacred Fire; Vayu, God of Air and Winds; and Indra, the mighty King of all the Gods who were perplexed by their inability to dispense with the straw using their respective powers. Goddess Uma, wife of Lord Shiva, daughter of Himavat[li], also known as the Goddess Parvati, appears before the gods to highlight their folly.

The Cobra Around Lord Shiva's Neck

The tale of the churning of the oceans features in multiple parts of Hindu scripture. The Matsya Purana refers to the poison as halahala[li], stating that it was created when the ocean of milk became agitated. Vasuki, the Lord of Serpents, fulfilled the role of a magnificent rope to rotate Mandar[lii] Mountain to churn the ocean. Whilst Lord Shiva was drinking the poison at the behest of the deities, he looked down and noticed that there were snakes within the water who were assisting him by also drinking the poison and Vasuki was among them. Lord Shiva smiled in appreciation of this act and as such Vasuki was given pride of place around Pasupathi's neck for eternity (readers will recall that Pasupathi is Lord Shiva's persona as the Lord of Animals).

The Bhagavat Purana features Lord Shiva drinking the poison with consistent elements such as Vasuki, King of Snakes lending himself as the rope with which to rotate the mountain. The Bhagavat Purana also suggests that scorpions, cobras and other poisonous animals and plants that exist to this day are the beings that ingested that little amount of poison that was scattered in the ocean as Lord Shiva drank from his palm. The Matsya Purana confirms that Lord Shiva, should be "garlanded" with snakes and Lord Shiva is oft depicted as such. Vasuki features in folklore versions of the adventures of Lord Shiva and the Tripurasura[liii] acting as the arrow with which Lord Shiva subdues the demon brothers (see chapter A8 of this book for the Shiva Purana version which does not mention Vasuki). Chapter A7 of this book relays the story of Lord Shiva as Nataraja, King of the Dance and this has an alternative version for the happenstance in which this deity came to have snakes around his neck and arms. These serpents were conjured by dark sages to attack Lord Shiva, but he effortlessly picked them up and wrapped them around him as ornaments where they remain.

Figure 6: Lord Shiva and the Cobra

Author's note: Lord Shiva is almost always pictured with a cobra around his neck in his meditative form; the cobra, being one of the deadliest animals known to mortals, adds gravitas to the indestructible nature of Lord Shiva. One lesson in the above chronicle of the churning of the oceans is that even the most capable of individuals may need help (or at least will appreciate the offer of help) at some point in their lives just as Lord Shiva was aided by the serpents and appreciated their assistance.

The River Ganges in Lord Shiva's Hair

Lord Shiva is oft pictured with the River Ganges flowing from his hair downwards to the Earth. There is reference to this in the Hindu Epic of The Ramayana: Bhageeratha[liv] was a valiant King but he was childless. In addition, it was suggested to him that Ganga the River Goddess should be brought down to the Earth from the heavens to bring peace to the souls of his ancestors who had been turned to ash by the wrathful glance of a powerful sage (but that is another story...). Desiring progeny and hoping to bring Goddess Ganga down to aid the souls of his forefathers, Bhageeratha left his Kingdom and the comforts of a regal life to perform penance and severe austerities in the wilderness. He undertook tapas (austere religious ceremonies not to be confused with the Spanish delicacy...) with fire on all sides and with his head exposed to the hot sun, taking food only once per month. Lord Brahma was pleased with his devotion and he appeared before Bhageeratha asking what he desired. Bhageeratha responded:

"If you have pity on me Lord Brahman then bless me with a child to continue the line of my forebears. Secondly, may you please order Goddess Ganga down so that the souls of my ancestors can be purified with her holy waters."

Lord Brahma replied that the wishes would be granted; however, there was a complexity in that the Earth could not withstand the force of Goddess Ganga's descent. Lord Brahma stated that Lord Shiva alone can stand this celestial force and so Bhageeratha was instructed to direct his penance toward Lord Shiva. Bhageeratha continued without food and water until he at last won Lord Shiva's grace and he agreed to receive the River Goddess upon his head. The River Goddess began her descent but, in her arrogance, she thought that she could fall upon the head of the Lord Shiva and sweep him away towards Patala[lv] (the underworld). Lord Shiva decided to teach the River Goddess a

Introduction – a "Primer" on Lord Shiva

lesson (readers will be starting to see a trend here in his distaste for arrogance...) and, at the moment he willed it, the flood of waters that fell upon him became trapped by his matted hair in an infinite receptacle.

Though she tried, not a single drop could emerge from the tangled maze of Lord Shiva's dreadlocks. When Lord Shiva had removed all of Goddess Ganga's arrogance, he permitted her to flow to Earth where she remains as a sacred river for devotees. The aarti (religious ceremony) is an uplifting spiritual ritual performed by devotees on the River Ganges. One famous ceremony takes place at Varanasi[lvi]. Hindu priests use oil lamps circled in a clockwise direction as they spiral out onto the river and this is accompanied by sublime religious chanting in praise of Goddess Ganga. It is believed by devotees that after the ritual is complete, the Goddess showers her blessing on all present as the River becomes filled with lit lamps and aromatic flowers.

Author's note: Bhageeratha's selfless request on behalf of his ancestors and his dedication to the task at hand are critical elements for success. His name has become synonymous with a stellar effort to overcome an insurmountable problem. There is a common thread in the above anecdote whereby the Trinity of Hindu Gods often work together to achieve the necessary and ask each other for assistance when required (as true leaders should). Readers will note the forgiveness of the Goddess Ganga by Lord Shiva once she had been trapped for a time. In other versions, Goddess Ganga had fallen in love with Lord Shiva, and this prompted her desire to wash him away to be with her in the netherworld. One of Lord Shiva's many names is Gangadhara (bearer of the River Ganges). The geographical aspects contained in this parable are consistent with the source of the River Ganges in the Himalayas where Lord Shiva is resident. The Ramayana states at the close of this episode that those who bathe in the holy waters of the River Ganges or read/listen to this divine tale with devotion, will be cleansed of sin and endowed with virtue, strength, and unflagging zeal[lvii] (may this be so for all readers).

The Crescent Moon Adorning Lord Shiva

The Shiva Purana sets out an interesting origin as to why Lord Shiva is oft depicted with a crescent moon in his hair. The Moon God (referred to in the Upanishads as Chandra) had twenty-seven wives, one of whom was Rohini. He loved Rohini very much, which made the rest of his wives jealous and angry. They went to their father, Daksha (it appears that they were all sisters...) and complained about the Moon God's behaviour in placing Rohini above all of them. Daksha, son of Lord Brahma, went to his son in law and advised him to give proper attention to each of his wives in equal measure (note that a Moon "day" - i.e., the time it takes the Moon to rotate on its axis, lasts twenty-seven Earth days which may have made things easier for Chandra in dividing his time among his wives...).

However, the Moon did not acquiesce to the request of his father-in-law. Chandra continued giving special treatment to his true love Rohini. When Daksha realized that Chandra had not paid him any attention, he cursed him to become weak and devoid of radiance. The Moon God then appealed to the other deities to petition Lord Brahma to intercede on his behalf. At first, Lord Brahma became angry with the Moon (presumably for not resolving the matter himself when he had the chance or maybe he was upset at the treatment of his granddaughters...); however, in time Lord Brahma's anger subsided and he instructed the deities that the Moon God would be liberated from Daksha's curse if he were able to chant the "Mahamrityunjaya Mantra" (a verse from the Rigveda often referred to as the more pronounceable "Rudra Mantra"):

"Om tryambhakam yajamahe sugandhim pushti vardhanam urvarukam iva bandhanan mrityor mukshiya maamritat"

Introduction – a "Primer" on Lord Shiva

(we offer our respect to the three-eyed Lord who is fragrant and who nourishes all living beings. As the ripe cucumber is freed from its stalk, we pray for you to move us away from the ensnare of death and put us on the path of salvation).

The Moon went to a sacred area and commenced his penance to appeal to Lord Shiva. Chandra chanted the Rudra Mantra one hundred million times (see comment above about the length of a Moon day being twenty-seven times as long as an Earth day...). Lord Shiva was duly satisfied with this devotion and he appeared before the Moon God and asked him to demand anything he wished. Chandra requested for Lord Shiva to liberate him from the curse laid down by Daksha; however, Lord Shiva told him that the words of Daksha, son of Lord Brahma can never become untrue. Lord Shiva offered a reconciliation. He blessed Chandra and commanded that he would forever wane during the dark lunar phase due to the curse, but forever wax during the dark lunar phase due to Lord Shiva's blessings. Further to this, Lord Shiva stated that the Moon God would be near to him and Goddess Parvati for all time as their faithful devotee. Thus, Lord Shiva established himself as Somnath (Lord of the Moon) and the Moon God secured an eternal place close to Lord Shiva.

Author's note: Readers will have noticed the specific number of twenty-seven wives. As mentioned above, the Moon takes twenty-seven earth days to rotate on its own axis and it takes twenty-seven earth days to orbit the Earth. In addition, there are twenty-seven lunar constellations in the Hindu astrology calendar. Therefore, this is a number associated with the Moon in a variety of ways. The moral from the above parable includes the importance of having regard to the feelings of one's family members, be they in-laws or spouses. Daksha is to be praised for not putting any one of his children above the others and attempting to talk to his son-in-law in the first instance before any further retribution is sought. There is an important lesson about communication between individuals and the perils of ignoring a problem in the hope that it will go away. Finally, Chandra took on a responsibility that was too much for him to handle effectively and this is an important lesson that all should take into consideration.

Lord Shiva's Third Eye – the Bravery of Kamadeva

Lord Shiva has a third eye on his forehead that opens when he is angry[lviii] consuming transgressors in fire. Instances on which Lord Shiva utilizes this terrible weapon of judgment are rare as he prefers the use of the Trident in combat (perhaps this is a sense of fair play for his opponents – who are defeated swiftly in any case...). There is an oft told story of Lord Shiva's use of the third eye involving Kamadeva, Lord of Pleasure, God of Love (he has his own Sutra...). The deities were tormented by the seemingly invincible Tarakasura (see chapter A3 of this book for the full chronicle of this diabolical Demon).

They went to Lord Brahma to seek his help who dispatched Kamadeva to disturb the meditation of Lord Shiva so that he would fall in love with the Goddess Parvati and sire a champion who would ultimately kill Tarakasura. Indra, King of Gods, decided to speak to Kamadeva also (it appears that the God of Love needed a lot of reassurance before firing an arrow at the Lord of Destruction...). Lord Indra confirmed that the Demon King Tarakasura could be killed only by such a person who was the son of Lord Shiva and Goddess Parvati. Lord Indra therefore instructed Kamadeva to arouse passion in Lord Shiva with an arrow of pleasure. Kamadeva, accompanied by his wife Rati, went to Lord Shiva to accomplish his mission (one is not sure why Kama took his beloved wife Rati with him – perhaps to strengthen his resolve or perhaps he hoped that she would talk him out of this fatal errand...).

After reaching the location where Lord Shiva was engrossed in his meditation, Kamadeva made repeated attempts to gain Lord Shiva's attention, but these were to no avail. One can picture poor Kamadeva at a loss for what to do. Suddenly, he saw Goddess Parvati arriving accompanied by her companions. She was looking divine in her beauty and at that same moment Lord Shiva had come out of his meditational trance. Kamadeva reflected that this was the most appropriate moment to achieve his task, so he struck Lord Shiva with his "Kamabana[lix]" (arrow of love) which had the desired impact; Lord Shiva was hit (quite literally…) by the unparalleled beauty of Goddess Parvati and his heart became full of passion for her. However, he was surprised at the sudden loss of his control over his emotions given his intense mastery over such feelings and many years of penance to achieve sensory control. He realized the truth: that this could only be an act of the God of Love influencing his mind with his arrows of desire. Lord Shiva looked all around him and, as he had suspected, he saw Kamadeva with a bow and arrows in his hands (in hindsight, it was probably ill advised for Kamadeva to have remained in the area with the bow still in his hands – this is probably why cupid has wings…).

Kamadeva, Lord of Pleasure, became absolutely terrified as the third eye of Lord Shiva opened letting out an eruption of fire reducing the heroic God of Love to ashes within an instant. After these terrible events, the deities went near to Lord Shiva (as near as they dared in any case…) and they paid homage to him. They relayed the fact that it was not the fault of Kamadeva, as he had acted in accordance with the aspirations of the deities. They explained Lord Brahma's prediction that the only circumstances in which the evil Demon Tarakasura could be killed would be through Lord Shiva's son. Thus, there was the necessity for Lord Shiva and Goddess Parvati to be married at once. The deities requested for Lord Shiva to make Kamadeva alive once again and restore him to his devoted wife Rati who was inconsolable. Lord Shiva consented to restoring the Lord of Pleasure to life, but his fury did not subside fully after the death of Kamadeva and the whole world started to feel the effect of his wrath. All the living creatures on Earth trembled with abject fear. They went to Lord Brahma and prayed to him to save them from Lord Shiva's considerable rage. Lord Brahma discussed the matter with Lord Shiva and conveyed their request to him offering a potential solution. Lord Shiva agreed to relinquish his anger to Lord Brahma who carried the fury to Varuna, God of the Sea. Varuna possessed this fury until its final dissipation and all living creatures felt a surge of relief. Kamadeva was restored to Rati and he remains the God of Love to this day shooting arrows of desire at young (and old) single folk...

Author's note: The tragedy of Kamadeva is one of bravery and the diligent application of one's duty despite the consequences that one may face. Kamadeva was fully aware of Lord Shiva's wrath; however, he knew that only his sacrifice could bring about the destruction of the Demon Tarakasura. A sage in The Ramayana refers to The God of Love as being "foolish" to have aimed his arrow at Lord Shiva; however, it was not folly but valour and divine destiny that forced his hand. There will be times when one is faced with a choice to act for the greater good even though there may be personal suffering as a result. In such situations, may all be granted the strength of character to do what is right despite the difficulties faced. The fable of Kamadeva further demonstrates the unique love that Lord Shiva has for Goddess Parvati as this was the only lapse in a long history of his impregnable concentration.

In many respects, the God of Love was able to overcome Shiva, Lord of Destruction. This is a feat that no warrior has ever matched and in doing so, Kamadeva helped to usher in a new benevolent incarnation of the deity as a devoted and loving husband. Chapter A2 of this book explores this in more detail. Lord Shiva consented to marry Goddess Sati; however, he fell in love with Goddess Parvati, and these are two vastly different circumstances. The tragic tale of Kamadeva warns against rage and the impact this can have on others. The Vedas are firm on this point: once anger is given life to, then it can be almost impossible to destroy this feeling without causing harm to ourselves and to others. In Vedic writings, the third eye or inner eye is not just to be applied in wrath and it enables the enlightened to view higher consciousness as will be explored in Part D of this book. Finally, readers will note the similarities between Kamadeva and the Greek legend of Eros (or Cupid) who is the God of Love, armed with a bow and arrows to provoke love, passion, and desire in unsuspecting individuals. The adventures of Lord Shiva continue in Part A below with the full story of his triumph over the terrible Lord Yama, God of Death.

Figure 7: Lord Shiva in Meditation

Lord Shiva depicted in anthropomorphic form as the Primeval Sage with his most familiar characteristics. These include the crescent moon in his hair, rudraksha beads, a cobra coiled around his neck, a tiger skin robe, the trident, and the River Ganges flowing down from his hair as he sits in meditation in Mount Kailas. The dormant third eye is also displayed on his forehead with the tripundra mark of three lines of ash. This is to be contrasted with the warrior form of Lord Shiva as the Destroyer, or his form as Nataraja King of the Dance.

PART A: *BRAHMACHARYA*
THE TALES OF LORD SHIVA

PART A: BRAHMACHARYA – Tales of Lord Shiva

Chapter A1 – Victory over the God of Death

As set out in the introductory chapter to this book, Lord Shiva once rescued his devotee Markandeya from certain death at the hands (and the noose, and the sword, and the Rod of Chastisement, and the black buffalo, and the jackals...) of the merciless Lord Yama and his legions of devastation. The anecdote is set out below and the main sources for this are The Linga Purana and The Mahabharata.

A great sage and his wife were devout worshippers of Lord Shiva and they lived a life of indigence as aesthetics in the wilderness. They were unable to have children, but they longed for a son that they could raise in accordance with the laws of love, morality, and duty. The couple performed austerities in the name of Lord Shiva for many years in the hope that he would grant them the divine wish (or boon) of a child.

Lord Shiva was sympathetic to the plight of his ardent followers; however, the gods must ensure that the principles of karma (action) are adhered to. Karma is the universal law of destiny that impacts all individuals based upon their actions in this life and previous reincarnations. As a result, Lord Shiva granted the request of the couple, but they were given the choice of either: (i) a virtuous and righteous son who would live a short life on earth, or (ii) a child of low moral fibre and low intelligence who would live a long life.

The couple opted to select the righteous child in accordance with Vedic principles as opposed to an immoral individual who would live for many years (regrettably, readers will have encountered people like this everywhere...). Unto this pious pair was born Markandeya, a legendary figure from Hinduism who was blessed with strong ethical values and selfless instincts. However, he was destined to die at the age of sixteen as part of the terms of Lord Shiva's boon.

Despite this unfortunate inevitability, Markandeya did not squander his short years on Earth, and he grew up to be a virtuous devotee of Lord Shiva as his parents before him. He demonstrated a keen understanding of the Vedic scriptures from a young age, and he was as affable as he was wise. He was loved and respected by all who encountered him. Markandeya was an asset to his parents who were torn between feelings of love for the young man he had become and fear for the terrible day that he would become sixteen and be taken to Lord Yama's Kingdom of Death.

Markandeya decided to meditate on Lord Shiva on the eve of his sixteenth birthday as there was no other hope for this brave soul. He continued his tapas and on the day of reckoning, Lord Yama's harbingers of doom duly came for him. The Markandeya Purana expands on the terrible fate awaiting anyone who encounters Lord Yama: His dreadful and vicious-souled followers appear with maces in hand. Then these emissaries of the Lord of Death bind the ill-fated with dreadful nooses (made of snakes...) and drag them to the south. They let out dreadful, inauspicious yells through the ground rough with thorns, anthills, pins, and stones, glowing with flames, blazing with the heat of the sun, and burning with its rays. Dragged by the dreadful and eaten by hundreds of jackals, the sinful person goes to Lord Yama's house through a fearful passage indeed.

The Puranas do not expand on how the righteous are dealt with by Lord Yama and his minions, but one would hope it does not involve any of the above...thankfully, The Mahabharata has a passage that many of us can take solace from. Lord Yama is defined in the Hindu Epic as handsome, radiant, strong as the sun, with dark skin shining and red eyes (and of course noose in hand...). Lord Yama states the following about an individual who has reached the end of their life that he has come to take away:

"This man is righteous, an ocean of virtue; it would not be right for my servants to take him, so I have come myself."

Lord Yama binds the individual in question with his noose and the body loses its lustre and ceases to breathe being no longer fair to look upon. This extract from The Mahabharata states that the virtuous have nothing to fear from Lord Yama even in death. The virtuous practice eternal morality and never know despair or anguish. They work for others, expecting nothing in return.

Returning to the plight of Markandeya, Lord Yama's legions found themselves unable to drag him away from his superlative devotion and worship of Lord Shiva. These servants of Lord Yama are essentially his "back-up team" as being the Lord of Dharma is a fulltime position given the magnitude of departed souls, righteous or otherwise...

Lord Yama decided it was time for him to intervene in relation to this virtuous soul, so he gathered up his weapons, mounted his black buffalo, and set off to take Markandeya away as was pre-ordained by destiny. Lord Yama was nonplused about the penance of this young man for he had been charged with dominion over the deceased by the gods themselves. He threw his deadly noose with precision around the neck of the devotee.

However, it was at that instant that Lord Shiva erupted onto the scene with trident poised for a swift execution. He fortified himself between the God of Death and the young boy, yet he controlled his third eye from opening (somewhere in the heavens Kamadeva was feeling bemused...). Lord Shiva was incensed by Lord Yama's lack of compassion for Markandeya. He attacked with his trident of destruction. Lord Yama may have thought for a moment about attempting to appeal to Lord Shiva but when the God of Death is challenged by the Lord of Destruction then glorious battle shall be the only possible outcome. Lord Shiva was swift to defeat Lord Yama despite the terrible power of the God of Death (his emissaries and jackals scarpered from the scene as soon as they saw Lord Shiva...).

This devastating defeat of Lord Yama secured Lord Shiva as "Kalantaka" (the Ender of Death). Lord Yama was either dead or close to death after this encounter; however, the deities appealed to Lord Shiva and Lord Yama was restored to his former health and position. Markandeya was blessed with immortality and he is believed to this day to reside in the Himalayas in constant meditation for the eternal good of mankind.

Author's note: Markandeya performs an important role in The Mahabharata given his long years of virtue and wisdom. The Markandeya Purana includes a significant re-telling of The Mahabharata Epic. The story above about Lord Shiva's intervention in death has many lessons, the first of which is the importance of hope even though problems may seem insurmountable at the time. The fable confirms the importance and value of living a moral and virtuous life even in a few short years as opposed to living a long life without merit.

Lord Yama himself has much to teach us in his guise as the Lord of Dharma. The Katha Upanishad confirms that meditation upon death can be a powerful means of awakening and self-realization. In this Upanishad, the son of a Brahmin[ix] seeks out Lord Yama for answers about life; the Lord of Dharma confirms three essential duties that will lead to eternal peace: (i) Study – application of the mind to the acquisition of knowledge, (ii) Austerity – sternness of attitude, (iii) Giving to charity. Lord Yama argues that he who clings to the "Good" but chooses "Pleasure" is like an arrow which misses the mark. Fools choose Pleasure and the wise choose Good; however, he cautions that whilst the foolish dwell in the darkness of ignorance, the wise dwell only in the darkness of their own arrogance.

PART A: BRAHMACHARYA – Tales of Lord Shiva

Lord Yama argues that if a person has no understanding and no sensory control in life then they will be as a chariot where the charioteer does not hold the reins firmly and their mind will wander as wild horses which can become vicious. The wise seek not stability in an unstable word but look inward to what they can control within themselves. This is important advice from Yama the God of Death and the Lord of Dharma who holds dominion over the souls of the departed...

Figure 8: Lord Shiva Challenges Lord Yama

Lord Shiva is portrayed rescuing Markandeya from Lord Yama. Markandeya is in prayer at the feet of Lord Shiva who is erupting out of a Shivalinga idol. In many versions of the tale, Lord Shiva kills the God of Death but later restores him to his position in recognition of the important role he serves in the Hindu universe as the Lord of Dharma (moral duty). Lord Yama is pictured here riding a black buffalo and he has dropped his trademark noose so that he can bring his hands together in supplication to Lord Shiva who is about to unleash his trident. Lord Shiva's defeat of Lord Yama provides all with hope that devotion and a life of good deeds can gain the favour of the Gods. Lord Yama is the judge, jury, and executioner for all Hindu souls and the manner in which one is taken to his Kingdom will depend upon the deeds of one's life. A righteous life will be met with more restraint and accommodation than a sinful one.

Chapter A2 – Eternal Love and Goddess Parvati

The Lord Shiva Narrative could never be complete without the Goddess Parvati. This couple exemplifies eternal love, and they are devoted to each other in a partnership of equals as the stories in this chapter will demonstrate. Goddess Parvati (or Uma as she is often referred to) is the reincarnation of Goddess Sati and she shares interminable affection with Lord Shiva. The main source for the stories below is the Shiva Purana and the Padma Purana.

Goddess Sati

A great sage once enquired of Lord Brahma as to how Lord Shiva came to be married to Goddess Sati despite being a celibate yogi (a reasonable question...). He requested Lord Brahma to tell him how the Goddess Sati became the daughter of Daksha and how she became Parvati in her next birth as the daughter of Himavat. Lord Brahma narrated the following tale in response: On one occasion, Lord Shiva admonished Lord Brahma and ridiculed him about his character. He felt ashamed and became jealous of Lord Shiva. Lord Brahma decided to attempt to influence him to break his impenetrable concentration; however, he was unsuccessful in his attempts. Lord Brahma meditated on Lord Vishnu who tried to make Lord Brahma understand the futility of his attempts, for he knew that Lord Shiva was beyond the reach of human emotions of desire.

However, fate would appear to have been on the side of Lord Brahma for his son Daksha had sixty daughters (yes sixty daughters...) of significant beauty. One of these was Goddess Sati who was destined to win the hand of Shiva, Lord of Destruction. Ten of Daksha's daughters were married to Yama, Lord of Dharma, thirteen to a great sage, twenty-seven to Chandra (the Moon - see Introduction chapter to this book), six daughters to Garuda[lxi] (mighty King of all Birds) and the remainder were also married leaving Sati. With respect to Goddess Sati's birth, Daksha meditated on the form of Bhagwati[lxii] and was instructed by her to undertake devotional sacrifice. Daksha performed a tremendous penance and thus Goddess Sati was born to Daksha. She was brought up with love and affection and she worshipped Lord Shiva by singing devotional songs in his praise. When she attained marriageable age, Daksha started to worry (as most fathers do...). She understood the reason behind her father's concern, and she went to her Mother Virani and expressed her desire to marry Lord Shiva.

Virani made all the necessary arrangements so that she could worship Lord Shiva without interruption. Goddess Sati commenced her austerities which continued for a year. The deities were impressed by her devotion and they all descended from the heavens to see her. They decided to approach Lord Shiva, requesting for him to get married but Lord Shiva did not wish to curtail his freedom by getting married (this is an exact translation from the Puranas...). When the deities insisted (as many married couples do to their single friends...), he consented if they could identify a suitable match for him. Lord Brahma and Lord Vishnu told Lord Shiva about the devotion of the young maiden who was undertaking austerities in his name. Lord Shiva agreed to appear before Goddess Sati, and he asked her to demand anything in recognition of her sacrifices. She was bashful and unable to speak in the presence of Lord Shiva; however, he could see her love for him, and he decreed:

"You will have me as your husband."

She beamed with joy and requested Lord Shiva to take this proposal before Daksha. Lord Shiva agreed. Goddess Sati returned home and narrated the events to her parents who both became extremely happy with this news. Lord Shiva then instructed Lord Brahma to put a formal proposal to Daksha regarding the marriage. Lord Brahma duly informed Daksha about Lord Shiva's proposal who accepted.

Lord Shiva then proceeded towards Daksha's abode on the auspicious moment of Phalgun[lxiii]. He travelled on the back of his vahana (animal chariot) Nandi, and he was accompanied by all the deities including Lord Brahma and Lord Vishnu. This majestic marriage-procession was received by Daksha with respect. The deities eulogized Lord Shiva and danced in joy. Though Lord Shiva was free from all kinds of attachment, he enjoyed a blissful married life for an exceptionally long time. However, his father in-law upset this harmony... Daksha in his arrogance commenced condemning Lord Shiva.

On one occasion, Daksha organized a grand ceremony inviting the gods except for Lord Shiva and Goddess Sati. Despite Lord Shiva's disinclination for Goddess Sati to attend, she insisted on going. When the Goddess reached the celebrations, she was not given due respect by her father. Daksha made fun of Lord Shiva's appearance (Daksha ends up with the head of a goat for his transgressions so he probably regretted this between bleats...). Goddess Sati had such love, devotion, and respect for her husband that she gave up her life by jumping into sacrificial flames. The Padma Purana expands upon this with Goddess Sati admonishing her father before this sacrifice. She tells Daksha that Lord Shiva is the author, and the creator, and only by the favour of Lord Shiva, did Indra, King of Gods, ascend to heaven. Goddess Sati warns him that if Lord Shiva is omnipotent (which she knows he is...), then truly Daksha's ceremony will be destroyed.

Contemplating the supreme spirit, Sati then burns herself with the lustre residing in her body, while the gods stand watching. Finally, she casts her body on to the bank of the River Ganges. When Lord Shiva received the news of his beloved Goddess, he became furious (as readers will appreciate, this will not turn out well for Daksha...). Lord Shiva tore off a lock of his hair and threw it to the ground creating the monstrous Demon God Virabhadra who had two thousand arms each with a weapon ready to strike. Virabhadra smashed Daksha's armies and many of the deities who were caught in the crossfire when Virabhadra stormed

Daksha's palace. Virabhadra then closed in on Daksha and tore off his head. The deities became afraid and prayed to Lord Shiva to have mercy. Lord Shiva duly brought Daksha back to life (many versions of the account state that Daksha's head was replaced with that of a goat...).

Goddess Parvati

Lord Brahma continued in his narration of the events with the story of Goddess Parvati: In her next birth, Goddess Sati was reborn as Parvati to Himavat, King of the Himalaya Mountains. Himavat and his wife Maina engaged themselves in the worship of Lord Shiva and Shakti[lxiv]. After many days Goddess Parvati was born, and the mountainous region of Himalaya became illuminated by her radiance of brilliant white light. Great sages foretold of her destiny to marry Lord Shiva and she grew up into a beautiful and virtuous young lady. One day Lord Shiva accompanied by his Ganas (armed guards or attendants: referred to as the "Shivaganas" in scripture) arrived at Himalaya, with the purpose of undertaking penance.

Himavat came to know about his arrival, and he went to receive him. After he had made his salutation, he was instructed by Lord Shiva to ensure that he would not be disturbed while meditating. Himavat made all the necessary arrangements so that Lord Shiva could perform his penance without interruption. Himavat requested for Lord Shiva to keep Parvati with him so that she could be at his service. Lord Shiva refused, fearing her presence might cause hindrance in the path of his penance. Himavat became concerned about his daughter's future (however, he was wise enough to know when to stop pushing, especially with Lord Shiva The Destroyer...). Goddess Parvati decided to intervene and said the following:

"I am 'Prakriti[lxv]' (Nature) and you are the 'Purusha[lxvi]' (Almighty). You exist in the Sagun[lxvii] (physical god) form because of me. In my absence, you will find it impossible even to exist."

Lord Shiva was impressed by her knowledge and he allowed her to be present while he was in meditation. Goddess Parvati would arrive each day at Lord Shiva's ashram (area for conducting religious ceremonies) and on occasion her companions would accompany her. She engaged herself in the worship of Lord Shiva with supreme devotion; however, Lord Shiva continued his penance. As set out in the Introduction chapter to this book, Kamadeva, the God of Love intervened at the behest of the deities as the son of Lord Shiva and Goddess Parvati was destined to defeat the Demon Tarakasura.

Kamadeva shot Lord Shiva with his celestial arrow of desire and Lord Shiva at once fell in love with the beautiful Goddess. However, Lord Shiva turned Kamadeva into ash with his third eye after realizing that the God of Love had been responsible for disturbing him. As a result of this, Goddess Parvati became afraid and ran home but at the same time she was unable to bear the sorrow of her separation from Lord Shiva who she loved above everything. Goddess Parvati decided to commence her own penance which became more severe day by day. She undertook austerities for three thousand years by chanting the five-syllable mantra of *Om Nama Shivay*.

The deities all flocked to witness this tremendous sacrifice of Goddess Parvati surrounded by fires during the summer heat. When it was monsoon season, she undertook her penance without any shelter, and during the cold winter months she immersed herself in icy deep water up to her neck. Goddess Parvati's power created such heat in the atmosphere that the whole world started to burn. The deities approached Lord Brahma and told him about the effects of Goddess Parvati's devastating penance that was now impacting the three worlds[lxviii]. Lord Brahma accompanied by Lord Vishnu went to talk to Lord Shiva and they described the impact of Goddess Parvati's severe austerities and they set out the carnage being wreaked by the Demon Tarakasura (see chapter A3 of this book for his defeat at the hands of Lord Kartikeya).

PART A: BRAHMACHARYA – Tales of Lord Shiva

Lord Shiva summoned the Saptarishis[lxix] (seven sages) and instructed them to test Goddess Parvati's love for him. They went to Goddess Parvati and attempted to deter her from her love for Lord Shiva, but she was firm in her resolve. On hearing about the failure of the seven sages, Lord Shiva decided to visit Goddess Parvati in the guise of a brahmin (sage), and he asked her why she was engaged in such devoted prayer. Goddess Parvati told him that she wanted to have Lord Shiva as her husband due to her unending love and admiration for him. The brahmin laughed out loud and began to curse and ridicule Lord Shiva to see how the Goddess would react. He taunted the maiden about the rough and unattractive appearance of this deity.

However, Goddess Parvati admonished the brahmin that he was wrong to say that Lord Shiva did not possess any wealth or clothes on his body arguing that his knowledge was his wealth, and his powers were his clothes. She stated that there was no greater sin than condemning him. At that moment, Lord Shiva revealed his identity; he held the hand of the Goddess who had proven her love and he boomed:

"You have been my wife since time immemorial."

Goddess Parvati's heart was filled with extreme joy and she requested for him to approach her father Himavat with their marriage proposal. Lord Shiva agreed and on returning to Mount Kailash he relayed the good news to his Ganas and the deities who all rejoiced and awaited eagerly for the day Lord Shiva would be married. Himavat went to bathe in the River Ganges and meanwhile Lord Shiva arrived in his appearance of Nataraja and started to dance in front of Goddess Parvati's mother Maina. Lord Shiva was happy and danced with much vigour. Maina was pleased by this dance and wanted to present jewels to the dancer in appreciation, but Lord Shiva refused to take them. He expressed his desire to marry Goddess Parvati; however, this unannounced proposal from an unknown dancer angered Maina.

Himavat arrived and he became angry too and ordered his attendants to drive away Nataraja. Nataraja demanded once again that Goddess Parvati be made as his consort, but Himavat in his ignorance again refused to permit this. Nataraja then left but Himavat had a feeling that perhaps it was Lord Shiva himself who had arrived in the appearance of Nataraja. He realized what a grave mistake had been committed and commenced his own penance and prostrations in the name of Lord Shiva. Lord Shiva was pleased (given his last experience with a father in law…), and the marriage was arranged to the rejoicing of the universe. Lord Shiva invited all the Ganas, deities, sages, and other celestial beings to the marriage ceremony. There is a reference in The Ramayana Epic to this wedding of momentous celebration held at Mount Kailas.

Author's note: The stories above demonstrate the importance of love and devotion to one person above all others. Lord Shiva and Goddess Parvati are destined to be together for eternity. There are occasions when their fathers in-law create friction through their actions, and this highlights the importance of respect for family but also knowing whether to challenge unhealthy behaviour or simply to not react to it. Daksha himself offers a cautionary tale about not ridiculing others. Readers will recall from the Introduction chapter that Lord Shiva supported Daksha's wishes in the incident with Chandra (The Moon); however, Daksha crossed a line with his disrespectful actions and was no longer subject to the respect or protection of the deities, even his own father Lord Brahma.

Goddess Sati teaches us the importance of communication and listening to each other. Lord Shiva advised that attendance at Daksha's celebration would not be a good idea but was unable to get this point across. There will be occasions when one feels snubbed by others and may all have the wisdom to ignore this if it does happen. Goddess Parvati teaches us a strong lesson about keeping true to what one believes even though others may try to ridicule and change one's mind. Himavat teaches us the importance of admitting to being wrong and doing something about this in good time. The adventures of Lord Shiva, Goddess Parvati their formidable offspring continue in the next chapter.

Figure 9: Lord Shiva and Goddess Parvati

Lord Shiva and Goddess Parvati are a love story across time and space that should inspire any couple. These Deities have had their disagreements, but they come together for the greater good of the universe. They make sacrifices for each other, protect each other, and rely upon each other. Throughout their incarnations and different forms, they are never able to endure separation from each other and reside in eternal happiness together on Mount Kailas. One folklore legend sets out an incident in which Lord Shiva became angry when Goddess Parvati yawned during one of his regalements. He cursed her to be banished and born on earth and she was born as the daughter of a noble fisherman. However, Lord Shiva regretted his anger the moment Goddess Parvati disappeared. The loyal Nandi took the form of a great shark to aid him, in doing so the people of the fishing village prayed to Lord Shiva who appeared as a fisherman and subdued the shark reuniting him with his great love.

Chapter A3 – The Divine Progeny of Lord Shiva

This chapter sets out the enthralling exploits of Lord Shiva and Goddess Parvati's sons: Lord Ganesha and Lord Kartikeya. The story of their lesser-known daughter, Goddess Ashokasundari, is also included. The main source for these stories is the Shiva Purana and Lord Kartikeya features in chapters from both Hindu Epics of The Ramayana and The Mahabharata. Lord Ganesha and Lord Kartikeya are worshiped by hundreds of millions of devotees as the "Remover of Obstacles" and "The God of War", respectively.

Lord Ganesha

Lord Shiva and Goddess Parvati lived a blissful life together on Mount Kailas for eons. Once while the Goddess was going to take her bath, she instructed Nandi, Gana of Lord Shiva, to stand guard at the entrance and not to allow anybody to enter without her permission. Lord Shiva arrived home and Nandi explained the situation to him (perhaps this was a half-hearted attempt as Nandi did not wish to enrage Lord Shiva...). Lord Shiva laughed and entered. Goddess Parvati was not impressed with Nandi's inability to carry out her instructions. She knew that her husband's Ganas were loyal to him alone (and afraid of him...) and so she decided to make an idol by gathering paste from her own body. She brought this idol of a strong young man to life and she asked him to stand guard and not permit anybody into her boudoir without her permission. She armed him with a single staff for his protection.

Lord Shiva arrived once again and when he tried to enter, the boy, Ganesha refused to let him pass. Lord Shiva was amused by this impudent youth and he ignored him. As Lord Shiva walked forward, Lord Ganesha hit him with his stick. Lord Shiva became annoyed with the youth and he ordered his Ganas to kill him. The

PART A: BRAHMACHARYA – Tales of Lord Shiva

Ganas attacked with ferocity; however, they were no match for the warrior, and they were defeated with ease. The defeated soldiers approached their Lord and narrated these events. Lord Brahma, Lord Vishnu and some of the other deities arrived there at the same moment due to the thunderous barrage that had taken place on Mount Kailas. Lord Brahma approached Lord Ganesha to talk to him, but he was attacked by him. Brahmaji[lxx] came back regaling this to Lord Shiva who decided it was time for him to deal with this matter himself. Lord Shiva fought a fierce battle with Goddess Parvati's creation. There are few who can even attempt to equal the mighty God of Destruction in combat, but Lord Ganesha began to dominate the fight. Therefore, Lord Shiva was forced to deploy his trident to sever the head of the young warrior.

Goddess Parvati was furious at the death of her son. Her rage resulted in the manifestation of innumerable Goddesses, who started to wreak havoc on the deities and Ganas. All were terrified, and they sought the refuge of Goddess Parvati expressing their remorse at the way they had behaved. They eulogized her, prostrated themselves at her feet, and requested to be pardoned for their actions. Goddess Parvati told them that they could be saved only when Lord Ganesha becomes alive once again and is worshipped by all with equal status as the Hindu Trinity.

Lord Shiva instructed the deities to travel north and bring him the head of the first creature they encountered. They came upon a single tusked elephant and by the blessings of Lord Shiva, Lord Ganesha was brought to life with the head of this animal. All worshipped Lord Ganesha with devotion and to this day he remains the first deity prayed to when Hindus are undertaking a new venture as he is the Remover of Obstacles. Lord Ganesha is referred to by many as Ganapati (Lord of the Ganas) and his many interactions with the other deities in the Puranic tales show him to be a wise counsellor and worthy of this illustrious title. Lord Ganesha is one of the most worshipped of all of the Hindu gods across the Indian Sub-Continent. In folklore, Lord Ganesha is said to have been the scribe of The Ramayana Epic, having removed one of his tusks to use as a writing implement to document this Hindu Epic.

Lord Kartikeya

Lord Kartikeya, Lord of War, was destined to be born as the son of Lord Shiva and Goddess Parvati so that he could vanquish the powerful Demon Tarakasura, terror of the gods. Tarakasura was protected by a boon and it was foretold that only Lord Kartikeya could kill him. However, at the time of Tarakasura's rise, Lord Shiva was living as a yogi and unmarried. The Padma Purana details Tarakasura's deep devotion and penance in his quest for strength. He commanded his demon subjects to act in the same manner and in doing so he won the benediction of Lord Brahma who blessed him with a boon that he could only be killed by someone he was not afraid of. The arrogant Tarakasura accepted this limitation to his request for immortality; his reasoning was that anyone he was not afraid of could not possess the power to kill him.

Lord Brahma returned to the heavens and at once asked the armies to ready themselves (Lord Brahma knew what was coming next, for one does not ask for a boon of immortality to then retire to a life of peace in the mountains...). The demon army chariots were yoked with eagles, tigers, and lions. The army of gods was in four divisions: (i) Elephants, (ii) Chariots, (ii) Cavalry, and (iv) Infantry. Yama, Lord of Death was made the general of this invincible army. Indra, King of Gods; Vayu, Lord of the Air; Agni, God of Fire all led divisions as did the Sun and Moon Gods. However, Tarakasura jumped down from his chariot like a mountain and a thunderbolt combined (a big thunderbolt...). He attacked tens of millions of deities and demi-gods with his bare hands and those who were not killed fled in all directions.

PART A: BRAHMACHARYA – Tales of Lord Shiva

At the height of Tarakasura's powers, Lord Shiva duly produced six celestial sparks of his essence, and these were contained by Lord Agni and carried by the River Goddess Ganga to be established amidst the river reeds. On the sixth day of the lunar month of Margashirsha[lxxi], a beautiful child manifested from Lord Shiva's essence. The birth of this child made the heavens rejoice including Lord Shiva and Goddess Parvati. He was named Kartikeya. The great sage Vishwamitra[lxxii] arrived at the spot where the child had appeared. On the repeated insistence of the child, the sage performed his purification rites and named him Kartikeya.

The divine child blessed Vishwamitra and bestowed supreme knowledge to him. Six goddesses arrived and they all tried to feed the small child out of affection. They started to quarrel over the infant who then appeared with six heads enabling all of them to nurse him. They brought him up with love and care and the Fire God, Agni arrived also and bestowed a divine weapon upon him. Lord Kartikeya went to Mount Kroncha[lxxiii] and tested his weapon on this stone fortress. The mountain could not bear the force of the impact and started to crumble. A multitude of demons living in the area came to kill the child for his affront to their home, but he dispensed with them using his divine weapons.

When Lord Indra, King of the Gods, heard about the bravery of this boy, he arrived along with the other deities to test him on the battlefield (Lord Indra must have been unaware of his parentage...). Lord Indra assaulted the boy three times with his renowned Vajra[lxxiv] weapon, indestructible as a diamond and as irresistible as one thousand thunderbolts. The weapon struck him once on the right side of his body, once on the left side of his body and once on his chest. This resulted in three powerful entities being created. Lord Kartikeya accompanied by these three new allies attacked Lord Indra and his armies who were satisfied with the worth of the child in battle and backed down.

Lord Shiva then ordered his Ganas to bring Lord Kartikeya to him. This was most likely a polite offer to join him as opposed to a show of force... Lord Kartikeya happily took permission from his six mothers and proceeded to meet Lord Shiva and Goddess Parvati. He then climbed into a beautiful chariot which had been sent by Goddess Parvati and proceeded towards Mount Kailash. All the deities, including his father Lord Shiva, were awaiting his arrival. When Lord Kartikeya reached them, he was provided with a royal reception. The whole atmosphere was filled with joy and celebration. Each of the deities presented him with a gift of celestial weapons and Lord Shiva coronated him with honours.

The deities were encouraged by the presence of Lord Kartikeya who would accompany them into battle. The army of the gods was assembled at the seashore and awaited the Demon Tarakasura who arrived with his huge force. The epic encounter began and Tarakasura appeared to be unstoppable. Lord Indra fell down unconscious with other deities and even the fearsome Virabhadra, slayer of Daksha, fell unconscious. Lord Vishnu engaged the Demon to protect the other deities while Lord Brahma explained to Lord Kartikeya that it was his destiny to kill Tarakasura. Lord Kartikeya came forward to fight with Tarakasura and the Demon and his legions ridiculed the deities for trying to shield behind a small child. Tarakasura thundered the following (presumably to clear what little conscience he had...):

> *"When this small boy is killed by me, the responsibility will lie upon you who cower behind him."*

However, whilst Tarakasura was bellowing, Lord Kartikeya commenced a fierce assault. Both received injuries from the other, but Lord Kartikeya was patient and he waited for the opportune moment when Tarakasura's chest was exposed. He unleashed the celestial weapon granted to him by Agni, God of Fire and this blow was fatal to Tarakasura who fell dead.

Lord Kartikeya's feat was hailed by all the deities. After killing the Demon, Lord Kartikeya went to his mother Goddess Parvati, who sat the young boy on her lap with affection. He was praised by all the deities and is worshipped to this day in all parts of the Indian Sub-Continent.

Goddess Ashokasundari

The Padma Purana, one of the eighteen main puranas, sets out a vivid account of the Goddess Ashokasundari who is the daughter of Lord Shiva and Goddess Parvati. The divine couple journey to a grove that is "best among groves" mounted on Nandi and accompanied by tens of millions of followers. This celestial forest is rich with trees full of flowers, fruits, and fragrance. The land is adorned with desire-yielding trees with auspicious wells and hosts of celestial nymphs. Thus, Lord Shiva and Goddess Parvati arrived at the abode of the meritorious, endowed with the quality of tranquility.

Lord Shiva directed the beautiful Goddess to a tree of trees where the fruits are described as akin to masses of lustre of the sun. He explained that the fruits of this tree give to the deserving gods that which they resolve. The Goddess Parvati, on hearing this wonderful news and with the full consent of her husband mentally conceived a virtuous and beautiful child; so lovely that she could delude the universe itself with her charm. Her hair was bright in splendour, curly and long and she was adorned with pearls and fashioned with the characteristics of a lotus flower. She shone as the moon, a mass of cool rays and a canopy of light; her face, always joyous, was celebrated in the universe. She stepped forward and blessed her parents asking:

> "Oh Lord, O Mother, tell me the reason for which I was produced?"

Goddess Parvati explained that she was her daughter, blessed with good fortune and that she would be known as

Ashokasundari. The Padma Purana sets out the daughter of Lord Shiva's brush with the Demon Hunda who took one look at her divine form and then began to brag about his power and exploits, propositioning Ashokasundari to be his wife. He did not listen to her polite refusal as she was betrothed to another and attempted to deceive her by posing as a young maiden to win her trust. Hunda, still in disguise, managed to trick the young Goddess into accompanying him to his palace. But when she saw his true form, she cursed him that he would die for his actions. Ashokasundari then performed penance in the mountains and whilst Hunda tried many things to avoid his death at the hands of fate, he could not avoid his destiny that had been sealed by his actions that were contrary to the teachings of morality.

The Race Around the Earth

The Shiva Purana sets out a famous tale about Lord Ganesha and Lord Kartikeya and a competition between these two immortal heroes. The sons of Lord Shiva grew up to become handsome youths and in due course their parents started to think about their marriage. The young men quarreled in sibling rivalry as to which of them should get married first. Their parents devised a plan to address the problem. Whoever returns first after circumambulating the earth will be married first.

Lord Kartikeya and Lord Ganesha agreed and Lord Kartikeya, athletically leaped onto his chariot and proceeded on his journey around the earth. With no sign of Lord Ganesha, he was confident of his victory. However, Lord Ganesha decided to apply his intelligence to the situation (his own life was a reminder of the folly of using only strength and force). He requested for his parents to sit at a place together and then he circumambulated them several times. One would be forgiven for thinking that the Lord Ganesha, Remover of Obstacles, had misunderstood the rules of engagement... However, Lord Ganesha said to his parents:

PART A: BRAHMACHARYA – Tales of Lord Shiva

"According to the Vedas, circumambulating one's parents gives virtues equivalent to that of circumambulating the whole earth. So now I must be married first."

His parents were impressed by his intelligence, knowledge of the Vedas, and flawless logic. They decided that he would be married, and this was arranged. While Lord Kartikeya was returning after driving his chariot around the earth, he was told about the marriage of his brother and he became sad at the thought of being cheated by his parents. When the Lord of War reached Mount Kailash after his journey, he made salutations to Lord Shiva and Goddess Parvati and without uttering a word he went to Mount Kroncha[lxxv] to undertake penance. Goddess Parvati became disconsolate and went to see her valiant son accompanied by Lord Shiva. When Lord Kartikeya saw them coming he moved to another place, but they followed him and ultimately reconciled with him. To this day, having a darshan[lxxvi] ceremony in honour of Lord Kartikeya on the full moon day of Kartik[lxxvii] is considered to bestow immense luck and destroy all sins.

Author's note: The children of Lord Shiva teach us many lessons. Lord Ganesha has supreme devotion to his mother and in Hindu tradition the mother is often kept above the father in worship and prayers. Goddess Parvati demonstrates unparalleled protection over her children throughout these stories; even though they may be hardened in battle they rely upon her. She avenges Lord Ganesha and ensures he is restored to glory and she also displays sympathy for Lord Kartikeya when he feels let down by his parents. These are important traits that all parents should emulate. The story of Lord Ganesha teaches us the importance of communication and respect for each other's wishes, even if one may not agree with them.

There is a sound demonstration for the folly of anger and fighting. There is a lesson in forgiveness at the end of the account by all parties when Lord Ganesha is established as a deity. The chronicle of Goddess Ashokasundari is an important reminder of the correct way to approach a potential suitor in life – not with boasting but with real emotion and honesty. It is important to accept rejection with class and move on unlike the Demon Hunda who is condemned by his own actions. Both Lord Ganesha and Lord Kartikeya teach us the dangers of underestimating anyone just because they are younger in age and Lord Kartikeya is both fearless and controlled in his emotions which are characteristics all should aspire to.

With respect to the competition between the brothers there are two important lessons. The first is thinking (including the abstract thinking of Lord Ganesha) and planning before rushing headlong into a task (even a race). The second is the noble acceptance of judgment by Lord Kartikeya who is temperate throughout the above stories. Although he is saddened by the events, he accepts the wisdom of his parents and removes himself from the situation with class and restraint. He does not react with rage or retribution as most would do in the same circumstance. May all find the strength to keep calm when faced with decisions that are deemed are unfair.

PART A: BRAHMACHARYA – Tales of Lord Shiva

Figure 10: Lord Shiva and Family

Lord Ganesha (The Remover of Obstacles) is shown circumambulating his divine parents Lord Shiva and Goddess Parvati with Lord Kartikeya (The God of War) returning from his journey around the earth on a celestial peacock. Despite their youth, these are two revered heroes from Hindu Scripture.

Chapter A4 – Lord Shiva fights Arjuna

Chapter B1 of this book looks at the appearances of Lord Shiva in the Hindu Epic of The Mahabharata; however, the episode when Lord Shiva meets the mighty Arjuna in combat is worthy of separate attention as a tale of Lord Shiva. The source of these events is the Shiva Purana and The Mahabharata. Arjuna is one of the five warrior sons of King Pandu. Termed the Pandavas, they are of high moral stature but destined to fight in a war of astronomical proportions against their own cousins. They are demi-gods and Arjuna's divine father is Indra, King of Gods. Arjuna is one of the most honourable heroes from Hindu scripture.

The Bhagavad Gita (or Song of God) involves Lord Vishnu in the form of Lord Krishna reciting philosophical and religious poetry about love, honour, and duty to the young hero on the eve of the war. Arjuna is reticent to fight against his kin and be the bringer of death to many warriors. However, in the Bhagavad Gita, Lord Krishna speaks to Arjuna and all of mankind about the purpose of one's existence on this earth. The Shiva Purana and The Mahabharata set out the pivotal meeting between Arjuna and Lord Shiva long before the onset of the war.

After losing their whole kingdom to their Kaurava[lxxviii] cousins and their evil uncle Shakuni[lxxix] in a rigged game of dice (yes, they did…), the five Pandava brothers embarked on a journey to the forest to live a simple life away from the comforts and riches they had frittered away. However, the Kauravas were not content with the fact that they had swindled the kingdom from them, and they sought to torment the Pandavas further (the Kauravas were a relentless bunch…). They sent a sage with thousands of disciples to visit the Pandavas who demanded food from them.

The brothers were concerned as they had minimal food and would not be able to satiate the hunger of thousands. Lord Krishna came to their rescue and saved them from being disgraced; however, he urged them to pray to Lord Shiva. The Pandavas neglected that advice and as a result their sufferings increased in magnitude.

However, one day a great sage arrived at the woodland retreat of the Pandavas, and he received a welcome reception (no doubt this sage did not bring thousands of disciples to feed like the previous sage...). He instructed the brothers on a sacred method of Parthiva[lxxx] worship involving wearing rudraksha beads and with ash on the forehead. Armed with this divine instruction, Arjuna then journeyed to Mount Indrakeel[lxxxi] to offer devotion to his father Lord Indra. Bearing only his bow, Arjuna traveled far over the mountains and began his austerities.

The penance of this mighty hero generated so much heat that all the living creatures of the three worlds were unable to bear its scorching effect. Lord Indra decided to intervene, and he went to Arjuna in the guise of a sage and asked about the purpose for which he was undertaking such severe penance. Arjuna told him that he required celestial weapons to defeat his cousins who had usurped his Kingdom. Lord Indra revealed his true form but conceded to Arjuna that it was not within his capacity to help him achieve victory over the Kauravas, because of Asvatthama[lxxxii] who had been created with Lord Shiva's blessing and who was to fight on the side of the Kauravas.

Lord Indra advised his son to direct his penance to Lord Shiva so that his wishes could be fulfilled. Lord Indra stated that he would help Arjuna with the gift of weapons only after Arjuna has met Lord Shiva. Arjuna duly directed his penance towards Lord Shiva. He stood on one leg and concentrated his gaze upon the blazing sun (do not try this at home...). The deities were impressed by Arjuna's intense penance and they went to Lord Shiva and requested for him to bless Arjuna. Lord Shiva accepted their request. At the same time, the Kauravas had dispatched the Demon Mooka disguised as a wild boar to kill Arjuna (maybe a tiger, or an army of tigers would have been a more fearsome choice for Mooka in hindsight...).

Arjuna was engrossed in his meditation when his concentration was disrupted by a loud noise. He opened his eyes and saw the despicable wild boar being chased by a tribe of people indigenous to the Himalayas (the Kirats[lxxxiii]). These were the Ganas of Lord Shiva in disguise led by Lord Shiva also in disguise as a Kirat bowman. Both Arjuna and the bowman struck the boar with their respective arrows at the same time. As a result, the Demon Mooka, in the form of the boar, was killed. Lord Shiva dispatched his entourage to bring back his arrow. Similarly, Arjuna approached the dead boar to bring back his arrow. Arjuna found his arrow lying on the ground and he picked it up in his hand.

Lord Shiva's followers arrived, and they taunted Arjuna as to why he had shot a dead boar already killed by their master. They asked him to give them the arrow in his hand believing it to belong to their Lord. However, Arjuna refused to part with his arrow. Arjuna became enraged and threatened to kill the Kirat bowman (who was none other than Lord Shiva).

The warriors commenced raining arrows upon each other and mighty Arjuna was astonished that he was unable to dispense with this solitary opponent. When his supply of arrows was depleted, he used his bow as a sword and attacked the Kirat in vain. Arjuna began to throw colossal boulders and he uprooted trees to use as a club but the Kirat was able to counter these assaults with ease. Finally, Lord Shiva engaged Arjuna in hand-to-hand combat and after a rigorous competition between the two of them he overcame Arjuna and subdued him. However, impressed with Arjuna's valour, strength and skill, Lord Shiva revealed his real identity to the Pandava who was ashamed that he had fought with him.

Arjuna propitiated Lord Shiva who praised him and granted him the terrible Pasupatastra[lxxxiv] weapon. Lord Shiva instructed the young warrior in the use of the weapon and counseled him against the dangers of destroying the entire world if not applied correctly (that is a lot of pressure to get it right...). The Puranas confirm that this weapon is never to be used against lesser enemies or by lesser warriors. Arjuna, having faced Lord Shiva in accordance with the instructions of Indra, King of Gods was then able to journey to meet his divine father again and be granted the additional celestial weapons that would assist him in his victory in The Mahabharata war.

Author's note: The opening of this anecdote has a clear message about the dangers of gambling and the importance of setting limits. The Pandavas are wrong to neglect the advice of their counselor Lord Krishna when he tells them to pray to Lord Shiva. The encounter between Lord Shiva and Arjuna demonstrates the danger of letting ego and rage control one's actions when there is a dispute about who the arrow belongs to and who killed the wild boar. Better to ignore the taunting and relinquish the arrow. Aside from the moral lessons, the sheer act of engaging Lord Shiva in combat brings legitimacy to Arjuna's role as the protagonist in The Mahabharata.

Lord Shiva is the means to attest to Arjuna's greatness (the next chapter follows a similar arc with Rama in The Ramayana being tested by Lord Shiva's bow). Arjuna is a mighty warrior respected by all before the encounter but that fact that he fought so valiantly against Lord Shiva puts him beyond the other warring characters in the saga. The Pasupatastra weapon can destroy creation itself and vanquish all beings. It is the most powerful weapon mentioned in Hindu scripture and it is symbolic that Lord Shiva entrusted it to Arjuna by recognizing his virtue.

The Lord Shiva Narrative

This is an important lesson about diligence and precision when one is undertaking any task and ensuring that one is suitably trained and prepared beforehand. Finally, Arjuna is seen to be contrite and deferential as soon as he learns the truth about the Kirat bowman being Lord Shiva, and this is another important lesson to admit when one is wrong no matter what the circumstance. Whilst he was wrong to give into his anger, Arjuna sets a fine moral example of how one should conduct one's life.

PART A: BRAHMACHARYA – Tales of Lord Shiva

Figure 11: Arjuna in penance to Lord Shiva

Arjuna performs severe austerities standing on one leg and looking into the blazing sun. Lord Shiva is pictured offering his blessings as celestial beings bear witness to the great penance. Lord Shiva bestowed the terrible Pasupatastra weapon upon Arjuna demonstrating the respect afforded to this great warrior.

Chapter A5 – The Bow of Lord Shiva

One of the most memorable episodes from The Ramayana is when the hero Rama must string the Bow of Lord Shiva to win the hand of Princess Sita. Before Rama makes his attempt, he is informed that many lionhearted princes and warriors have tried, and no-one has had the strength to even lift the divine weapon up let alone string the bow. The story is set out here and the source is Valmiki's[lxxxv] Ramayana. Even though Lord Shiva is absent in person, he casts a monumental shadow over the events in the form of the Great Bow of Rudra (Lord Shiva The Destroyer).

Rama, avatar of Lord Vishnu, was a virtuous and unique man endowed with divine qualities. He was destined to fight and win a monumental victory over Ravana, the Demon King of Lanka[lxxxvi]. Ravana was protected by powerful boons from Lord Brahma and Lord Shiva that ensured he could not be killed by god or by demon. Rama is the embodiment of dharma (moral duty) in this Hindu Epic whilst Ravana is his adharmic opposite driven by ego, lust, arrogance, and obstinacy. Both Rama and Ravana have formidable skill and strength on the battlefield and the stage is set for an epic encounter when Ravana kidnaps Sita and takes her away to his palace in Lanka. Long before these events unfold, there is an important incident where Rama proves that he is worthy to marry the beautiful and virtuous Sita. Sita can be described with this passage from The Ramayana:

> "The beauty of the Goddess Earth mortal eyes cannot see in its fullness, but we get glimpses of it as we gaze with grateful hearts on the emerald green or golden ripeness of sprint-tide or autumn fields, or with awe and adoration on the glories of mountain and valley, rivers and ocean. This loveliness was Sita in its entirety."

PART A: BRAHMACHARYA – Tales of Lord Shiva

When Sita reaches the age of marriage, her father King Janaka was sad that he would have to part with her. He meditated on the important decision of who would be worthy of his virtuous daughter of divine beauty. Many princes and warriors came to the palace but none of them were good enough for King Janaka (this may sound familiar to some readers...).

The King came to a decision that would eradicate the lesser suitors. Long ago, pleased with a yaga (sacrifice) that King Janaka had performed, Varuna, God of the Sky presented the King with the Bow of Lord Shiva and two quivers (it is not clear how Varuna obtained Lord Shiva's bow, but the Lord of Destruction's weapon of choice is the trident in any event[lxxxvii]...). This was no ordinary celestial bow. Two great bows of equal quality were created for Lord Vishnu and Lord Shiva for these deities to battle demons who challenged the might of the gods. The stories in Part A of this book include examples of these legendary battles.

This was one of the two ancient heavenly bows which no ordinary man could even move, and no god or demon could grip, string, or attempt to shoot other than Lord Vishnu or Lord Shiva. King Janaka issued a proclamation that Sita would marry the prince who could lift, bend, and string the bow of Lord Shiva. The implication is that none, but Lord Shiva or Lord Vishnu would be suitable, or at least a man who possessed the characteristics of these gods. Many would be suitors journeyed from faraway lands to attempt this feat, yet none could fulfil the condition.

Then Rama arrived on the scene. He was camped out near to King Janaka's palace, on the banks of the River Ganges. He bathed in the sacred waters of the river and made "lustrations to his forbears" (i.e., he prayed to his parents...). The next day Rama and his heroic brother Lakshmana both entered the palace of King Janaka. The King was extremely impressed with these god-like youths who stood before him in his palace. King Janaka, who was wise enough to see what was transpiring, decided to help the fates to run their course. He issued a command to his many trusted generals to bring forth the bow and he added that if the young prince could string the bow then he would win Sita's hand in marriage. He continued that he would be happy if the prince succeeded where so many others had failed (King Janaka could teach Daksha a few things about being a father-in-law with reference to the anecdote of Goddess Sati at chapter A2 of this book...).

The Great Bow of Lord Shiva was stored in an iron box and was dragged out on an eight wheeled chariot pulled by five thousand tall men of illimitable energy. However, these men still struggled to drag the chariot and great bow of Lord Shiva. King Janaka stated that none in all the assemblages of gods, demi-gods, or demons was capable of taking aim with the bow. They had been unable to take a proper grip, twitch the bowstring, string the bow, otherwise move or brace it. Rama, with the confidence of young adulthood and secure in his devotion to the gods, took his permission from King Janaka and then he stepped forward to the iron box and threw it open with a resounding boom.

Rumour had spread of the divine warrior's arrival at the palace and a crowd of spectators had made their way into the court to see the young prince. Rama reached into the iron box and he lifted the bow effortlessly as if it were a garland of flowers. Then, pinning one end of it between his toe and the ground, he bent the bow back to string it. However, he drew the bow with such irresistible force that the mighty bow snapped in the middle with a crash like a one hundred claps of thunder. The earth shook with tremors as if a great mountain had exploded. A shower of lotuses rained down from the heavens upon the gallant hero and many of the onlookers swooned at witnessing these events.

King Janaka remained firm as all around him were shaking with the impact of the explosion. This great King was true to his word and did not delay in making the wedding arrangements for Rama and his daughter Sita. The Kingdom rejoiced at the auspicious events and at the appointed day and hour of their marriage, King Janaka said the following which to this day features in many wedding ceremonies in the Indian Sub-continent:

> *"Here is my daughter, Sita, who will ever tread with you the path of dharma. Take her hand in yours. Blessed and devoted, she will ever walk with you."*

Author's note: In the same way that Arjuna's fame was strengthened by his encounter with Lord Shiva in the previous chapter, so was Rama's fame strengthened by his unintentional destruction of Lord Shiva's bow when he was attempting to string it. This is how Rama shows himself to be beyond the prowess of ordinary men in the Hindu Epic of The Ramayana. Rama only needed to lift the bow to have demonstrated his superiority over others; however, he went further in bending the bow and then breaking it.

Rama teaches us to have temperance, respect, and humility despite the power one may possess. Rama also displays strength of mind and confidence in himself which are traits that all can possess and should aspire to. King Janaka is true to his word in arranging the marriage to his beloved daughter Sita once his impossible conditions had been met by Rama. King Janaka is a noble individual, mentioned in the Brihadaranyaka Upanishad, who offers his respect to anyone deserved of that respect, no matter what their age or background. He is both wise and fair; a sound example for any father or prospective father-in-law in how to treat others and how to conduct oneself according to the principles of kama (love), dharma (moral duty) and artha (purpose). The city of Janakpur in Nepal is named after him. It is fitting that the words of this legendary King can be heard spoken at Hindu wedding ceremonies around the world instructing couples to walk together in the path of dharma.

The Lord Shiva Narrative

Figure 12: Rama Breaks the Bow of Lord Shiva

Rama, breaker of the Great Bow of Lord Shiva, is pictured here in a temple carving with his brother Laxmana (far right) as King Janaka observes from his throne on the left. The episode from The Ramayana in which the hero lifts, strings, and breaks the Great Bow of Rudra (Lord Shiva) is a critical point in the story. The strength and divinity of Rama are demonstrated to all in this incident and in doing so he also wins the hand of his great love Sita. The bow of Lord Shiva is the means for which a mortal can demonstrate their power; it is the supreme test which provides the hero with legitimacy as the greatest warrior on earth. No other mortal could even lift the bow and no other mortal can rival Rama. Despite being absent from the story, Lord Shiva's presence is felt in the form of this great weapon which has been used in battle on many occasions by The Lord of Destruction. The Ramayana, and Lord Shiva's appearances in this Hindu Epic are explored further in chapter B2 of this book.

PART A: BRAHMACHARYA – Tales of Lord Shiva

Chapter A6 – Lord Shiva imprisons Ravana

There are many stories in folklore and temple carvings that set out the interactions between Lord Shiva and Ravana, Rama's antagonist in The Ramayana. Ravana is believed to have been an ardent devotee of Lord Shiva. There are minor mentions of these interactions in The Ramayana and the Puranas which may serve as the source for these tales which are set out below.

Ravana is referred to in Valmiki's Ramayana as the "Conqueror of Kailas" when his sister is boasting to Rama about the exploits of her family. However, this is indeed a boast and the converse is shown to be true with Ravana becoming imprisoned by the mountain. There are many temple idols in India that picture Ravana lifting Mount Kailas as Lord Shiva sits atop with indifference. The Ramayana makes mention of an encounter between Ravana and Nandi, Lord Shiva's faithful Gana. Ravana is attempting to seek out Lord Shiva and he is stopped by Nandi who explains that Lord Shiva is incapable of being approached as he is in severe meditation.

On hearing this, Ravana, Lord of the Demons became irate and came to the base of Mount Kailas. Nandi stopped him and Ravana derided Nandi stating that he has a monkey like face. Ravana roars with laughter (at his own joke...and besides, Nandi has the face of a bull not a monkey) but Nandi is calm, and he places a curse on Ravana that is as ironic as it is divine: The Varanas (Hanuman's[lxxxviii] race of anthropoids) will ensure the destruction of Ravana's race and crush his high pride. This fed Ravana's fury even more and he seized the mountain with his arms and lifted it up. The mountain trembled and shook the attendants of the deity in residence (a.k.a. Lord Shiva). Lord Shiva put out his divine toe and pressed lightly upon the mountain whereupon Ravana's mighty arms of stone gave way. He let out a shout of pain that shook the world, the sea, and the mountains.

Ravana then began many thousands of years of lamentations to Lord Shiva whilst trapped in his mountain prison. Lord Shiva eventually felt pity for the Demon King and released him bestowing upon him an effulgent sword.

There is a popular mantra with over one thousand verses named the Tandava Strotram that many devotes believe to have been composed by Ravana whilst he was imprisoned under Mount Kailas and offering adoration to Lord Shiva. The mantra refers to many of the aspects of Lord Shiva that have been referred to in the Introduction chapter and Part A to this book. Some of these are set out below:

> "With neck consecrated by the flow of water from his hair...glorified by the moving waves of the River Ganga..."
> "...On his neck, a snake hung like a garland..."
> "...The crescent moon as a jewel on his head...in the tangled strands of Shiva's hair..."
> "...Lord Shiva, who has three eyes, who offered the powerful God of Love to fire, the terrible surface of his forehead burns..."
> "...Companion of Parvati, daughter of the mountain King..."
> "...Whose neck is dark as midnight on a new moon night..."
> "...Who destroyed the Tripura, the Demon Andhaka, and who overwhelmed the God of Death, Yama..."

The above extracts cover many of the familiar characteristics of Lord Shiva and many of the triumphs in battle (the stories of the Tripura and Andhaka are covered in chapters A8 and A10 below). In addition to the blessings granted by Lord Shiva, Lord Brahma had already bestowed the boon upon Ravana that he could not be killed by god or demon; however, Rama (the avatar of Lord Vishnu) ensured that Ravana's treacherous life was ended at the hands of a man.

The Shiva Purana sets out an additional story in relation to the penance that Ravana performed in the name of Lord Shiva to receive a boon: After many years of penance from Ravana, Lord

PART A: BRAHMACHARYA – Tales of Lord Shiva

Shiva still did not appear, so the Lord of Demons took out a huge sword and began to offer his ten heads to Lord Shiva one by one. Ravana had sacrificed nine of his ten heads and was about to lop off the tenth when Lord Shiva finally appeared and blessed Ravana with unparalleled power and strength. Lord Shiva restored his ten heads once again. There are two lakes that exist in proximity to Mount Kailas to this day. One is sacred freshwater Lake Manasarovar (Lake of the Mind) and the other lake adjacent to it is the curious saltwater Lake Rakshatal (Demon Lake). Rakshatal is believed to be the location where Ravana performed penance in the name of Lord Shiva.

Author's note: In the above anecdotes, Ravana embodies many negative traits of adharma that all should avoid including ignorance, ego, arrogance, anger, lust, disrespect, and obstinacy. The interaction with Nandi, in which Ravana's disrespectful comments come back to haunt him in the form of the destruction of his city, teach us an important lesson about treating others the way one would wish to be treated ourselves. One may wonder why Lord Shiva blessed the Demon Ravana with strength despite all the above negative characteristics displayed and why Lord Brahma blessed him with the boon that he could not be killed by god or demon.

This is an example of how the Hindu Trinity often come together to restore balance between the three worlds as Lord Vishnu is born in human form as Rama to defeat Ravana and to set an example of how to live one's life according to ethical and moral principles. One strives to be like Rama, and one strives to distance oneself from the behaviour of Ravana. The Tandava Strotram contains an elegant summary of Lord Shiva's many characteristics that are covered in this book including Lord Shiva as Somnath (Lord of the Moon), Gangadhara (Lord of the River Ganges), Nataraja (King of the Dance - see chapter A7) and Pashupati (Lord of Animals).

One can picture Ravana trapped under the mountain and attempting to placate Lord Shiva by chanting many accolades and adulations. There is a vast amount of scripture within the Hindu Universe; however, the more one reads, the more the different aspects of Lord Shiva conform to a consistent narrative.

Figure 13: Lord Shiva Imprisons Ravana Under Mount Kailas

The ten-headed Demon King Ravana is pictured above lifting Mount Kailas with Lord Shiva and Goddess Parvati atop the mountain. This is a remarkable feat of strength demonstrating the power and resolve of this monstrous King. It is also a remarkable act of defiance. The other Deities and Ganas of Lord Shiva are depicted around the central characters. This scene is shortly before Ravana's imprisonment for thousands of years after his arms give way under the might of Lord Shiva's single toe pressing down on the mountain. Lord Shiva forgives Ravana for his insolence after many years of his lamentations from under the mountain and bestows a divine sword upon him plus invincible strength. Further to this, Ravana is protected by a boon from Lord Brahma also that he cannot be defeated by God or Demon and this sets the scene for the epic encounter with Rama, Avatar of Lord Vishnu in human form to put an end to the evil practices of the Demon King of Lanka. The above carving is from the impressive Ellora Caves in Maharashtra, India.

PART A: BRAHMACHARYA – Tales of Lord Shiva

Chapter A7 – Nataraja "King of the Dance"

The Shiva Purana sets out the popular recital of how Lord Shiva acquired the name Nataraja (King of the Dance). This depiction of Lord Shiva is a stark contrast to the demon slaying Lord of Destruction that are explored in the other stories in this book.

A group of sages were engaged in dark rituals (that old black magic...). They had convinced themselves that they could manipulate the three worlds and the deities with the use of spells and magic wands and so they spent many hours practicing their craft with dedication. They conducted anti-Vedic mantras that fed the power of this growing dark force. However, this began to have a negative impact on mankind and all the creatures of the earth. Lord Shiva observed these events and he decided that he must put an end to the suffering that was being caused by the sages. He left behind his trident of destruction and he took the form of Bikshadana, the mendicant.

However, despite his lack of wealth and worldly possessions, the appearance of Bikshadana was spectacular, beautiful, and soothing to all eyes. His divine appearance caused all creatures to follow him in a trance-like state and this included the wives of the sages... The sages were interrupted from their base incantations and they became concerned on seeing that their spouses had fallen under the positive spell of divinity exuded by Lord Shiva. They focused their magical powers to attack Lord Shiva and in doing so the creatures of the earth were freed from the negative effects. The dark magic had no impact on Lord Shiva who has mastery over his emotions. The evil wizards decided to intensify their attack and released dreadful serpents on him from all directions.

Lord Shiva picked them up and wore them as ornaments around his neck and hands. The sages increased the severity of their chanting even more and created a fierce demonic tiger with their magical powers. Lord Shiva tore the hide off the evil beast with ease and used it as his robe. The sages continued and materialized more demon animals from their sacrificial fires. The beasts fell upon Lord Shiva, but with effortlessness he pushed them back into the flames. The relentless sages then combined all their evil powers to give birth to the Demon Apasmara. He was the ultimate symbol of arrogance and ignorance (he was arrogant about his ignorance and was ignorant of his arrogance…).

However, Lord Shiva stepped on the Demon's back and then began an exquisite dance[lxxxix] of artistry the like of which had never been seen before and never shall be seen again. It was the dance of dances and has become known as Tandava, or the ecstatic cosmic dance. All of the three worlds stopped to watch the resplendence and the deities all rejoiced in this wondrous sight of the Lord of Destruction transforming into the King of the Dance. The realization dawned on the sages (finally…) that this lowly beggar who shone like the sun, defeated all their beasts, and who danced on their demonic creation was none other than Lord Shiva.

The divine vision of Lord Shiva dancing upon the back of the Demon Apasmara removed the arrogance and ignorance of the sages, drew in all their dark powers, and liberated the three worlds from potential destruction. The sages came to understand that their devotion to evil practices was ill-advised and they began Vedic austerities for the good of all creatures.

The Shiva Agamas also describe the different aspects of the Nataraja Tandava dance symbolized by the protruding limbs of Lord Shiva:

- Creation (shrishti), Lord Brahma.

PART A: BRAHMACHARYA – Tales of Lord Shiva

- Preservation (sthiti), Lord Vishnu.
- Destruction (samhara), Rudra.
- Illusion (maya[xc]), Maheshvara[xci].
- Liberation moksha), Sadashiva[xcii].

The Tandava is referred to as the cosmic dance that perpetrates the cycle of the universe through the above five aspects.

Author's note: The above story warns against the misuse of powers and knowledge for adharma. The episode created an enduring, compelling visual image of Lord Shiva triumphing through dance and not through warfare with his trident. Lord Shiva decided in this instance to not annihilate the transgressors but to distract them and demonstrate the folly of their actions by neutralizing with ease, ridiculing, and humiliating their greatest demon creation by performing the Tandava dance upon his back.

Lord Shiva was the Ender of Destruction in this fable. The cosmic dance of Lord Shiva has inspired countless artwork, idols, and dance recitals in honour of this deity. Often the Nataraja figure is depicted with a circle of fire around him. The author, Ananda Coomaraswamy wrote fourteen essays on "The Dance of Shiva" published in 1918 and summarized the importance of the Nataraja form to the ongoing cycle of the universe.

The Tandava dance can also be seen performed to this day at the Chidambaram Temple in Tamil Nadu in Southern India which has Lord Shiva, King of the Dance, established as the prime deity. The link between the Tandava and the basis for Creation and existence can be seen at the CERN[xciii] particle acceleration plant in Geneva which has a statue of Lord Shiva as Nataraja. The statue was gifted by the Government of India. The CERN website refers to the statue on the FAQ (frequently asked questions) section as follows: "The Shiva statue was a gift from India to celebrate its association with CERN, which started in the 1960's and remains strong today. In the Hindu religion, Lord Shiva practiced Nataraja dance which symbolizes Shakti, or life force. The deity was chosen by the Indian government because of a metaphor that was drawn between the cosmic dance of the

Figure 14: Nataraja – King of the Dance

Lord Shiva pictured as Nataraja, King of the Dance. Lord Shiva dances at many junctures in the stories set out in this book, dancing for his potential in-laws and dancing on his vanquished opponents. However, the dance portrayed above is the dance that saved the universe from destruction by overcoming evil, ignorance, and arrogance. This is a dignified display from Lord Shiva who for once puts down his trident and edifies us through supreme artistic form and power.

PART A: BRAHMACHARYA – Tales of Lord Shiva

Nataraja and the modern study of the "cosmic dance" of subatomic particle."

Chapter A8 – The Three Demon Brothers

One of the most popular triumphs of the Lord of Destruction is that over the Tripurasura, three demon brothers. The source for this story is the Shiva Purana in which Lord Shiva annihilated these demons to protect the three worlds. These three brothers were the children of the Demon Tarakasura who had been slain by the young Lord Kartikeya (as told in chapter A3 of this book). The three sons of Tarakasura began immense religious penance after his death.

The eldest among the brothers was Tarkasha, next was Viddyunmali, and Kamalaksha was the youngest. Lord Brahma was pleased by their devotion and their austerities for one cannot try the children for the sins of their father (but then these three apples did not fall far from the tree as readers shall soon discover...). Lord Brahma asked the brothers what he could bestow upon them for their devoted prayers. They asked him to create three forts as magnificent as they were invincible. They should be laden with all kinds of wealth and splendour and nobody should be able to impenetrate these fortresses. Lord Brahma acquiesced and a golden fort was constructed for Taraksha; a silver fort for Kamlaksha, and an iron fort for Viddyunmrt (probably stronger than bronze...).

One of these forts was constructed in the sky, one on earth, and the third in the netherworld (tough break for the youngest brother...). Lord Brahma, having overseen the construction of these mighty palaces then told the three brothers that despite the protection of the forts, they were destined to be slain by Lord Shiva the Destroyer, Vanquisher of Demons. Lord Brahma departed having issued his warning. However, impressed with their new palaces and impressed with themselves they began to torment the deities in arrogance (they should have just enjoyed their palaces and wealth...).

The deities went to Lord Brahma to complain about their treatment at the hands of these terrors and he told them to seek out Lord Shiva who would resolve the issue. The deities relayed their concerns to Lord Shiva and asked him to eliminate these brothers of doom and desolation. Lord Shiva replied that the Tripurasuras were virtuous in many of their actions so they could not be killed. He suggested that Lord Vishnu could help and so the deities went to The Pervader and made the same request to slay the demons. Lord Vishnu performed an oblation and a spirit with one thousand arms appeared. The spirit attacked with the force of multiple gods; however, it was no match for the might of the Tripurasura stockades.

The deities who had been observing returned to Lord Vishnu and narrated the chain of events; he sent back the deities and meditated to discover the means in which the Tripurasuras could be killed. After careful reflection, Lord Vishnu concluded that the Tripurasuras could not be killed while they remained virtuous and religious in their practices (despite the tormenting of the gods). They were different to the many demons who had come before them, including their own father, as they were practiced and well versed in the scriptures. Therefore, he created an illusionary entity from his body. The entity asked Lord Vishnu about the purpose of his existence and his name. Lord Vishnu told him that his name was Arihan and instructed him to create a "trick" scripture which stressed upon the importance of short-term pleasure (which is distinct from the spiritual rituals explained in the Vedas and the distinction between what is "pleasurable" and what is "good" for us).

Lord Vishnu told him to keep the language of that scripture as simple and degenerated as possible (some of the demons were not that smart...). Lord Vishnu then preached Arihan on the science of illusion for this new scripture which stressed that heaven or hell does not exist anywhere else, but only on this earth itself. Arihan was instructed to initiate the Tripurasuras with this philosophy so that the demon brothers would become irreligious.

Arihan duly created illusionary entities from his being who were to act as his followers. They entered the forts of the Tripurasuras and, in a gradual manner, started increasing their influence with the demon brothers. As a result of their teachings, the Tripurasuras became irreligious as Lord Vishnu had commanded to Arihan. Their demon subjects all followed in a short space of time and forsook their religion and worship of the gods for base pleasures. When the deities observed that the Tripurasuras had completely abandoned their religion and penance, they went to Lord Shiva and requested him to now kill the Tripurasuras.

However, he was with Goddess Parvati, Lord Kartikeya and Lord Ganesha and they did not wish to disturb him. The deities approached Lord Vishnu to seek his counsel who reminded them of the sacred Om Namah Shivaya mantra suggesting that they chant this prayer ten million times (and so prayer wheels were invented...). The deities duly undertook this, and Lord Shiva became pleased and appeared before them. He assured the deities that their wishes would be fulfilled and that he would dispense with the demons. Lord Shiva proceeded towards the forts of the Tripurasura on his great chariot (see chapter A13) followed by a huge army of the deities.

Lord Shiva unleashed his celestial weapons, but they were unable to penetrate the robust forcefield. The army of the gods were stunned that the Lord of Destruction was unable to break these forts. Lord Shiva went to his son Lord Ganesha, Remover of Obstacles, for his blessings and his advice who told him that he must not hesitate to use the Pasupatastra, most devastating of all weapons ever created. Lord Shiva knew that this was the correct way to proceed, and he released the missile in the direction of the three forts of Tripurasura which at once became penetrable. The Gold, Silver and Iron forts were obliterated (as if they were made of bricks, wood, and straw...).

On seeing the death and destruction all around them, the Tripurasuras woke from their arrogance with a jolt, and they remembered their religion. They prayed to Lord Shiva to have mercy on them. Lord Shiva assured them that after their death (which was about to occur...) that they would be re-born as his faithful Ganas. The Tripurasuras were burnt to death by the Pasupatastra but were reincarnated as Ganas so their good deeds in the next life could obliterate sins in this life.

Authors note: The story provides a lesson that one should not hide behind religion and devotion on one hand and then commit unethical and arrogant acts (i.e., the tormenting of the deities just because the Tripurasura are protected in their fortresses). The leaders of the Hindu Trinity work together once again to achieve the salvation of all and do not attempt to fix problems on their own which is something one must always bear in mind when undertaking difficult tasks.

Only by working together can the formidable demons be defeated. These demons have learned from the errors of those who have been slain before them in that they do not ask to become invincible, but they ask for invincible protective buildings. In addition, they are more practiced in scriptures than some of other demons slain by Lord Shiva. Lord Shiva at one point goes to his own son Lord Ganesha for support and advice reminding one that help can be enlisted from all different sources. Lord Ganesha delivers simple but effective advice like all good counsellors. The behaviour of the Tripurasura instructs to keep one's faith even when times are good.

The demon brothers are quick to renounce their religion when they see the pleasures that action can bring them; however, they are wrong to stop being thankful for what they have been bestowed. Many find themselves in this position at some point and may all have the wisdom to be thankful in equal measure when things are going well and when they are not.

Finally, one must forever be wary of the path of adharma that is known to be incorrect even if such a path is preached by those who are supposed to be counsellors. As the Vedic texts stress, one must forgo short term pleasures for long term good.

Figure 15: Lord Shiva with Trident

PART A: BRAHMACHARYA – Tales of Lord Shiva

Chapter A9 – The Decapitation of Shankachuda

Many illustrious battles have been waged between Lord Shiva and the demon armies and one tumultuous example was his contest with Shankachuda. This tale from the Shiva Purana describes the defeat and decapitation of this Demon who was born to King Dambha. When Shankachuda grew up, he travelled to Pushkar[xciv] (in Rajasthan) and he undertook a tremendous penance to please Lord Brahma. Lord Brahma blessed his devotee and said that he would remain invincible. His father, Dambha had also undertaken a penance lasting many thousands of years in the name of Lord Vishnu at the same site and Lord Vishnu had blessed Dambha with the boon of a valorous son (sadly not a virtuous son or he may have kept his head on his shoulders...).

Shankachuda's invincibility soon saw him crowned King of the Demons and immediately after his coronation, he attacked Lord Indra's Kingdom. With his massive army, he smashed all who opposed him and in a noticeably short space of time the three worlds were under his command (fear not as The Hindu Trinity are exempted as they survive beyond and between the various worlds). After their crushing and swift defeat, the deities went to Lord Brahma (it seems that Lord Brahma is always "first counsel" of the Trinity...). The deities implored the wise Lord Brahma to assist them in eliminating the menace named Shankachuda.

Lord Brahma then took them to Lord Vishnu; however, as mentioned above, Shankachuda and his father had been granted boons by this deity and by Lord Brahma, so all approached Lord Shiva who was free of such restrictions and could deal with the matter at hand. They set out the predicament and Lord Shiva listened with patience. He assured the deities that he would certainly kill Shankachuda and that they should not worry about the Demon King from that moment onward. The deities were happy, and they returned to their respective abodes (except those who had been evicted by Shankachuda...). In an act of diplomacy, Lord Shiva sent a messenger to the Demon Lord to ask him to return the Kingdom of the Gods to them. Shankachuda refused to oblige, on the contrary he expressed his willingness and readiness to fight Lord Shiva in a battle he had dreamed about since his childhood. Lord Shiva's messenger returned, and the challenge of the King of Demons was relayed to the Lord of Destruction. Lord Shiva appointed his two mighty sons as generals of his grand army of Ganas. Lord Kartikeya, Lord of War and Lord Ganesha, Remover of Obstacles (obstacles such as Demon Kings...), proceeded towards the battlefield with a huge army following them.

The sons of Lord Shiva engaged Shankachuda in a war that shook the three worlds. The assault between the gods and demons grew in intensity. Each side attacked the other with every destructive weapon at their disposal. However, after a glorious stalemate, it was time for Lord Shiva to take up arms. Armed legions from both sides parted while he drove his chariot through the skies to engage his opponent. The deities including Lord Kartikeya and Lord Ganesha all turned to Lord Shiva who was ascending into the air with his trident in hand commanding a challenge for Shankachuda to come forward and meet his destiny (i.e., his death...).

A spectacular battle was fought between Shankachuda and Lord Shiva and after a titanic struggle the Demon King's head was removed with the devastating throw of Lord Shiva's trident. The heavens rejoiced at this glorious victory.

Author's note: This story is not associated with the usual displays of arrogance on the part of the demon antagonist. Shankachuda merely challenges the might of the gods after being empowered with a boon of invincibility. At one point he is given a chance to back down but by then it was too late which teaches us about the dangers of not knowing when to back down in life.

PART A: BRAHMACHARYA – Tales of Lord Shiva

The Demon Lord soon finds out that no-one is invincible which is an important lesson for all. As a final and important lesson, the apologue demonstrates the trust and respect Lord Shiva places in his sons to fight on his behalf. One should always show such support to children when they are ready.

Figure 16: Lord Shiva Triumphant in Victory

Lord Shiva has triumphed many times in battle over the Demons that threaten the universe with their ways of adharma (especially with their ignorance and arrogance). He is pictured above with his trident of destruction. The Demon Kings defeated by Lord Shiva in the stories set out in this book are Ravana, Andhaka, Jalandhara, Shankachuda, and the Tripurasura Demon brothers. Lord Shiva is victorious in these glorious encounters; however, the adventures of this Deity caution that, if one is not careful, those demons can be created through one's own actions for Jalandhara and Andhaka are both creations of Lord Shiva.

Chapter A10 – Lord Shiva The Merciful

Despite his terrible wrath, Lord Shiva is known to show mercy to those who challenge him, and he has been known to provide an opportunity for them to redeem themselves. One fine example from the Shiva Purana is that of Andhaka.

On one of many happy occasions in the life and love of Lord Shiva and Goddess Parvati, the beautiful Goddess playfully surprised her husband by placing her hands over his eyes. Lord Shiva's sweat fell on the ground and Andhaka was born, a creature without sight. The Demon Hiranyaksha had performed tapas for a son and Lord Shiva granted him the powerful Andhaka to raise as his own. Hiranyaksha is the Demon who was slain by Lord Vishnu in the form of a boar after the Demon had accosted Mother Earth and pulled her deep into the oceans of space (not a good role model for a son...).

After the death of Hiranyaksha, Andhaka was crowned King of the Demons. He was the demonic son of Lord Shiva and as such he had incredible skill and power. However, his brothers (as brothers frequently co...) teased him about his lack of sight and his parentage. They taunted him that Lord Shiva and Goddess Parvati had created him by accident and did not want him thereby abandoning him to Hiranyaksha. Though they may have told him this in good humour, Andhaka was saddened by their remarks which hurt him. He relinquished his throne and went to a deserted place in the forest and started to undertake a severe penance. Lord Brahma was pleased by his adulations and offered a boon; however, he was astonished by the soulful request of this tragic Demon:

PART A: BRAHMACHARYA – Tales of Lord Shiva

"I only long for the love and affection of my brothers. O Lord! Bless me so that nobody should be able to kill me except Lord Shiva."

Lord Brahma blessed him thusly.

Andhaka returned to the Demon Kingdom and with the co-operation of his brothers, he challenged the deities and brought them under his control in a short but effective military campaign. However, forgetting his initial feelings of sadness, he became drunk with power and he became very arrogant. He commenced tormenting all the creatures of the earth (sadly there were high hopes for this Demon…).

Andhaka did not show any respect to the deities and he even dishonoured Goddess Parvati (this is the nail in the coffin, or the trident in the neck…). Lord Shiva became furious; however, Andhaka attacked Lord Shiva with his huge army in a demonstration of defiance. The Demon did not care that he was invincible to all except Lord Shiva, and he rushed ahead to his inevitable death. Lord Shiva sent his Ganas to manage the situation but Andhaka defeated them under the protection of Lord Brahma's boon. Lord Shiva was undertaking his Pasupathi austerities and in his absence, the war raged for a thousand years. Lord Shiva returned from his prayers and saw Lord Vishnu locked in combat against the mighty Andhaka.

Andhaka zeroed in on the Lord of Destruction and he attacked him. Lord Shiva in his fury swallowed armies of demons as he lifted the other deities to safety. Finally, Lord Shiva raised his trident and attacked Andhaka. Blood fell on the ground from Andhaka and manifested as thousands of Andhaka-like demons, equal in might to the Demon King. Lord Vishnu slayed all of these manifestations who were not protected by his boons of invincibility and then Lord Shiva lifted Andhaka into the sky with his trident.

There Lord Shiva held the Demon King between the earth and the heavens, suspended for an age. Andhaka remained in this predicament for an eternity bearing the fiery heat of the sun and the icy cold showers of the rain (readers please bear with me as the mercy from the title of this chapter is soon to arrive...). Andhaka did not perish throughout this ordeal and ultimately, he decided to take the refuge of Lord Shiva to spare his life. Andhaka remembered that his initial request from Lord Brahma was that he would be loved and respected by his family. Lord Shiva became pleased by Andhaka's change and he appointed him as the leader of all the Ganas, Lord Shiva's formidable army. Andhaka, freed from ego and arrogance, became an effective general of Lord Shiva throughout the ensuing ages.

Author's note: The story of Andhaka conveys many lessons and the first is the importance to ignore the torments of others, no matter how cruel this may be, and to not let anyone else control us. Andhaka allows his brothers to lead him down the path of adharma. Equally, one must take care when making fun of others in jest as they may take things to heart. This is an important lesson for all to bear in mind. Andhaka felt abandoned by Lord Shiva and the taunting of his brothers exacerbated his feelings of rejection creating much misery and suffering for himself and for others.

The fact that Andhaka exempted Lord Shiva from his boon demonstrated that his intention was to get the attention of his creator through conquering the three worlds. The tale covers familiar themes of the dangers of arrogance but the importance of forgiveness and redemption. Andhaka's "adopted" father Hiranyaksha did not set a good example, however, Andhaka was his own man and could have chosen a more righteous path in the first instance.

Andhaka demonstrates remorse when he is at last subdued by his creator and the mercy shown by Lord Shiva enables Andhaka to redeem himself as a Gana through a virtuous life. This is an important lesson for us all in that it is never too late to commence living one's life according to the principles of dharma, no matter what has transpired in the past. Lord Shiva's forgiveness of Andhaka is a lesson for us all in not bearing grudges. Andhaka was created from the happiness of Lord Shiva and Goddess Parvati and as such it is fitting that his story does not end in tragedy. The next chapter tells the story of a Demon created by Lord Shiva in anger and this has a markedly different ending...

Figure 17: Lord Shiva, Warrior

Andhaka is a tragic figure who is tormented by his family for his appearance and who harbours feelings of abandonment. With the power of Lord Shiva, he conquers the three worlds in a short space of time, and he forces a final showdown with his creator and is defeated. However, Lord Shiva shows mercy to Andhaka and he is appointed the leader of the Shivaganas, Lord Shiva's fearsome army. This is a common thread in the tales of Lord Shiva where he is merciful and provides the possibility of redemption for those that see the error in their ways and return to the path of dharma.

Chapter A11 – Scourge of the Three Worlds

This chapter chronicles Jalandhara who conquered the three worlds requiring Lord Shiva to take up his weapons of destruction once again. This story is also from the Shiva Purana. As with the mighty Andhaka from the previous chapter, this Demon was created by Lord Shiva. However, while Andhaka was born out of happiness, Jalandhara was born from Lord Shiva's considerable wrath.

Lord Indra, King of the Gods was on his way to Mount Kailash to honour Lord Shiva. He was accompanied by a great sage. Lord Shiva sensed the arrival of these honoured guests and he took it upon himself to test their devotion towards him for the deities had been known to be arrogant in eons gone by. Lord Shiva met them on their way in the guise of a hermit; however, Lord Indra did not recognize the fact that this hermit who was sitting in humble meditation was none other than Lord Shiva. Lord Indra inquired of his sage companion as to who this person was in the perilous climate of the Himalayas and then he asked the hermit where he lived. The hermit sat quietly with no response to the mighty Lord Indra.

The King of the Gods repeatedly asked the same question, but each time Lord Shiva remained quiet. Lord Indra became furious and attempted to attack the hermit with his celestial weapons (this may have been an overreaction...). The hermit used his divine power to paralyze the raised hands of Lord Indra. Lord Shiva's eyes reddened due to his wrath and the sage and Lord Indra realized the terrible truth that this was the Lord of Destruction. The sage and Lord Indra both offered their apologies for the lack of patience they had displayed and for the aggression towards the hermit.

PART A: BRAHMACHARYA – Tales of Lord Shiva

Lord Shiva was appeased, and he diverted the power of his radiant eyes to the ocean. The trio all retired to their respective abodes after this near catastrophe. However, the effulgence, which had been diverted to the ocean resulted in the manifestation of a small child. This occurred at the sacred place where the River Ganges submerged into the ocean and which is known as Gangasagar[xcv]. The child began to cry with such ferocity that an environment of fear was created throughout the three worlds. The deities went to Lord Brahma to satisfy their curiosity about this uncommon noise. Lord Brahma assured them and then to investigate the matter he traveled to the location of the harrowing screams of the child.

Lord Brahma picked up the child and set him on his lap. However, the ungrateful infant pressed Lord Brahma's neck with such power that tears rolled down from his eyes. For this reason, he named the child Jalandhara (strongman of the road). Lord Brahma told Varuna, the Sea God that the child will become the mighty ruler of the demons and that no deity would be able to kill him except for Lord Shiva. The Sea God was pleased with this divine prediction and brought the child up with affection. Jalandhara was crowned King of the Demons and he sent for a sage to provide him with a history of the Demon Kingdom that he ruled over (he had been raised away from the other demon boys and girls and needed some catch up sessions...).

The sage told Jalandhara of the history of Demon Kings that had been slain by Lord Vishnu and Lord Shiva. Jalandhara was furious after hearing these stories about his ancestors; he was unaware that he had been created by Lord Shiva's rage. Lord Indra, King of the Gods, was first to draw the wrath of the Demon. Jalandhara sent an emissary and instructed him to enquire of Lord Indra, as to why had he misappropriated all the wealth and power of Jalandhara's father (the Sea God). Jalandhara was referring to the nectar which had emerged during the churning of oceans (see Introduction chapter for this full story).

The Lord Shiva Narrative

The messenger issued a challenge to Lord Indra to take refuge elsewhere or else Jalandhara would rain combat upon the heavens. Lord Indra sent this poor wretch back to the Demon Kingdom (most likely with a good kick to the hind parts...). Jalandhara's fury was fueled and grew more potent. He raised his army into the skies and attacked Lord Indra's Kingdom with a violent onslaught. A fierce battle was fought between his demons and the gods.

Many warriors were killed on both sides. However, the gods were able to administer herbal medicines from Mount Drongiri[xcvi] to the wounded and return them to the battlefield. On seeing this, the mighty Demon King smashed the mountain into the sea with his fist, so that it became impossible for the gods to obtain the healing plants. On seeing this demonstration of supreme strength, the gods became demoralized and fled from the battlefield. And so Jalandhara captured the Kingdom of the Gods.

The terrified deities sought the refuge of Lord Vishnu who gave them a patient hearing and agreed to help them; however, there were two problems (readers can decide which was the bigger problem...). (i) Only Lord Shiva could kill Jalandhara as foretold by Lord Brahma, and (ii) Lord Vishnu's wife Goddess Laxmi considered Jalandhara as her brother as they were both born from the sea. Lord Vishnu promised to Goddess Laxmi that he would not kill Jalandhara, but he set off to engage the Demon to protect the other deities.

An epic encounter ensued between Lord Vishnu and the Lord of Demons which remained indecisive till the end. Lord Vishnu became very much impressed by the valiance of Jalandhara and asked him to demand any boon he wanted. Jalandhara requested him to make his dwelling in the sea along with his sister the Goddess Laxmi which Lord Vishnu consented to. Jalandhara became the ruler of all the three worlds. Many of his subjects were satisfied by his just and virtuous rule, except for the deities who now approached Lord Shiva to seek his help in defeating

Jalandhara who had usurped the heavens. A great sage was sent by Lord Shiva to Jalandhara, and the sage praised the splendour and prosperity of Jalandhara's Kingdom. However, he added that it was nothing in comparison to Lord Shiva's splendours and his long years of happiness with a devoted wife which is essential to complete one's prosperity. Jalandhara asked with curiosity as to where he could find a fitting consort and the sage duped Jalandhara by stating that only Goddess Parvati was worthy of him.

The Demon King sent a messenger to Lord Shiva with a proposal to part with Goddess Parvati (Jalandhara may as well have sent a messenger to Lord Yama King of Death saying "come and get me..."). Lord Shiva was incensed with this despicable and deplorable request and his anger manifested a ferocious creature which ran towards the emissary to devour him. The messenger prayed to Lord Shiva to spare his life (and for the creature to not eat the messenger...). Jalahandra attacked Mount Kailash with the full fury of his ferocious forces. Lord Shiva's Ganas fought a lengthy assault with the demons and began to dominate the battle. Jalahandra then created beautiful creatures with his illusionary powers to divert the attention of the Ganas who became enchanted by the intoxicating creatures and stopped fighting to watch them dance.

Jalahandra then went to Goddess Parvati in the guise of Lord Shiva but was recognized by her immediately. The poor Demon King was enchanted by her beauty and he was immobilized by her powerful wrath. The illusionary powers created by Jalandhara eroded and the Ganas recommenced his onslaught. Lord Shiva decided that the engagement had raged for long enough and he created a chakra[xcvii] (spinning disc weapon) from his toe and severed the head of Jalandhara. After his death, Jalandhara's soul was united with Lord Shiva.

Author's note: One of the principal lessons here is that once one gives life to anger then it can be almost impossible to destroy. Lord Shiva's anger takes the form of Jalandhara in this tale. There are many chances to stop the tragic events: Lord Indra's impatience; Lord Shiva's fury; Jalandhara's ignorance; Jalandhara's reactions without having the facts; and Jalandhara chasing after the unobtainable Goddess Parvati. Jalandhara is defeated by a lack of mental discipline long before Lord Shiva removes his head on the battlefield. Goddess Parvati is shown to have immense power once again in immobilizing the Demon and seeing through his illusions the other deities had succumbed to.

Figure 18: Lord Shiva Dances Upon a Subdued Demon

The look of joy on Lord Shiva's face as he dances on the subdued Demon is a warning to all who would challenge his might. Conversely, the Demon looks on in anguish and regret.

PART A: BRAHMACHARYA – Tales of Lord Shiva

Chapter A12 – Collaboration of the Trinity

The above tales include many instances in which Lord Brahma, Lord Vishnu, and Lord Shiva work together to achieve balance in the universe and to protect all souls. There is a fable told to us as children involving Lord Shiva, the mighty Mahadeva, seeking help from Lord Vishnu at one point when he was let down by his trust in one of his devotees. The source of this is the Bhagavat Purana (one of the eighteen main Puranas).

Lord Shiva covers the three natural modes with his characteristics of (i) sattva (emotion), (ii) rajas (authority), and (iii) tamas (darkness). However, Lord Shiva is said in this Purana to be quick with his condemnations and his blessings. A Demon named Vrika[xcviii] had heard the story about Lord Ravana receiving blessings from the gods (see chapter A6 of this book) and so he took it upon himself to perform penance to please Lord Shiva. Vrika was the son of Shakuni who is one of the chief villains in The Mahabharata War. Vrika made the treacherous voyage to Kedara[xcix] in the Himalayas and began to make intense sacrifices in the name of Lord Shiva. Vrika took a huge cleaving sword and began to carve his flesh and his limbs offering them to Lord Shiva in a sacrificial fire. Out of frustration, he wet his hair in the sacred waters of this holy place and raised his sword to cut off his own head in offering to Lord Shiva.

Lord Shiva was compassionate for this devotee and he rose from the sacrificial fire and grabbed the hand of the Demon. One touch of the hand of the Mahadeva and Vrika was restored to full health and body. Lord Shiva shouted "enough" and offered a benediction, promising to bestow whatever boon he desired. Lord Shiva explained to this seemingly ignorant individual that tormenting one's body was useless for Lord Shiva is pleased by a simple offering of water. The evil Demon asked for a boon that shook all living beings with terror: he requested that anyone upon whose head he placed his hand would perish. Lord Shiva at once knew the grave mistake he had made but in accordance with dharma he could never renege on his promise. The request was granted and Vrika held his impudent and oafish hand out to place it on the head of The God of Destruction.

Lord Shiva disappeared at once knowing that he must enlist the help of Lord Vishnu who was not bound by an oath to the vile son of Shakuni. Lord Vishnu received his Trinity partner with open arms and said he would arrange the necessary: for Lord Shiva had come to the aid of the gods on many occasions so he was happy to assist in vanquishing this foe. Lord Vishnu transformed himself into a young brahmin sage complete with a rope belt, deerskin, and prayer beads. He sought out the Demon and greeted him with humility. Vrika had been running all over creation (figuratively and literally in this case…) and was exhausted so the brahmin told him to rest for a while and catch his breath.

The brahmin asked Vrika why he was circing around in all directions and searching aimlessly. Vrika recounted the circumstances of the boon he had been granted by Lord Shiva after nearly sacrificing his life and how the deity had disappeared when Vrika attempted to place his hand on his head. The brahmin smiled and said that Lord Shiva had been cursed by Daksha and that such powers were no longer at his domain. The young man suggested to Vrika that the very reason Lord Shiva had disappeared was because he knew that Vrika would be unsuccessful and that Lord Shiva's fame would be destroyed, and all would come to know that Lord Shiva's powers had been removed from him. Vrika had heard the stories about Lord Shiva and Daksha and this all resonated with him. In addition, he could not believe that Lord Shiva would grant him such power of life or death over the gods themselves.

PART A: BRAHMACHARYA – Tales of Lord Shiva

The brahmin continued in his necessary deception and said that it was folly to believe that the boon had been bestowed and that Vrika only needed to put his own hand on his head to see that the no such power existed in his hand. Lord Vishnu in the guise of the sage was convincing, and the Demon placed his hand upon his head (Vrika was clearly not one for using his head...until this moment) whereupon it was instantly shattered as if hit by one hundred bolts of lightning. And so perished Vrika, son of Shakuni and the heavens released a rain of flowers upon Lord Vishnu and Lord Shiva.

Author's note: Lord Shiva demonstrates compassion for his devotee no matter what their background and this is laudable. However, this is an elegant example about the dangers of placing one's trust in someone who does not live their life according to ethical and moral principles. Despite this, Lord Shiva is quick to enlist the help of Lord Vishnu in the same way as Lord Vishnu and Lord Brahma have relied upon Lord Shiva in the stories set out above. This is an admirable quality in any leader (and any one of us) to get help when required and to empower others to be involved in the solution. There are many instances in life in which things would be improved instantly if one asked for assistance. Vrika teaches us the additional lesson of not squandering a divine gift (i.e., life) and to ensure that one thinks before one acts. He displays remarkable ignorance in placing his own hand upon his head.

On occasion, stories about the Hindu Trinity and their interactions can cause friction between different divisions of Hinduism who attempt to compare one member of the Trinity with the other (like comparing which of the sides of an equilateral triangle is the longer...); however, the Vedic scripture is clear that the Trinity is one Supreme collective. The stories in which they work together are reminiscent of Milton's Paradise Lost[c] when in the Archangel Wars, the Archangel Michael could have struck the fatal blow to

Satan, but this privilege was reserved for the Son of God in accordance with his pre-ordained destiny. In the same way, the Hindu Trinity each have their role to play in the unfolding of events within these stories.

Figure 19: The Hindu Trinity

The above photo is a depiction of the Hindu Trimurti (Trinity) of Lord Brahma, Lord Vishnu, and Lord Shiva as one Supreme being as opposed to three separate Deities. Whilst they possess different roles of Creator, Pervader, and Destroyer, they are considered to be one supreme Brahman or divinity. The Hindu scriptures contain many references to this, and the philosophy that everything is one, including one's inner self or soul is termed Advaita (which means "not two"). This idol can be found at the remarkable Elephanta Caves which is discussed in chapter C3 of this book. Lord Shiva and Lord Vishnu are worshipped more readily by devotees; however, Lord Brahma appears more prevalently in the early Hindu Scriptures as discussed in Part B of this book. In the tales of Lord Shiva, Lord Brahma is the wise counsellor who has knowledge of how events are to unfold, and he is the first port of call for the Deities when there is an issue. Lord Vishnu and Lord Shiva are depicted in the Puranas as the enforcers of manifest destiny.

PART A: BRAHMACHARYA – Tales of Lord Shiva

Chapter A13 - The Great Chariot of Lord Shiva

The Linga Purana includes a detailed description of the Great Chariot of Rudra, deployed by Lord Shiva on many occasions in the battles that have been chronicled so far in this book. There is no moral lesson in this chapter; however, the description of this mighty chariot is included for readers to obtain a sense of the magnificent poetry contained within the Hindu scriptures.

The Chariot was constructed with assiduity by the architect of the gods. The sun was the right wheel with twelve[ci] spokes, and the moon was the left wheel with sixteen[cii] spokes. The constellations were the ornaments, and the seasons were the rims. The interior of the chariot was Mount Mandara, mountain of the rising and setting sun. The wind was its velocity, and the two transits of the sun were the joints of the wheels. The sky was the fender of the invulnerable vehicle and the heaven and salvation were its flags.

Virtue and detachment were the staffs. Dharma (duty) and Kama (love) were the tips of the two yokes; the unmanifest principle[ciii] was the pole shaft and cosmic intellect was the connecting shaft. The ego was its angular points, the elements were its strength, and sraddha (faith) was its movement. The unshakeable Chariot was pulled by the Vedas as its horses. The Puranas, Mimamasa (treatise on holy rites), Dharmasastras (ethical literature), and Nyaya (science of logic) were its perfect screen cloths on all sides.

The mantras and four stages in life (Brahmacharya student- Grihastha householder- Vanaprastha hermit- Sannyasa ascetic) were its bells. The oceans formed the blankets spread on its surface. The Charioteer was Lord Brahma, and he held the reins and Pranava (the cosmic sound) as the whip.

Himavat, King of Mountains was the bow and Vasuki Lord of Serpents the bowstring. Soma (the Moon God) was the arrow. Lord Vishnu, in the form of a leading bull, lifted the Chariot and Lord Shiva mounted it. Accompanied by the gods he shook heaven and earth by his movements. He requested Lordship of the Animals and in return he would defeat the demons. The gods offered prayers to Lord Ganesh, the son of Lord Shiva, to remove all impediments. Nandi went ahead of the chariot as chief of the Ganas and the gods mounted elephants, huge bulls, and stately horses. They carried their celestial weapons with them. Virabhadra rode a huge bull to the south of the Chariot in service of the three-eyed Lord who had created him from a lock of his hair.

Goddess Kali[civ] moved ahead of the armies with the gait of an elephant in rut. She had skulls adorning her as ornaments and held in her hand the whirling trident that shone like fire. She was intoxicated by drinking the blood of demons which tasted to her as wine. The demon armies trembled at the site of the army of gods before them Lord Vishnu mounted Garuda, King of Birds, and flew alongside the Chariot. He shone like the thousand-rayed fierce sun. The six-faced Lord Kartikeya served the Chariot and his father Lord Shiva. Goddess Parvati was seated on the left side of the trident bearing Destroyer and she shone with the lustre and colour of the golden lotus. Lord Shiva looked at the armies of demons and they burned to ashes, he fired his arrow and it returned to him after destroying the demon fortresses in his path.

Author's note: The detailed description of this heavenly chariot places one at the scene of battle as an observer. The Chariot being pulled by the Vedas as the four horses speaks volumes about the importance of these writings in the Hindu universe. The story is consistent with Advaita philosophy of all the deities combined into one supreme force.

PART A: BRAHMACHARYA – Tales of Lord Shiva

Figure 20: The Great Chariot of Rudra

The story of the Great Chariot of Rudra from the Linga Purana contains a lucid representation of Lord Shiva's imposing vehicle deployed upon the celestial battlefield. The Chariot has been utilized in the annihilation of Demon armies. Virtue and detachment were the staffs. Dharma (duty) and Kama (love) were the tips of the two yokes; the unmanifest principle was the pole shaft and cosmic intellect was the connecting shaft. The elements were its strength, and sraddha (faith) was its movement. The Chariot was pulled by the four Vedas as its horses. The Puranas, Mimamasa (treatise on holy rites), Dharmasastras (ethical literature), and Nyaya (science of logic) were its perfect screen.

Chapter A14 – The Creation of the Universe

Whilst Lord Shiva is most often associated with the role of annihilator, the accounts from Hindu scripture set out below contain a distinct version of the events of Creation and Lord Shiva's role. The relevant Hindu texts were written well over one thousand years ago but there are many consistent elements with modern day scientific theories coming to light in this century and the last century. This chapter has more scientific content and less destroying of demons than prior chapters...

The Upanishads set out the circumstances of Creation as follows:

> *"In the beginning there was darkness alone. It was moved by Brahman, it became agitated, it became obscure, then it became goodness. The essence flowed forth..."That" part belonging to darkness is called Rudra, the Wild God, "That" to obscurity is Brahman, the Creator, "That" to goodness is the God, Lord Vishnu The Preserver."*

The Padma Purana and the Linga Purana add the following cyclical analysis to the events of Creation: The "characterized", Shakti[cv] is said to be endowed with smell, colour, taste, sound, and touch. This is the Prakriti. The "non-characterized", Lord Shiva, is devoid of smell, colour, taste, sound, and touch. This is the Purusha. The characterized is the physical body of the worlds and the non-characterized, thus, becomes characterized through maya (illusion) and the three important deities took shape. The entire universe began thusly and at the time of creation, from mahat (the cosmic mind) evolved the cosmic egg[cvi] and the five elements (i) earth, (ii) water, (iii) fire, (iv) air, (v) ether and thus the nucleus for all creation. Ether is the pure essence, the cosmic element leading to air, then fire, then water, then earth. These constituents of creation begin with the cosmic mind and end with earth. The destruction of the universe is subject to the behest of

PART A: BRAHMACHARYA – Tales of Lord Shiva

Lord Shiva and when Creation is annihilated, the non-characterized and the characterized come to a standstill and remain inactive. Creation occurs when there is no equilibrium of the characterized and non-characterized. When they are in equilibrium the universe will be dissolved after every kalpa (cycle of creation, protection, and destruction). One thousand kalpas represent one "year" for the Hindu Trinity of gods. One kalpa or "day of Brahma" is four billion years. This makes one feel quite miniscule…. The Rig Veda also has the following passages in relation to Creation:

1. THEN was not non-existent nor existent: there was no realm of air, no sky beyond it. What covered in, and where? and what gave shelter? Was water there, unfathomed depth of water?
2. Death was not then, nor was there aught immortal: no sign was there, the day's and night's divider. That one thing, breathless, breathed by its own nature: apart from it was nothing whatsoever.
3. Darkness there was: at first concealed in darkness this all was indiscriminate chaos. All that existed then was void and form less: by the great power of warmth was born that unit.
4. Thereafter rose desire in the beginning, desire, the primal seed, and germ of spirit. Sages who searched with their heart's thought discovered the existent's kinship in the non-existent.
5. Transversely was their severing line extended: what was above it then, and what below it? There were begetters, there were mighty forces, free action here and energy up yonder.
6. Who verily knows and who can here declare it, whence it was born and whence comes this creation? The gods are later than this world's production. Who knows then whence it first came into being?
7. He, the first origin of this creation, whether he formed it all or did not form it, whose eye controls this world in

highest heaven, he verily knows it, or perhaps he knows not.

Author's note: The above version of Creation from Hindu scripture gives one a lot to ponder with the concepts of matter ("characterized") v anti-matter ("non-characterized")[cvii], the fifth element of "ether", the "cosmic mind", and the cyclical nature of the universe. The most widely accepted scientific theory relating to the universe is the Big Bang[cviii] theory which relates more to the ongoing expansion of the universe and has less to do with creation itself.

The rate of acceleration of certain galaxies away from us has enabled scientists[cix] to (i) postulate that the universe is expanding and (ii) wind back the clock to assert that at the outset there was an atom sized dense point that exploded. This is consistent with the cosmic "egg" from Hindu scriptures as a pregnant atom. The cyclical aspect of creation and the destruction over successive kalpas (cycles) is consistent with the Pulsating Theory[cx] of the universe expanding to a point and then contracting when a critical point is reached. The current state of the universe is believed to be the expansionary phase with ongoing death and birth of stars.

The above scriptures set out the destruction of the universe when there is an equilibrium, consistent with modern day theories on matter and anti-matter annihilating each other if they come into contact and leaving behind energy. The reverse will have occurred at inception where energy created matter and anti-matter. If they were created in equilibrium then there would be no universe so there must be non-equilibrium, no matter how small, for matter to have sustained to form the stars and planets.

The Rig Veda is one of the oldest religious books written in the world and the section re-produced here in relation to Creation has *such depth that it takes the reader back to the beginning of time itself. The text composed four thousand years ago brings science, philosophy, and religion together in an elegant manner.*

Figure 21: The Creation of the Universe

Hindu scriptures postulate that the universe was formed from and contained within the cosmic egg (or atom) which created ether (the fifth element), then air, then fire, then water, then earth. Modern day scientific theories suggest that at the point of the Big Bang, the universe had zero size and was infinitely hot[cxi] at which time a pregnant atom exploded to create the universe. Modern scientists[cxii] theorize that a "super-liquid" of zero viscosity was created an instant before sub-atomic particles were formed. Destruction of the universe is said to occur when there is an equilibrium of the characterized and non-characterized. This is consistent with modern day theories on matter and anti-matter annihilating each other if they come into contact and leaving behind energy. The reverse will have occurred at Creation where energy created matter and anti-matter. If they were created in equilibrium then there would be no universe so there must have been non-equilibrium at inception, no matter how small, for matter to have sustained to form the stars and planets.

Chapter A15 – Fifty-Two Morals

This chapter collates the key morals from the above tales of Lord Shiva into one handy reference of rectitude for readers. The fifty-two moral lessons set out below are applicable at home in personal interactions with family and friends, and at work in professional interactions with colleagues, clients, and advisers. They can be applied wherever one encounters others and are of equal value with existing and new relationships.

Whilst Part A of this book and the Tales of Lord Shiva should be enjoyable and instructive to all, there is much content that should assist the younger Brahmacharya student who is developing their moral compass (e.g., one lesson per week). Parents, grandparents, uncles, aunts, teachers can all assist by reading these stories to them or discussing the moral lessons with them after they have absorbed the contents. As for the non-Brahmacharya readers who already know the correct path...sometimes it is good to have a weekly reminder.

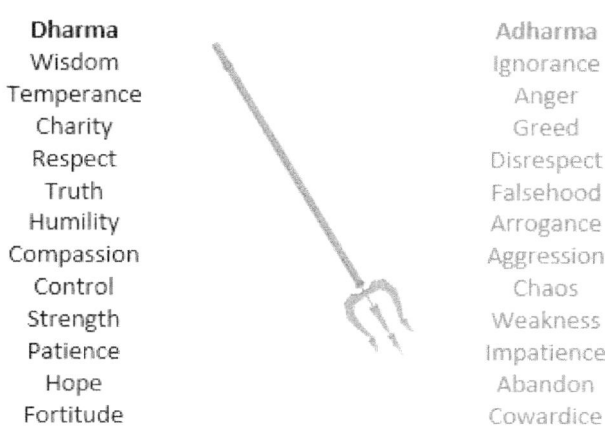

Dharma	Adharma
Wisdom	Ignorance
Temperance	Anger
Charity	Greed
Respect	Disrespect
Truth	Falsehood
Humility	Arrogance
Compassion	Aggression
Control	Chaos
Strength	Weakness
Patience	Impatience
Hope	Abandon
Fortitude	Cowardice

PART A: BRAHMACHARYA – Tales of Lord Shiva

Fifty-Two Morals from the Tales of Lord Shiva

1. Put the needs of others first. Selfless acts can attract the benevolence of others.
2. Be aware of undertakings that appear too easy as there may be hidden dangers.
3. Even the strongest may need help and will appreciate the offer of such.
4. Good leaders work together for the benefit of all.
5. Grant forgiveness to others no matter what the offence.
6. Have regard to the feeling of all family members, do not put one above the others.
7. Communicate with each other and do not ignore problems.
8. Do not take on more responsibility than one can handle.
9. Act for the greater good even though one may suffer for it.
10. Be temperate. If one gives life to anger, then it is difficult to destroy without hurting others and oneself.
11. Have hope even if problems appear insurmountable.
12. A short life of virtue is preferable to a long life of immorality.
13. Study, austerity, and charity will lead to eternal peace.
14. Fools choose pleasurable lives whilst the wise choose good lives.
15. Do not succumb to ego and arrogance. Fools dwell in the darkness of ignorance but even the wise may fall into the darkness of arrogance.
16. A person with no sensory control is as a charioteer who does not hold the reins firm -the horses can become vicious.
17. The wise seek not stability in an instable world but look inward to what they can control.
18. Respect one's family; however, know when to challenge unhealthy behaviour and when to ignore it.

19. Do not ridicule or disrespect the few for this may lose the favour of all.
20. When one is snubbed or taunted by others, have the wisdom to ignore it. Do not let others control one's actions.
21. Hold on to one's pure beliefs despite the challenge of others.
22. Admit when one is wrong and help address the issue in good time.
23. Worship one's mother above all others.
24. Protect one's children from all those who would oppose them.
25. Communicate with one another before unthinkable tragedies occur.
26. Respect the wishes of others even when one does not agree with them.
27. Approach others with honesty and true emotion, not through boasting.
28. Accept failure and rejection with grace as one would accept success.
29. Do not underestimate anyone based on their age or background.
30. Be fearless and controlled in one's emotions.
31. Think and plan before one acts (including abstract views of the situation).
32. Find the strength to accept decisions that one deems to be unfair.
33. Be aware of the dangers of excess and accept one's limits.
34. Do not neglect the advice of others, particularly one who is already one's counsellor. But be aware of those who preach acharma.
35. Have diligence and precision in undertaking any task. Ensure one is suitably trained in advance.

36. Even the most powerful should have patience, humility, and respect for others.
37. Always hold true to one's word.
38. Offer respect to all no matter what their background.
39. Do not hide behind religion to commit unethical acts.
40. Never be too proud to request assistance, it can come from all directions.
41. Offer simple but effective advice when asked for counsel.
42. Have the wisdom to be thankful for the gift of life in equal measure when times are good and when tragedy strikes.
43. Know when to concede, especially if afforded the opportunity to do so. No-one is invincible.
44. Respect one's children to do the necessary when they are ready, and back them up if required.
45. Take care when making jokes at the expense of others, they may take this to heart.
46. Live a life of love, morality, and purpose even when those around are not.
47. It is never too late to commence living a life of love, morality, and purpose, no matter what has transpired in the past.
48. Exercise mental discipline and educate oneself against ignorance. It is folly to covet the unobtainable.
49. Have the wisdom to see through the falsehood of others.
50. Have compassion for others but take care when interacting with immoral individuals.
51. Do not misuse knowledge and power.
52. Do not squander a divine gift (i.e., life).

**PART B: *GRIHASTHA*
THE HINDU SCRIPTURES**

PART B: *GRIHASTHA* – The Hindu Scriptures

Introduction to Part B

Part B of this book is for the Grihastha (householder). One continues to be a student in the pursuit of knowledge; however, there are now responsibilities to others. The adventure stories of Lord Shiva are still of great interest and the core Hindu scriptures contain a plethora of philosophy that can assist with one's interactions at work and at home. There are two types of sacred text: (1) Shruti – realized through meditation, conveyed by word of mouth, and written down; and (2) Smriti – remembered and written down. The four Vedas fall into the former category of Shruti scriptures, as do the two hundred Upanishads.

The mentions of Lord Shiva within these texts are not frequent but have been set out below for completeness for the reader along with the associated philosophy and characterizations of this deity. Lord Shiva is referred to as Rudra in these texts and over time, Rudra has become synonymous with Lord Shiva as the Destroyer. The Hindu Epics of The Mahabharata and The Ramayana are considered by many to be core scripture, in particular the Bhagavad Gita (Song of God) which forms part of The Mahabharata. Therefore, an analysis of Lord Shiva's role in these stories is included here as a segue from Part A. The other Hindu texts not discussed in Part B include the following:

- Sutras – these include the Dharma Sutra, Brahma Sutra, Kama Sutra, Yoga Sutra, and the Shiva Sutras. The Shiva Sutras are covered in Part D of this book.
- Puranas - there are thirty six Puranas and the Shiva Purana, Linga Purana, Padma Purana, and Skanda Purana make up the bedrock of stories in Part A of this book.
- Agamas – there are over two hundred Agamas and the Shiva Agamas[cxi] are not covered in Part B of this book due to the significant portions of these texts that relate to practical tasks from performing ceremonial rituals to building temples.

Chapter B1 - Lord Shiva in the Mahabharata

This chapter sets out the appearances of Lord Shiva in The Mahabharata. Whilst Lord Vishnu is the main deity in this Hindu Epic, the stories below demonstrate the key role that Lord Shiva plays in the events that unfold throughout the story. The Mahabharata of Vyasa[cxii] is set out in eighteen main book chapters and tells the story of warring cousins for the throne. The characters from the tales of Lord Shiva in Part A of this book, bar a few exceptions, fall into the categories of gods or demons. It is clear what the moral lessons are as summarized in chapter A15. However, The Mahabharata features more complex characters on both sides who are prone to human emotions and mistakes.

Birth and Divinity of the Pandavas

The Mahabharata tells us the story of how Lord Indra saw a woman weeping into the Ganges and each of her tears became a golden lotus. He asked her who she was and why she was weeping, and she told him to follow her leading him to a youth playing a game of dice with some young women. The youth ignored the mighty Indra, King of Gods who began to bluster angrily at this perceived slight; however, at a single glance from the youth (who was none other than Shiva), Lord Indra became paralyzed and collapsed to the ground. The four other deities who were present with him were transported away and became imprisoned in a mountain[cxiii].

When Lord Indra, divested of his pride, begged for their freedom Lord Shiva told him that all five of the deities would return to their own world in the heavens only after being born as men. Lord Shiva agreed to their stipulation that in their human form they must be begotten by deities[cxiv] and thus the five Pandava demi-gods were born on earth. There are several similar tales in the Puranas in which the deities are penalized for their arrogance by the Hindu Trinity of gods.

Lord Shiva v Arjuna

As set out in chapter A4 of this book, Arjuna meets Lord Shiva in the guise of a bowman, and they fight an engaging encounter. Lord Shiva is impressed with Arjuna's skill and blesses him. This is a common thread to both the Hindu Epics as the central heroes of Arjuna and Rama are both tested in accordance with Lord Shiva's power to provide credence to their position as dominant and deserving protagonists.

Asvatthama

Asvatthama is a fearsome character in The Mahabharata who is one of only three survivors of the Kaurava army when the war is reaching its climax. Asvatthama plays a central role in the epic as he slaughters the majority of the Pandava[cxv] armies in one single night after learning that his father Drona was killed with deception (and by using Drona's love for his son Asvatthama[cxvi]). There are a multitude of heroes and villains in this Hindu Epic; however, Asvatthama's devastating incursion in a one night offensive is a memorable event indeed. Asvatthama is born from a devout penance performed in honour of Lord Shiva. Drona performs many years of severe austerities to please Lord Shiva and obtain a son who possesses the same valiance as Lord Shiva. The Mahabharata includes the following:

> *"From a fusion of the great God Shiva and Death, Desire and Anger, there was born Drona's son Asvatthama, the brave afflicter of his enemies; that mighty hero appeared on earth, lord of men, as a lotus-eyed destroyer of enemy forces".*

The above quote implies that Asvatthama possesses more than just the characteristics of Lord Shiva, he may have been created from Lord Shiva. Despite the above passage, Asvatthama is linked with Lord Shiva in folklore but he is not held out to be a son of Lord Shiva in the same way that Lord Ganesha and Lord Kartikeya are. The above extract does explain why Asvatthama is able to smash the Pandava armies in one night. Preceding the moment of Asvatthama's attack on the camp, he prays to Lord Shiva for protection and offers himself as a sacrificial victim. A golden altar appears with a host of extraordinary beings who are the Ganas of Lord Shiva. They wield weapons and they leap about in a terrible sight. Lord Shiva addresses Asvatthama saying that the time has come for those who must die[cxvii], and he places a sword in the hand of the warrior before entering his body and proceeding to destroy the Pandava soldiers.

Birth of the Kauravas

Gandhari, the mother of the Kauravas, was a devout worshiper of Lord Shiva who granted her a boon that she would have one hundred sons who became the Kauravas.

The Pandavas marry Draupadi

The Mahabharata mentions that Draupadi received a boon from Lord Shiva in a past life that led to her marrying the five Pandavas. She was a lovelorn girl who asked for a virtuous husband five times and Lord Shiva said in a next life she would have five husbands.

The Pasupatastra Weapon

As referred to above, Lord Shiva meets Arjuna in combat in one episode in The Mahabharata. After their encounter, Lord Shiva bestows the apocalyptic Pasupatastra weapon on Arjuna. The weapon is not used in The Mahabharata for to unleash it upon a mortal would destroy all living things and end creation. Therefore, the donning of the weapon to Arjuna demonstrates the restraint and discipline of this hero. At a prior juncture in the Hindu Epic, Arjuna dreams that he and Krishna journey to the heavens to worship Lord Shiva and obtain the Pasupatastra. Lord Shiva directs the two to the lake of nectar where his weapons are stored, and they are confronted by two fierce snakes; they sing Vedic hymns to Lord Shiva and the snakes turn into a bow and an arrow which they take to Lord Shiva.

Lord Shiva sings a mantra and then shoots the arrow back into the lake and returns the bow. Arjuna's resolve is strengthened and the stories of Lord Shiva's exploits with his celestial weapons are recounted to include his disruption of Daksha's sacrifice (chapter A2 of this book) and his destruction of the triple city (chapter A8 of this book).

Jayadratha

One interesting character in The Mahabharata is Jayadratha, brother-in-law of the one hundred Kauravas who is beaten and has his head shaved by the Pandavas after he has attempted to kidnap their wife Draupadi. Jayadratha desires to avenge his humiliation by defeating them on the battlefield. He performs a rigorous tapas to please Lord Shiva who appears before him. Jayadratha asks for the ability to smash the Pandavas; however, Lord Shiva replies that such a boon is impossible. However, he grants Jayadratha the ability to check the advance of the Pandavas and their forces for one whole day. On this fateful day, Abhimanyu, the valiant son of Arjuna is killed as a result of the boon granted to Jayadratha.

The Slaying of Bhishma

Bhishma is a righteous and valiant warrior who finds himself impelled to fight against the Pandavas as the leader of the Kaurava army. He is finally mortally wounded by Shikhandi, who is born as Draupadi's sister but fights in The Mahabharata War as a man. Shikhandi was granted a boon in a previous life from Lord Shiva that she would kill Bhishma who she held responsible for her misfortunes in life.

Lord Krishna's Praise for Lord Shiva

There are many points as set out above at which Lord Shiva assists both the Kauravas and the Pandavas in preparation for the war. After the Mahabharata War has concluded, Lord Krishna talks to the Pandava brothers about Lord Shiva and mentions his own travels to the Himalayas where he had seen Lord Shiva's glory, surrounded by the gods and other steadfast beings. Lord Krishna offered praise to Lord Shiva and was granted boons after concluding that the entire universe has its origin in Lord Shiva.

Figure 22: The Mahabharata War Begins

PART B: *GRIHASTHA* – The Hindu Scriptures

Author's note: The Mahabharata details a war between rival cousins the Pandavas and the Kauravas. Dhritarashtra and Pandu were brothers; Dhritarashtra had one hundred sons (the hate-filled Kauravas) and Pandu had five sons (the righteous Pandavas). Dhritarashtra, the older brother, was born blind and Pandu was made King. However, Pandu died at an early age leaving the stage set for a power struggle between the cousins. A chain of events leads to a sixth (older) brother of the Pandavas named Karna finding himself on the side of the Kaurava army.

The five Pandava brothers and Karna are all demi-gods. Arjuna, the main hero in the fable is reticent to fight against his cousins and Lord Vishnu, in the form of Krishna sets out the Bhagavad Gita (Song of God) to Arjuna reminding him of the importance of love, honour, duty, and looking beyond one's own life to see a broader universal plan. As set out in this chapter, Lord Shiva plays an important role in the Hindu Epic. Firstly, he punishes the five deities (Indra, King of Gods; Yama, Lord of Death and Dharma; Vayu, the God of the Wind; and the Asvins (twin Gods of the Dawn) for their impatience and rage, and they are reborn as demi-gods in the form of the Pandava brothers. Secondly, Lord Shiva tests Arjuna and bestows upon him the devastating Pasupatastra weapon.

Arjuna does not use this weapon in the battle as he was instructed not to use it against lesser mortals; in doing so Arjuna demonstrates his virtuosity in being entrusted by Lord Shiva and shows restraint in not using the weapon. The third important role played by Lord Shiva in the story is to imbue his powers for one night into Asvatthama in the Kaurava army enabling him to wipe out the Pandava armies in one assault (except for the five brothers who were away that night). This is part of the broader universal plan in the Mahabharata War which led to the annihilation of both armies leaving only a handful of survivors on both sides.

Chapter B2 - Lord Shiva in the Ramayana

This chapter sets out the appearances of Lord Shiva in Valmiki's Ramayana[cxviii]. This Hindu Epic features Lord Vishnu more prominently than Lord Shiva; however, an important function is performed by Lord Shiva as this chapter will summarize. The Ramayana was composed by Valmiki in 600-300 B.C. and has six main parts spanning four hundred chapters:

1. Bala (youth),
2. Ayodhya (the city),
3. Aranya (forest),
4. Kishkindha (empire of the Varana anthropoids),
5. Sundara (beauty),
6. Yuddha (war).

The story of Rama, avatar of Lord Vishnu, is relayed through the above sections and this magnificent work is considered to be a core Hindu scripture. The characters from the tales of Lord Shiva in Part A of this book, bar a few exceptions, fall into the categories of gods or demons. It is clear what the moral lessons are as summarized in chapter A15. However, The Ramayana features more complex characters on both sides who are prone to human emotions and mistakes.

Viswamitra

Viswamitra was a King who attained sainthood and mastery of celestial weaponry through the practice of severe austerities. On one occasion, he entrusted his Kingdom to one of his sons and proceeded to the Himalayas to perform tapas, directing his devotions to Lord Shiva who was pleased with how steadfast his devotion was. Viswamitra asked to be blessed with divine arrows and to be the master of every weapon; Shiva duly granted this boon which included all the celestial weapons available to the gods. It is Viswamitra, in the Ramayana Epic, who takes Rama and his brother Lakshmana as young adults on their first (of many) conquests to slay the Rakshasas Mareecha and Subahu. He takes Rama to the Court of King Janaka where Rama meets Sita for the first time and wins her hand in marriage. Viswamitra becomes impressed by the bravery and skill demonstrated by the brothers in their first engagement with demons and he teaches Rama the use, control and recall of the various divine weapons he was granted mastery over by Lord Shiva.

The above story demonstrates an important role of Lord Shiva in the Ramayana epic despite not featuring in the main interactions between the characters. It is Lord Shiva's boon gifted to Viswamitra that enables Rama to obtain the necessary skills in warfare to overcome his enemies and triumph in the final terrible battle with Ravana.

The Churning of the Oceans

This popular story featured in the Introduction chapter to this book is told in The Ramayana. The gods were seeking immortality and freedom from ill-health, so they decided to churn the milky ocean. Vasuki, Lord of Serpents, was the rope and Mount Mandara was applied to mix the waters creating soma, nectar but also halahala, poison. The universe was in great danger of being burned by the force of this poison, so the gods approached Lord Shiva to save them, and he duly drunk the halahala. Lord Vishnu, on seeing this feat praised his Hindu Trinity member and called him omnicompetent god among gods.

The River Goddess Ganga

The Ramayana sets out in detail the story of the descent of the River Goddess Ganga upon the head of Lord Shiva. Rama happens upon the location of this descent and the yarn is narrated to him by a sage. This is a fine example of how the different Hindu scriptures are interconnected like threads in a tapestry. Valmiki's Ramayana sets out the penance undertaken by the noble King Bhageeratha standing on the tip of one of his big toes, by day and by night, sustaining himself only by the air until Lord Shiva acquiesces to receive the force of Goddess Ganga upon his head. The River Goddess attempted to wash Lord Shiva away to the underworld and to punish her ignorance, Lord Shiva entrapped her in his matted locks. The full account of Goddess Ganga and Lord Shiva is set out in the Introduction chapter to this book.

The Great Bow of Lord Shiva

As set out in chapter A5 of this book, the supreme test for any man on earth is if he can lift and string the bow of Lord Shiva. Rama was not only able to lift the bow, but he broke it when attempting to string the bow. The fact that this bow belonged to Lord Shiva demonstrates the divinity of Rama. This is a common thread to both the Hindu Epics as the central heroes of Arjuna and Rama are both tested in accordance with Lord Shiva's power to provide credence to their position as dominant and deserving protagonists.

Rama being blessed by Lord Shiva

The Shiva, Skanda, Linga, and Padma Puranas chronicle Rama's prayers to Lord Shiva at Mount Maryada[cxix]. Rama is described as receiving a virtuous feeling having cast off ignorance. He joins the palms of his hands and with his body horripilated (goosebumps) having made respectful obeisance by the prostration of his body to Lord Shiva, the trident-holder, the god with three eyes. Rama says in honour of this deity:

"I seek the refuge of that Sankara (Lord Shiva), who affords protection, and who held on his head, like a garland of unsteady flowers, Ganga with her water at once pure, charming, and rolling, and having fearful waves, falling from the sky."

Lord Shiva duly bestows his blessings upon Rama at this point and confirms that all men who follow him will be in happiness on earth and in heaven. In Valmiki's Ramayana, Lord Shiva blesses Rama before he undertakes the assault on the city of Lanka. There is mention of an Island located in the middle of an ocean where Rama's troops are stationed and where Lord Shiva blesses the warrior. The Temple of Rameswaram (see chapter C11) is dedicated to this episode of the Ramayana. Rameswaram is one of the closest drop-off points one can reach Sri Lanka[cxx] from and this would be consistent with a military incursion into Lanka.

In other versions of The Ramayana, Rama offers prayers to Lord Shiva on the banks of the River Ganges after constructing a clay image. Rameswaram is one of the twelve sacred Jyotirlinga Temples (see Introduction to Part C of this book). Lord Shiva also addresses Rama after the war has been won to confirm that his father had reached the heavens with honour. He states that Rama will live long and that his reign will be a happy one.

The Wedding of Lord Shiva and Goddess Parvati

The auspicious wedding of these Hindu gods is referred to in The Ramayana and a ceremony attended on Mount Kailas by all the rishis and deities. One sage of great virtue had to remain behind in the south to balance the Earth. Chapter A2 of this book sets out the interactions between Lord Shiva and Goddess Parvati in more detail and chapter A3 chronicles the tales of their offspring.

Ravana and Lord Shiva

As set out in chapter A6 of this book, Ravana, key antagonist of The Ramayana is a devotee of Lord Shiva. Ravana is referred to in this Hindu Epic as the Conqueror of Kailas (Soorpanakha, the demon sister of Ravana, makes mention of this title when announcing herself to Rama to woo the hero). The Ramayana, the Shiva Purana, the Padma Purana, and many Temple idols/carvings contain the stories of Ravana and both his penances on Mount Kailas and his affront to Mount Kailas which are summarized in chapter A6 of this book.

The fight between Lord Shiva and Lord Vishnu

Part A of this book includes a selection of stories in which Lord Shiva and Lord Vishnu work together. The Puranas also contain tales in which one is able to meet the challenge of the other as great and powerful warriors who none can rival or challenge. Valmiki's Ramayana details one such encounter in which Lord Shiva is immobilized by Lord Vishnu. The powerful warrior sage Parasurama[cxxi], also an avatar of Lord Vishnu, arrives to challenge Rama upon hearing that he had smashed sensationally the great bow of Lord Shiva.

Parasurama narrates the origin of the bow of Lord Shiva and the bow of Lord Vishnu that he himself is carrying. The two celestial weapons were fashioned for the gods by the divine architect Vishwakarma[cxxii]. One was given to Lord Shiva for combat with the Demon Tripura and their impenetrable fortresses (see chapter A8 of this book). The second bow was given to Lord Vishnu and is an indestructible, citadel conquering longbow. It is identical in its efficacy with Lord Shiva's longbow. Parasurama continues in his narration and mentions that long ago, the gods asked Lord Brahma who is more powerful out of Lord Vishnu and the blue-throated Lord Shiva. Lord Brahma decided to test them, and he enraged Lord Shiva with comments that Lord Vishnu had to save him from the Demon Vrika (see chapter A12 of this book). Lord Brahma also suggested that it was the bow that defeated the Tripura and not the bowman.

Lord Shiva grew angry, and a fierce war took place between him and Lord Vishnu using the great bows that were bequeathed to them. They rained arrows upon each other for an eon; however, Lord Vishnu was in this instance able to render Lord Shiva and his bow motionless to coincide with a reduction in Lord Shiva's

PART B: *GRIHASTHA* – The Hindu Scriptures

wrath. The two deities reached a state of agreement and Lord Shiva gave his bow away in compensation for losing his temper whereupon it found its way to King Janaka who stored the weapon in an iron box in his Kingdom.

Figure 23: Rameswaram –Rama's incursion into Lanka

The Lord Shiva Narrative

Author's note: The Ramayana Epic sets out the story of how Lord Vishnu's avatar Rama was born as a mortal on earth to rid the world of the evil Demon King Ravana. Ravana kidnaps Rama's beautiful wife Sita and Rama leads an offensive into the Island of Lanka to rescue his virtuous bride. As mentioned above and in Part A of this book, Rama represents a righteous way to live one's life and Ravana represents the opposite. As set out in chapter B3 above, Lord Shiva plays an important role in the Hindu Epic.

Firstly, he bestows Rama's military teacher, the sage Viswamitra, with knowledge of all celestial weapons. This knowledge is imparted to Rama who is triumphant in the final battle with Ravana. Secondly, Rama is tested by Lord Shiva's bow and is able to demonstrate his strength and divinity when he breaks it. Thirdly, Ravana is an ardent devotee of Lord Shiva after he had been imprisoned under Mount Kailas for one thousand years for his insolence. Lord Shiva bestowed a divine sword and invincibility onto Ravana after he was satisfied with his penance making Ravana a formidable Demon King that even the gods could not challenge thanks to a boon from Lord Brahma. This necessitated a hero among men, Rama, that would be born to slay the evil Ravana.

Both of the Hindu Epics take the moral lessons from the detailed and complex Vedas and Upanishads and make these lessons more accessible to us all through the adventures of the core characters. It is much easier to tackle these books than it is to wade through tens of thousands of mantras. Therefore, the Hindu Epics, including the Bhagavad Gita, are of equal importance to the Vedas and Upanishads and are considered alongside these works as the core of Hindu scripture. The next two chapters of the book consider the mentions of Lord Shiva in these early Hindu texts and draws out some of the key elements of his character and philosophy. Readers will be going further back in time as some of these texts were recorded four thousand years ago...

PART B: *GRIHASTHA* – The Hindu Scriptures

Chapter B3 - Lord Shiva in the Vedas

This chapter explores the four Vedas and highlights the mentions of Lord Shiva that help to confirm our understanding of this Hindu God's appearance and philosophy. Veda means "to have knowledge". This body of divine intelligence contains comprehensible wisdom, and the teachings are the earliest recorded of the Hindu texts (of similar age to the Egyptian Book of the Dead[cxxiii]). The spiritual beliefs, incantations, philosophy, and rituals are set out into four main sections:

- Rig (meaning "verses"),
- Sama (meaning "chants"),
- Yajur (meaning "formulas"), and
- Atharva (named for the sage Atharvan).

The Vedas include references to several deities including Lord Indra and those deities that are associated with natural forces to include Aditya[cxxiv], God of the Sun; Agni, God of Fire; Vayu God, of Wind; Varuna, God of the Sky; and Yama, God of Death. Lord Shiva is referred to as "Rudra" in the Vedas and Lord Vishnu and Lord Brahma also feature. Each Veda has two parts: (i) Samhitas (mantras) and (ii) a Brahman part with theories. The Upanishads (see chapter B4 below) are connected by content to each of the Vedas. Hence the Upanishads are often referred to as Vedanta – the end of the Vedas.

There are elements of instruction in the Vedas in relation to karma (action), and jnana (knowledge). They are believed to have been passed down through generations by great sages, seers, or rishis over an unknown period; however, they were arranged and compiled in written form around 1800 B.C. to 800 B.C. They are acknowledged to have existed for many thousands of years prior to this date. This chapter will explore each of the four Vedas in turn and the references to Lord Shiva.

Rig Veda

The Rig Veda is believed to have been recorded as early as 1800 B.C. It was written before any of the other Hindu scriptures reviewed in Part B of this book. In addition to some minor references, there is a "Book of Rudra" in the Rig Veda that contains verses praising this deity that is now synonymous with Lord Shiva. The text of the Book of Rudra is set out below:

1. FATHER of Maruts[cxxv], let thy bliss approach us: exclude us not from looking on the sunlight. Gracious to our fleet courser be the Hero may we transplant us, Rudra, in our children.
2. With the most saving medicines which thou givest, Rudra, may I attain a hundred winters. Far from us banish enmity and hatred, and to all quarters maladies and trouble.
3. Chief of all born art thou in glory, Rudra, armed with the thunder, mightiest of the mighty. Transport us over trouble to well-being repel thou from us all assaults of mischief.
4. Let us not anger thee with worship, Rudra, ill praise, Strong god! or mingled invocation. Do thou with strengthening balms incite our heroes: I hear thee famed as best of all physicians.
5. May I with praise-songs win that Rudra's favour who is adored with gifts and invocations. Never may the tawny god, fair-checked, and gracious, swift hearing, yield us to this evil purpose.
6. The Strong, begirt by Maruts, hath refreshed me, with most invigorating food, imploring. As he who finds a shade in fervent sunlight may I, uninjured, win the bliss of Rudra.

7. *Where is that gracious hand of thine, O Rudra, the hand that giveth health and bringeth comfort, Remover of the woe that gods have sent us? O Strong One, look thou on me with compassion.*
8. *To him the strong, great, tawny, fair-complexioned, I utter forth a mighty hymn of praises. We serve the brilliant god with adorations, we glorify, the splendid name of Rudra.*
9. *With firm limbs, multiform, the strong, the tawny adorns himself with bright gold decorations: The strength of godhead never departs from Rudra, him who is sovereign of this world, the mighty.*
10. *Worthy, thou carry thy bow and arrows, worthy, thy many-hued and honoured necklace. Worthy, thou cut here each fiend to pieces: a mightier than thou there is not, Rudra.*
11. *Praise him the chariot-borne, the young, the famous, fierce, slaying like a dread beast of the forest. O Rudra, praised, be gracious to the singer. let thy hosts spare us and smite down another.*
12. *I bend to thee as thou approach, Rudra, even as a boy before the sire who greets him. I praise thee bounteous giver, Lord of heroes: give medicines to us as thou art lauded.*
13. *Of your pure medicines, O potent Maruts, those that are wholesome and health-bestowing those which our father Manu hath selected, I crave from. Rudra for our gain and welfare.*
14. *May Rudra's missile turn aside and spare us, the great wrath of the impetuous one avoids us. Turn, bounteous god, thy strong bow from our princes, and be thou gracious to our seed and offspring.*

> 15. O tawny Bull, thus showing forth thy nature, as neither to be wrath, O god, nor slay us. Here, Rudra, listen to our invocation. Loud may we speak, with heroes, in assembly.

In addition, the Rig Veda gives us the sacred Rudra Mantra:

"we offer our respect to the three-eyed Lord who is fragrant and who nourishes all living beings. As the ripe cucumber is freed from its stalk, we pray for you to move us away from the ensnare of death and put us on the path of salvation)".

Author's note: Lord Shiva, in the form of Rudra, is praised in the above hymns and extracts with some attributes that are not referred to in the later Hindu scriptures. The mention as father of the Maruts (or Rudras) is interesting as there are many of these warriors referred to in the Vedas as violent and aggressive with golden weapons and chariots. Father may be a reference to leader rather than parent.

The Maruts may have been carried over into the Puranic tales as the Ganas (Shivaganas), but they are not referred to as the sons of Lord Shiva In the above hymns, Rudra is a healer with many references to medicines, strengthening balms, best of physicians, health-bestowing etc In addition to the above, there is mention of the more familiar traits for Lord Shiva of being armed with thunder, mightiest of the mighty, sovereign of this world, mightier than thou there is not. With respect to the Lord of Destruction, there are references to the anger and wrath, chariot-borne, slayer of dreaded beasts, and for Rudra's missiles to turn aside and spare us.

There is also a mention that Rudra is armed with bows and arrows and that he will cut each fiend to pieces. Many of the above traits were imbued into Lord Shiva in the form of the Destroyer and as mentioned above, Rudra is now synonymous with that characteristic of Lord Shiva. There is beauty in the Rig Veda verses which are practical for the Grihastha householder in giving thanks *and asking for protection for daily aspects of their life. Agriculture may have been the main profession at the time, but these verses remain current for all professions and endeavour. Whilst readers may be put off by the length of the Rig Veda, it is worth a visit as one of the oldest religious texts ever recorded.*

Sama Veda

The Sama Veda is believed to have been recorded in 1200-800 B.C. As is the case for the Rig Veda, the "nature" or "elemental" gods feature more prevalently than the Hindu Trinity. Lord Shiva appears in minor sections as Rudra where upon Agni, God of Fire, is stated to know the manner of praise in which to procure the favour of Rudra. Rudra is referred to as the causer of grief and the Rudras and the Maruts are also referred to in the text as deities to which to perform sacrifices in the name of. In the Sama Veda, Indra, King of the Gods is referred to as the Lord of the Maruts and the Rudras are said to sing to their own primeval divinity.

Author's note: The Sama Veda does not refer to Lord Brahma or Lord Shiva other than the minor mentions of Rudra set out above. Some of Lord Vishnu's avatars are referred to, but again these are sparse mentions. Lord Indra and Lord Agni feature most heavily in this Veda along with the Moon (Chandra referred to here as Soma), Lord Mitra and Lord Varuna (Gods of the Sky). There are some two-thousand verses in the Sama Veda that cover music and elevating one's consciousness through the mantras. Whilst, filled with magnificent poetry, the Sama Veda does not provide much additional exploration into the character and philosophy of Lord Shiva.

However, this Veda includes melodious mix of devotional verses and spirituality that should be sung and heard as opposed to being just read. It is the root of much of the classical music and dance to be found across the Indian Sub-Continent.

Yajur Veda

The Yajur Veda (composed in "White" and "Black" sections) is believed to have been recorded in 1200-800 B.C. and contains multiple references to Rudra as set out below. In this Veda, one sees the familiar hallmarks of Lord Shiva:

- Let Rudra's dart avoid you. Abide, with this lord of cattle.
- May Rudra guide thee hither in the path of (Lord) Mitra.
- May Rudra with the Vasus (attendants to the gods) be favourable to thee.
- Rudra with the taniman (garden)...Rudra with the blood.
- He eats of the wild, the wild is power, and so he bestows power upon himself.
- Rudra alone yields to no second.
- O Rudra; rejoice in it; with it for food, do thou go away beyond the Mujavants[cxxvi]. With unstrung bow, thy club in thy hand, clad in skins.
- Rudra is his dread form; verily he cuts him down to him; swiftly he reaches misfortune.
- Tisya (auspicious) is Rudra.
- The fire becoming Rudra would leap after him and slay him.
- He tramples with the thunderbolt on the evil foe; from the lordship of Rudra.
- Rudra in the fire, in the waters, in the plants, the Rudra that hath entered all beings, to that Rudra be homage.
- Rudra overlord of animals.
- Now the fire is Rudra, the beast the sacrificer; if he were to produce the fire after offering the beast, he would place the sacrificer in the power of Rudra.

In addition, there is a substantial "offering to Rudra" chapter in the Yajur Veda which has the following references that readers will recognize as traits of Lord Shiva:

- *Homage to thy bow and arrow.*
- *O liver on the mountains, confounding all the serpents.*
- *Blue-necked and ruddy.*
- *To him of all creatures.*
- *Him of the braided hair.*
- *Armed leader of hosts, lord of assailers, to you that are destructive.*
- *To the hero and the destroyer.*
- *Lord of the fields.*
- *To him of the drum, the unconquerable.*
- *Destroyer of men.*

Author's note: The Yajur Veda provides multiple references to Lord Shiva in the form of Rudra. These include his position as the Destroyer and the Lord of Animals. There is reference to the familiar characteristics of his wrath, his blue-neck, serpents, his being clad in skins, his braided hair, his abode in the mountains and his bow and arrow. The trademark trident does not feature in the Vedas for Rudra. The Yajur Veda contains two-thousand mantras dealing with sacrificial formulas and rites to appease the gods and the hymns to Lord Shiva in the persona of Rudra include multiple elements of devotion to win the favour of this deity.

The accolade of Lord of the Fields can be seen in chapter C5 of this book to be consistent with Kedarnath Temple (Kedarnath means "Lord of the Fields"). The Vedas were composed in advance of the Puranas and the Hindu Epics; however, already the many traits of Lord Shiva were being formed. The Yajur Veda is upbeat in many ways confirming that "he who sees all existence in the self and the self in all existence. Falls not into the trap of blighting and weakening despondency".

The mantras themselves can help to develop sensory control and will power to be free of ignorance and to offer one's devotion to the heavens. One other critical point to note is that the Yajur

Veda, like the other Vedas, is not instructing us to follow a life of asceticism; instead, a more practical and balanced approach is considered to control and self-improvement alongside the Grihastha's daily responsibilities. The mantras highlight at many junctures that there is great beauty to be seen in everyday life.

Atharva Veda

The Atharva Veda is believed to have been recorded in 1200 -800 B.C. There are six thousand hymns with mantras to guard against number of items including but not limited to:

- bad weather,
- ill health,
- anger,
- jealousy, and
- serpents...

There are also mantras for winning the favour of the heavens for finding:

- a spouse,
- having a child,
- driving away demons, and
- triumphing in battle.

These are mantras and procedures for every imaginable real life situation. Some of these come across as spells or incantations alongside the religious rituals; however, one of the central philosophies of the Vedas is to provide an exercise for control of the mind and senses through focus and concentration. The Veda also sets out in a number of locations that all the Vedic gods are one giving rise to the inclusive Advaita philosophy of Hinduism.

Lord Shiva, in the form of Rudra features in a few minor locations in the prayers. Some examples have been set out below:

- *Whoever treateth us as foes, be he our own or strange to us, a kinsman or a foreigner,*
- *May Rudra with his arrows pierce and slay these enemies of mine,*
- *Reverence be to Rudra, reverence to the takman (fever),*
- *Adoration be to thee, O Rudra, as thou casteth (thy arrow),*
- *Adoration to the (arrow) when it has been placed upon (the bow); adoration to it as it is being hurled,*
- *Adoration to it when it has fallen down!*
- *Rudra has broken your necks, may he also break your ribs, ye spooks!*

Author's note: In the Atharva Veda one does not gain additional insight into Lord Shiva's characteristics and philosophy but there is reverence to Rudra to help deal with everyday practical problems and to gain their favour for everyday wishes. There are references to Prajapati with respect to being a lord of animals. However, these have not been set out above as these may relate to Lord Brahma as he is referred to in the Puranas. Prajapati may also refer to Lord Vishnu and is distinct from Pasupathi as a concept. The Atharva Veda contains many thousands of mantras for different situations and includes medical and scientific practices also. There are positive hymns in favour of world peace and even though these may lose something in the translation from the original Sanskrit, these are words to admire: "May the earth be peaceful, may the atmosphere be peaceful…may all the enlightened persons be peaceful, may all the actions be peaceful". In addition to the above there is a benediction for all readers to take away with them:

"May you see a hundred autumns, may you thrive a hundred autumns, and may you remain pure a hundred autumns".

Figure 24: Original Vedic Mauscripts

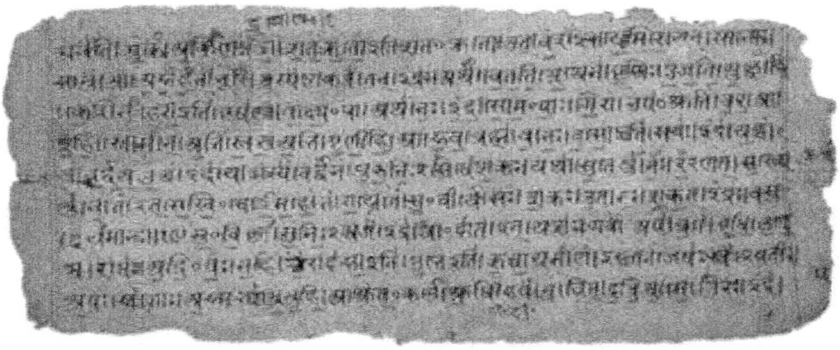

The Vedas are the earliest recorded of the Hindu Scriptures and one of the oldest religious books in the world. They combine poetry, religion, philosophy, science, and ritual in equal measure and are an important part of life in the Indian Sub-Continent. The four Vedas are (i) Rig, (ii) Yajur, (iii) Sama, and (iv) Atharva. The Rig Veda contains over ten thousand mantras dealing with the forms of prayer, existence, and human evolution; the Atharva Veda contains almost six thousand mantras dealing with medicine, science, and protection from evil spirits; the Sama Veda contains two thousand mantras dealing with music and elevating one's consciousness to achieve the Parabrahman state; and the Yajur Veda contains two thousand mantras dealing with sacrificial formulas and control of the universe. The earliest known surviving copies of any of the Vedas are the copies of the Rig Veda and Atharva Veda that are stored in the Bhandarkar Oriental Institute in the State of Maharashtra in India. The earliest written scriptures are believed to have been recorded in 1800 B.C. Lord Shiva is referred to in the early Vedas as Rudra, a Deity that became subsumed into the forms of Lord Shiva as The Destroyer. The next chapter of this book looks at the Upanishads which extend the philosophy of the Vedas and explore in more detail the path to moksha and liberation of the self.

PART B: *GRIHASTHA* – The Hindu Scriptures

Chapter B4 - Lord Shiva in the Upanishads

This chapter explores the eighteen Principal Upanishads and the fourteen Shiva (Saiva) Upanishads and highlights the mentions of Lord Shiva that help to confirm our understanding of this Hindu God's appearance and philosophy.

The Principal Upanishads

There are two hundred[cxxvii] Upanishads (commonly referred to as the Vedanta) These are central elements of Hindu scripture that relate to meditation and philosophy when compared to the symbology and ritualism of the Vedas discussed in the above chapter. Twelve of these Upanishads are referred to as the Mukhya or Principal Upanishads and attached to the Vedas. These core Upanishads were believed to have been written in the first millennium B.C. The word Upanishad could be translated into "secret teaching" or it could also be translated as "sit close by" (as a student may sit by a teacher).

A summary of the deities mentioned in these Mukhya Upanishads is set out in the table overleaf. This chapter considers Lord Shiva as mentioned in the twelve Principal Upanishads. Readers will note from the table below that there are many more references to Lord Shiva/Rudra and Lord Vishnu in the Principal Upanishads than in the core Vedas explored in the previous chapter. In addition, this chapter looks at the fourteen Shiva (or Saiva) Upanishads which contain multiple references to Lord Shiva. Readers should note that there is a rich body of philosophy contained within the Upanishads that is not discussed below as this is beyond the focus of this book. However, the author encourages readers to examine these sacred teachings if they get an opportunity as the information has inspired a significant amount of Eastern and Western philosophy, poetry, and literature over the years.

Summary of the Principal Upanishads

Principal Upanishad	Deities and other concepts referred to in the prose
Isa	Dakshinamurti (the primeval sage), Brahman, Agni, Maya
Kena	Shiva, Uma, Parvati, Indra, Agni, Vayu, Brahman
Katha	Yama (Death), Brahman, Agni, the primeval Tree of Life, Ethereal Angels
Taittiriya	Mitra (God of Wisdom), Varuna, Aryaman (Eye of the Sun), Indra, Brihaspati (of Ancient Speech), Vishnu, Brahma, Vayu, Brahman, Celestial Angels, Ananda (Bliss), Dakshinamurti, Prajapati
Aitareya	Brahman, Agni, Vayu, Aditya, Prajapati
Mundaka	Brahman, Atharvan (son of Brahman), Kali, Dharma, Agni
Mandukya	Brahman, Indra, Indra's Pantheon, The different states of (i)Vaisnavara, (ii)Taijasa, (iii)Prajna, (iv)Turiya
Prajna	Indra, Rudra, Brahman, Isvara (The Personal God)
Brihadaranyaka	Aditya, Vayu, Prajapati, God of Death, Brahman, Indra, Varuna, Soma, Rudra, Parganya, Yama, Mrityu, Isvara, Dharma, Maya, Chandra, Prajapati, Akshara (ether), Vasus (elements and celestial bodies), Gautama
Chandogya	Brahman, Agni, Soma, God of Rain, King of Plants, Ganges, Indra, Prajapati
Maitri	Brahman, Angels & Devils, Yama, Prajapati, Rudra, Vishnu, Agni, Varuna, Vayu, Indra, Chandra
Svetasvatara	Brahman, the three tendencies (i) Rajas (activity), (ii) Tamas (passivity), (iii) Sattva (clarity), Savitri (God of Seers), Agni, Maya, Rudra

PART B: *GRIHASTHA* – The Hindu Scriptures

The Isa Upanishad

The Isa Upanishad contains the following passage mentioning Dakshinamurti who is believed to be Lord Shiva (and is to this day portrayed as such in temple carvings and artwork).

> *"So, worship of the Immanent without the worship of the Transcendent leads to different consequences. This we have learned from the Ancient Rishis and the primeval sage Dakshinamurti who taught by silence".*

Lord Shiva is oft depicted in meditation as Part C to this book examines in more detail. There is no specific mention of Lord Shiva or Rudra in the Isa Upanishad beyond the reference to Dakshinamurti.

Author's note: The above passage considers the distinction between (i) immanent devotion to god within oneself and within the universe when compared to (ii) transcendent devotion without forms or limits. Vedic teachings argue that it is possible to reconcile the practice of both forms of worship.

The Kena Upanishad

Lord Shiva is referred to in passing in the Kena Upanishad when introducing the Goddess Uma who is confirmed as Goddess Parvati, wife of Lord Shiva:

Then in that same place Indra came toward an incredibly beautiful woman, highly bejeweled, and smelling sweetly of perfumed fragrance. It was Uma, wife of Lord Shiva, daughter of Himavat, once known as Parvati".

The extract confirms the relationship between Lord Shiva and Goddess Parvati (and confirms that Goddess Uma is Goddess Parvati). Himavat is confirmed as Goddess Parvati's father providing consistency with the Shiva Purana stories set out in Part A of this book.

Author's note: The above story is summarized in the Introduction chapter to this book (the battle between the gods and the demons over who was entitled to drink the nectar of immortality that was produced when the ocean was formed). The events can also be found in the Kena Upanishad and the Shiva Purana (Lord Shiva features more prominently in the latter version).

The Katha Upanishad

There is no mention of Lord Shiva or his different forms in the Katha Upanishad.

Author's note: This Upanishad belongs to Lord Yama, God of Death and Lord of Dharma (see chapter A1 of this book).

The Taittiriya Upanishad

The Taittiriya Upanishad contains the following passage mentioning Dakshinamurti once again:

"Prajapati is one drop of the blissful love of Brahman, like the Supreme Sage Dakshinamurti."

Scholars[cxxviii] have argued in their analysis of the Principal Upanishads that the following passage from the Taittiriya Upanishad may refer to Lord Shiva as the cook who devoured egos:

"He who sacrifices me, he alone preserves me. He who eats food I too eat as food. I overcome the whole world; I am endowed with golden light like the blazing sun."

Author's note: The tales of Lord Shiva are replete with instances in which the ego, ignorance, and arrogance of demons and other deities are destroyed (or devoured) by Lord Shiva.

PART B: *GRIHASTHA* – The Hindu Scriptures

The Aitareya Upanishad

There is no mention of Lord Shiva or his different forms in the Aitareya Upanishad.

Author's note: As with many of the Upanishads, the Aitareya Upanishad references Brahma plus Agni, Aditya, and Vayu (Gods of Fire, Sun, and Air).

The Mundaka Upanishad

There is no mention of Lord Shiva or his different forms in the Mundaka Upanishad.

Author's note: Many of the Upanishads including the Mundaka Upanishad refer to both Brahman (the Supreme Lord) and Lord Brahma (of the Hindu Trinity). This Upanishad includes a discussion of the "word of appearance" or the phenomenal world as one perceives it. It also reinforces the importance of good deeds within one's life alongside realization of the "higher good" to be free from ignorance and arrogance.

"Fools live in darkness, the wise in their own conceit."

The Upanishad teaches that one should be conscious of reality, love, and the self through concentration, attention, and apperception without craving or desire.

The Mandukya Upanishad

There is no mention of Lord Shiva or his different forms in the Mandukya Upanishad.

The Prajna Upanishad

The following reference to Time may be a reference to Lord Shiva as Pasupathi, the Lord of Animals:

> "He has twelve limbs corresponding to the lunar months. He is the pull of water and their tides, the substance above the

heavens, above the sky. Other calculators of apparent time say that the whole universe is fixed like the spokes on the nave of a wheel, who as the embodiment of illusory Time is possessed of seven wheels in the form of seven horses, endowed with six spokes of six seasons. Whether possessor of five feet, twelve limbs, seven wheels or six spokes, it is the Aeon, the embodiment of the mystery of Time, Ruler of Creatures led by the Sun and the Moon which causes a world of illusion."

Lord Shiva is referred to in the Prajna Upanishad as Rudra with the following passage:

"By thy strength you are Rudra as guardian, you move in the atmosphere of space as a Sun, the Lord of Lights. When you shed rain, the creatures sigh blissfully knowing there will be the substance they desire. You are ever pure, Oh Life Force, The One Seed, The Devourer, The True Lord of All. We give our food to be eaten, all pervading Space you are our Father."

Author's note: This is consistent with Lord Shiva's depictions as Pasupathi, Lord of the Animals; and Rudra, The Destroyer (and Devourer). Lord Shiva is the devourer of ignorance and delusions once again.

The Maitri Upanishad

This Upanishad mentions the Hindu Trinity of deities and the circumstances of Creation:

"In the beginning there was darkness alone. It was moved by Brahman, it became agitated, it became obscure, then it became goodness. The essence flowed forth. This is "That" the self, intelligent, reflected in men and women as the sun in jars of water. Knowing this body affirmed by his conception, willing, being, you are Prajapati, called Viva. "That" part belonging to darkness is called Rudra, the Wild God, "That" to obscurity is

Brahman, the Creator, "That" to goodness is the God, Lord Vishnu The Preserver."

Author's note: This is the traditional view of the Hindu Trinity with the roles of Creator, Preserver and Destroyer. The initial passage of text alludes to the "one-ness" of Lord Shiva and Lord Vishnu (darkness...became goodness). The references to "darkness" and "The Wild God" are consistent with Lord Shiva's Rudra form as the Lord of Destruction. Chapter A14 of this book explores the Hindu version of Creation of the universe in more detail.

The Svetasvatara Upanishad

This Upanishad develops the lore of Rudra/Lord Shiva in more detail:

"The non-dual One who casts the net of Maya rule through His powers. They who perceive this reach Immortality. For there is One Rudra without a second who rules all with his Power he dwells within every creature. After projecting all world illusion, he becomes the Guardian withdraws his powers for the dissolution of the end of an Aeon. He is omniscient, his eyes, his face, his arms, his feet everywhere. The One God creating heaven and earth bestows hands on humans and birds with wings. Rudra, the Origin and Source of Divine Powers, Guardian of our Universe, projected his brilliant knowledge as His inner essence in the beginning."

This Upanishad discusses the following elements of Rudra (who is confirmed in the Svetasvatara Upanishad to be the "Omnipotent Shiva"):

- *Divine form which is not frightening but shows us True Virtue through a joyful form,*
- *Lives on a mountain peak* (a potential reference to Kailas),

- *Wields an arrow* (there is no mention of the trident or battle axe),
- *Envelopes the whole universe and extends beyond it tenfold with thousands of heads, eyes, and feet* (this may be a reference to the cosmic dance of Nataraja),
- *One reaches peace by realizing Lord Shiva as subtler than the subtle, in the middle of the unknowable and imperishable ignorance,*
- *There is only Shiva, the Supreme, as potential energy, a rest, in stillness,*
- *Protector of our sons, husbands, wives, daughters, and grandchildren. Do not wreak destruction on our lives. In wrath do not slay your fearless servants.*

Author's note: *This Upanishad confirms many of the characteristics of Lord Shiva that have been explored in this book to include the celestial mountain top abode, Lord of Animals, Nataraja (with arms and feet everywhere), and the conflicting personas of "Destroyer" and "Benevolent God". There are hymns of prayer and devotion to Lord Shiva to ensure that one has his favour. The reference to Maya is in relation to the illusion one must overcome to achieve liberation.*

The Svetasvatara Upanishad refers to the creation of the universe once again and Lord Shiva's role in this (see chapter A14 of this book). The Shiva Upanishads in the next section deal expand on these concepts in more detail. The concept of the creation and destruction of the universe encourages one to look beyond the world we live in.

In this main Upanishad, Lord Shiva is the Supreme, in some of the main Upanishads it is Lord Brahma and in others it is Lord Vishnu.

The Brihadaranyaka Upanishad

There is no mention of Lord Shiva or his different forms in the Brihadaranyaka Upanishad beyond a cursory reference to Rudra.

Author's note: This Upanishad lists out many deities that are mentioned throughout the other Principal Upanishads, but it does not provide any specific details about them. There is an interesting discussion within this Upanishad relating to the route to moksha (liberation) of the self with many lucid analogies such as salt dissolving in water being comparable to the self dissolving in the sea of pure consciousness. The Upanishad also sets out that as a person acts, so they become in life. Those who do good become good; those who do harm become bad. One is what one's deep, driving desire is.

The Chandogya Upanishad

There is no mention of Lord Shiva or his different forms in the Chandogya Upanishad.

The Shiva Upanishads

The Shiva (or Saiva) Upanishads are fourteen in number. The Kaivalya, Atharvashiras, and Athavashikha Upanishads are believed to have been written in the first millennium B.C., many of the other Saiva Upanishads were recorded after this date. These Upanishads contain several references to Lord Shiva that are set out below and they also explore the practices of devotion to and meditation upon Lord Shiva as a means to achieve moksha (liberation) a so referred to as the Parabrahman state.

Summary of the Shiva Upanishads

Shiva Upanishad	Main concepts explored with respect to Lord Shiva
Kaivalya	Inter-relatedness of the states of consciousness
Atharvashiras	Attainment of the Parabrahman
Atharvashikha	Freedom from illusion and delusion
Brihajjabala	Shiva and Shakti relationship and the universe
Kalagni Rudra	The use of the tripundra[cxxix] marks in devotion
Dakshinamurti	Mantras for the attainment of knowledge
Sharabha	Summary of main characteristics
Akshamalika	Rudraksha beads in meditation and prayer
Rudrahridya	The Hindu Trinity and the Parabrahman state
Bhasmajabala	Liberation from samsara (reincarnation)
Rudrakshajabala	Why the rudraksha beads are considered sacred
Pancabrahma	Non-dualist, formless character of Lord Shiva
Jabali	The use of the tripundra marks in meditation
Gahapatya	The four aspects: dharma, artha, kama, moksha

Kaivalya Upanishad

The Kaivalya (meaning solitude) Upanishad is represented as a discourse between Lord Brahma and a sage who asks what is good for them and how to reach the Parabrahma (the highest, supreme state). It has a useful summary of the "aims" in life of dharma, kama, artha, and finally moksha.

The Upanishad states that while useful for purifying the mind, karma alone cannot help one to obtain enlightenment. This is only possible through detachment of freedom, emotional attachments, clinging, leaning on people, material things, situations, power, fame, position, and psychological weakness. The Upanishad states the following:

> "I do not fear death, as I do not have death. I have no separation from my true Self, no doubt about my existence, nor have I discrimination based on birth. I have no father or mother, nor did I have a birth. I am not the relative, nor the friend, nor the guru, nor the disciple. I am indeed, "That" eternal knowing and bliss, Shiva, love, and pure consciousness... By meditating upon Lord Parameswara consorted by Mother Uma, the Highest Lord, the all-powerful, the three-eyed, the blue-necked and the ever tranquil, a true man of reflection reaches Him, who is the Source of all the manifested world, the Witness-of-all, and who is beyond all darkness".

This Upanishad also suggests that to meditate it is important to self-abnegate, i.e., remove all distractions for the mind and body. This will facilitate control of the inner (heart) and outer (mind) senses. It points towards the meditation of a tranquilized Lord Shiva and his three eyes which are referred to as the sun, the moon, and the fire. The Upanishad also discusses the four states of consciousness (awake), sub-consciousness (dreaming), unconsciousness (asleep), and the Parabrahman (supreme state of liberation) that can be attained through meditation. There is an exploration of the link between the three primary states, by way of example the dream state being influenced by the awake state and vice-versa.

Author's note: There is an elegance to the prose in the Upanishad which through Lord Shiva is informing us to mentally free ourselves from attachment by remembering that all are spiritual children of Lord Shiva and Goddess Parvati. There is reference once again to the three-eyes and the blue neck of Lord Shiva, unmistakable characteristics discussed in other chapters of this book. The Upanishad also covers scientific and psychological ground in its exploration of the different states to assist the devotee in recognizing the differences and the inter-relatedness.

Atharvashiras Upanishad

This Upanishad is represented as a discourse between Lord Shiva/Rudra and the gods relating to the attainment of Parabrahma (the highest, supreme state).

The Devas (i.e., gods) journey to Mahakalaisa (Mount Kailash) and meet Lord Shiva referred to as Rudra: the one who drives away the diseased of delusion. They ask who he is (one would think that they would know this) and Lord Shiva indulges them with a summary of his non-duality):

"I am the one absolute existence, the innermost Atman that is the basis of the apprehension "I" and the like. I was in existence long before the creation, even prior to beginningless time. I am at present in existence".

Lord Shiva continues:

"I am the Brahman, and I am the Abrahman (the prime cause and the myriads of its effects); I am also the Atman and the Anatman; I am the one inclining towards the east and towards the west; I am the one inclining towards the south and towards the north."

There is further confirmation in the Atharvashiras Upanishad of the roles of Lord Shiva as Mahadeva, Lord of the Animals

(Pasupathi), and The Destroyer (Rudra - in particular, the destroyer of the creatures of ignorance).

Author's note: This Upanishad highlights the different persona of Lord Shiva and sets out the importance of freeing ourselves from the illusion and delusion/ignorance of one's lives to attain liberation.

Atharvashikha Upanishad

The Atharvashiras Upanishad sets out the root of the sacred sound AUM with the Hindu Trinity embedded within:

- A – the colour of red and yellow with Lord Brahma as the presiding deity. The "A" also encompasses the state of being awake,
- U – the colour of the sheen of lightning with Lord Vishnu (the All Pervading) as the presiding deity. The "U" encompasses the dream state,
- M – the colour of white with Lord Rudra (Prosperity and Adversity) as the presiding deity. The "M"" encompasses the state of being asleep.

This is a unique reference to Shiva as a potential Lord of Prosperity and Adversity, not a common trait associated with this deity. This Upanishad suggests that by completely dissolving the prana (life force/breath) along with the organs of perception and action in the mind, and remaining with the mind alone as the residuum, the state of Rudra can be obtained. When a state of a deity is referred to, this means achieving the highest state of mind and liberation of the soul. Lord Shiva is mentioned as one who is exclusively worthy of being meditated upon as he brings about the well-being of all his devotees and this is evident from many of the tales about Lord Shiva who in, his generosity to devotees, is often referred to as Bholenath (the down to earth

Lord). The above extracts are consistent with the stories in this book where austerities are undertaken in the name of Lord Shiva.

Author's note: It is interesting to see the letters of the spiritual sound AUM (sometimes written as OM) being linked to the Hindu Trinity and three of the four states of consciousness (awake, in dream, asleep, and the Parabrahman highest state). There is a recommendation for achieving the state of Rudra (or Shiva) –i.e., achieving liberation and the Parabrahma or Supreme state. This recommendation is to free ourselves of perception and action through meditation upon Lord Shiva.

Brihajjabala Upanishad

This Upanishad is a discourse on creation of the phenomenal world as one perceives it. The creation and destruction of the world left behind ignorance and concomitants which assume the form of the belief in the existence in the phenomenal world. Sacred ash and rudraksha beads are reiterated as important tools to help protect us and to help with one's journey to moksha (liberation). The Upanishad explores Lord Shiva's relationship with Shakti (divine feminine power) creating balance in the universe. Lord Shiva is referred to as the conqueror of death in relation to the ignorance of the atman.

Author's note: The Upanishad tells us that the truth of creation and life cannot be seen by the ignorant naked eye. Only the creative minds of poets and seers, which lies deep in their hearts can provide this vision and that is the place to look for truth. As with the other Shiva Upanishads, there is a movement away from the characteristics of Lord Shiva as a warrior who defeated Lord Yama, and instead one is presented with the formless Lord Shiva ensuring the death of ignorance.

PART B: *GRIHASTHA* – The Hindu Scriptures

Kalagni Rudra Upanishad

This Upanishad commences with a discussion of the tripundra (three marks) of Lord Shiva which is worn by devotees as body art on the forehead, most often with three straight lines of ash and on occasion with a red dot at the centre. The Upanishad states to wear the three marks on the forehead, the chest, and the shoulders and that these represent the following:

1. The syllable A, the fire, the atman (Self), the power of sentient action (Lord Brahma), the Rig Veda, the early morning austerity,
2. The syllable U, the rhythm, the anatman (mind and body), the power of truth (Lord Vishnu), the Yajur Veda, the noon-tide austerity,
3. The syllable M, the inertia, the Paramatman[cxxx] (supreme state), the power of knowledge (Lord Rudra), the Sama Veda, the evening austerity.

It is set out that the devotee who dons this mark of Lord Shiva, be he Brhamacharya, Grihastha, Vanaprastha, or Sannyasa, becomes hallowed from the effects of sins. He becomes one who has had his ablutions in all the sacred waters even without resorting to them. He attains the fruit of having studied all of the four Vedas. He becomes the reciter of all the Rudra-mantras in perpetuity.

Author's note: The wearing of the tripundra marks as an act of devotion is practical for those who have not the time to study the Vedas or the access to the sacred rivers. It is a simple act of faith to keep close to Lord Shiva and to keep him close. There is no reference in the Kalagni Rudra Upanishad to the third eye of Lord Shiva; however, in idols and artwork, Lord Shiva is oft pictured with three lines across his forehead with the vertical third eye closed within the tripundra.

Dakshinamurti Upanishad

The Dakshinamurti (Primeval Sage) Upanishad sets out mantras to be employed in the attainment of knowledge. The legendary and immortal Sage Markandeya (see chapter A1 of this book) features in a discourse in glorification of Lord Shiva as the means to achieve the Parabrahman state. Sage Markandeya explains that his long life and sate of bliss come from meditation on Lord Shiva as the Paramatman (supreme Self). Lord Shiva is referred to as the primeval sage, being resplendent with the beams of the crescent-moon, destroying all ignorance, the import of the foremost worlds.

Knowledge is said to be achieved through non-differentiated perception of Lord Shiva through meditation. A number of mantras are listed for this purpose. Such knowledge is acquired by surrendering the entire functioning of the body to Lord Shiva. The innermost atman (self or soul) is referred to as a lamp of knowledge filled with the oil of detachment, furnished with the wick of devotion; and having the full receptacle (oil-can) as intense silence. This will irradicate the darkness of delusion.

Author's note: The Upanishad confirms Lord Shiva's form of the primeval sage, Dakshinamurti. One helpful aspect is the analogy that assists in the visualization of the commitment required to meditate on Lord Shiva. The starting point is the oil-can which is likened to intense silence into which the oil of detachment is stored. Only in this intense silence and concentration can we hope to store detachment. The oil is then poured into the lamp which symbolizes the knowledge we are seeking to obtain. The knowledge is the receptacle and also the means to which light is focused so that it is not just intense heat. The wick is one's devotion that absorbs detachment and is lit to remove one's delusions. Whether one has practiced meditation before or not, the above analogy is simple and effective in guiding the devotee.

Sharabha Upanishad

This Upanishad confirms that the route to moksha (liberation) is through meritorious deeds and freeing oneself from delusion by meditation on Lord Shiva, Lord of the Mountain (see Introduction chapter of this book), armed with the trident, to reach the recesses of the heart. Many of his exploits are celebrated including his blue neck from drinking poison to save the three worlds (see Introduction chapter), the creation of Virabhadra (see Introduction chapter), the story of Nataraja in which the Demon Apasmara is vanquished (see chapter A7), the annihilation of the Tripurasura (see chapter A8). The universe is also said to have been destroyed by a single spark of fire from Lord Shiva's forehead prior to Creation (see chapter A14).

Author's note: The Sharabha Upanishad sets out a summary of all the main characteristics of Lord Shiva we have considered in this book. After these adulations and summaries of the heroic tales of Lord Shiva, there is instruction that righteous behaviour is an essential tenet in the search for moksha (liberation). This is not possible for a lewd, wicked person, puffed up with pride, a sycophant, a rouge, and a liar. A true person of upright conduct, possessed of self-control, mental composure, sincerity, and full of appreciation will be able to obtain this being released from the recurrence of births and deaths over and over again (samsara).

Akshamalika Upanishad

The Akshamalika Upanishad commences with a discussion between Lord Brahma and Lord Karitkeya (referred to as Guha, the six faced son of Lord Shiva) about how meditation and mantra with the aid of fifty Rudraksha beads can purify the mind and purge one of all sins. Lord Brahma responds that the thread is Lord Brahma, the right side of the beads Lord Shiva and the left side of the beads Lord Vishnu. Each of the fifty beads corresponds to one of the fifty letters of the Sanskrit alphabet and to a particular goal: by way of example, one bead will represent the destruction of evil spirits, another will be the curer of all diseases, another will bestow wealth, and so the mantra continues. Concentration on the beads is said in this Upanishad to assist with overcoming ignorance by focusing attention and overcoming the obstacles to spiritual elevation.

The Akshamalika Upanishad also introduces the following attributes for the Hindu Trinity:

- Lord Brahma, Mobility
- Lord Vishnu, Rhythm
- Lord Shiva, Inertia

Author's note: The use of meditation and the rudraksha beads as an aid for concentration is set out in this Upanishad as a guide for those who wish to attain moksha (liberation). The fifty beads each have a purpose. The Brahmacharya student benefits from a consolidation of the fifty letters of the Sanskrit alphabet which must be chanted (one for each bead). Those further along the life cycle such as the Grihastha householder benefit from the purpose of each bead as a means to address a particular and practical wish for their everyday lives. As one moves further along the life cycle, the beads become a means to achieve absolute concentration and mute out distractions from meditation.

Rudrahridya Upanishad

This Upanishad revisits Lord Shiva's role within the Hindu Trinity and continues the non-dual contention that they all function as one Supreme Parabrahman. Lord Shiva is held as the character of Lord Brahma and Lord Vishnu and all are accredited with Creation. Lord Shiva is the male form of all and the unmanifest and Goddess Parvati (called Uma in the Upanishad) is the female form of all and the manifest. What has to be done is by Lord Vishnu, what is being done is Lord Brahma, and the cause is Lord

Shiva. The Trinity have infinite existence, pure sentience, unsurpassed bliss, lying beyond the range of speech of the mind. Invisible, ungraspable, formless, eternal, omnipotent, and immanent in all. Lord Shiva is again referred to as the devourer, experiencing worlds by eating them and the various experiences afforded by the phenomenal world of ignorance. The Upanishad instructs to be well grounded in the Vedas to attain the Parabrahman state. The analogy is provided that satya (truth) is realized by aiming our atman (self or soul) as an arrow toward the centre of the target which is Lord Shiva. There should be deliberate aim from a practitioner who has experience and practice.

Author's note: The above Upanishad accords with chapter A14 of this book and the Puranic view of Creation where Lord Shiva is termed the "non-characterized" form. There is a helpful analogy in relation to an archer needing to practice at length before aim becomes accurate. In the same way one is instructed to practice meditation and immerse oneself in Vedic philosophy so that the atman will be able to hit the mark of the Parabrahman state. This is a sensible, practical, and reasonable way to approach this subject.

Bhasmajabala Upanishad

The Upanishad takes the rare form of a discourse with Lord Shiva on Mount Kailas, who shares his diadem with Goddess Parvati, is clad in the skin of a tiger, has the three parallel lines of the tripundra, has five faces relating to the five elements, is devoid of attachment, and who has the moon, the sun and fire as this three eyes. Lord Shiva instructs on a number of mantras and the importance of rising early to bathe before meditating on the rising Sun. The Upanishad also covers the union of Lord Shiva and Goddess Parvati as the creator of the Earth, and the generator of the Sun, the Moon, fire, and the three worlds. The Upanishad also confirms that the world of persons ignorant of the real nature of the atma (self of soul), on coming to realize Lord Shiva shall attain immortality and liberation. Lord Shiva states:

"The wind wafts only out of fear for me, the Sun rises only out of fear for me, the God of Fire discharges his duties only out of fear for me...I am the controller of all, the earth, the waters, the fire, the air, I am Kala (time), I am the Liberator."

The Upanishad also explores the subject of samsara (reincarnation) unless the self or soul can obtain moksha (liberation). One will be reborn multiple times in multiple forms until the cycle can be broken by obtaining moksha (liberation).

Author's note: This Upanishad commences with a reminder of Lord Shiva's many physical characteristics and is more seated in prayer and ritual than the philosophy of some of the other Shiva Upanishads. The discussion in relation to samsara is of interest. The relationship with Goddess Parvati is explored as a partnership of two equal halves making up the whole.

Rudrakshajabala Upanishad

The Upanishad sets out an interesting origin story for the sacred rudraksha beads that are used by many across the world in prayer and meditation. The beads come from the rudraksha trees. Lord Shiva was tasked with bringing about the destruction of the Tripurasura. The deity had to close his eyes once his task was complete and drops of water fell on the earth which became the rudraksha trees bearing the beads. They are sacred and will absorb sin and convey great religious merit to the wearer and whoever uses the beads in prayer and meditation. Wearing the beads, in particular on auspicious days, will convey wealth, perfect health, clear intellect, purity of mind, and wisdom.

Author's note: Many of the Shiva Upanishads look at the use of the sacred rudraksha beads to aid meditation. They are unique to look at and complex, but beautiful in shape and colour. The beads

PART B: *GRIHASTHA* – The Hindu Scriptures

are readily available from trees across the Indian Sub-Continent which makes these obtainable for all devotees who would wish to use them. They are easily placed on a thread due to the hollowing in the centre.

Figure 25: The Sacred Rudraksha Bead

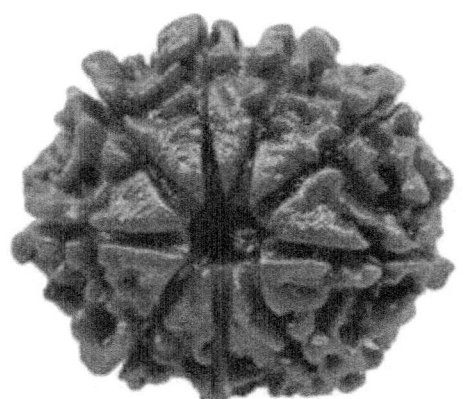

Pancabrahma Upanishad

This Upanishad looks at the non-dual, sentient character of Lord Shiva who is referred to as Mahadeva (the great god), controller of the three durations (past, present, and future). Keeper of the profound secrets of the universe. The East face of Sadashiva (perpetual Shiva – see chapter C1) is the character of the earth; the west face is the character of water, the south face is the character of fire, the north face is the character of air, the midpoint of the faces is the character of ether. Lord Shiva's body is said to be vast and indivisible as the macrocosm, granting all desires, healing all ills of the mind and body, wielding all powers, and transcending the three states of waking, dreaming, and sleeping. The unmanifest who is thoroughly tranquilized, having destroyed its own maya (illusion) becomes established in its own peerless non-dual existence (the Parabrahman) long before the phenomenal world as one perceives it came to be. Immune from the conception of things apart from itself. He who knows this becomes immortal and liberated.

Author's note: The Upanishad refers to the five elements as the faces of Lord Shiva and discusses creation and destructions of the universe at the end of each kalpa (see chapter A14). The Upanishad argues that the form of the radiance of Lord Shiva does not stand within the range of vision of persons deluded on account of their ignorance. Therefore, one is leaving behind the Brahmacharya's (student's) perception of Lord Shiva and his anthropomorphic characteristics discussed in Part A of this book. The five syllabled mantra of om-nam-ah-shiv-ay is referred to as an important tool in meditation on the formless, Advaita (non-dual) Lord Shiva as the Parabrahman. Most major religions believe in a similar, formless, non-dualist being as the Supreme.

Jabali Upanishad

This Upanishad also explores the tripundra mark discussed above in the Kalagni Rudra Upanishad. However, the discussion here relates to the wearing of the three lines of ash on the forehead as a means to acquire knowledge of the Parabrahman. The Kalagni Rudra Upanishad sets out the use of the mark for devotional prayer. The Jabali Upanishad sets out the use of the mark for intense mediation of Lord Shiva and profound silence through austerities is considered to be one critical means to achieve enlightenment. This Upanishad also discusses all living beings (men and animals) under Lord Shiva's title of Pasupathi, Lord of Animals. As one moves through the life stages, one may move from prayer and devotion to meditation.

Author's note: This Upanishad covers the same material as the Kalagni Rudra Upanishad setting out the manner in which to apply the tripundra mars, where to place it on the body, and what the three lines represent. However, this Upanishad suggests the use of the mark to assist with meditation on Lord Shiva to achieve the supreme state. The Kalagni Rudra Upanishad suggests the mark as an act of devotion. In meditation, the mark may assist in focusing the mind on Lord Shiva.

Gahapatya Upanishad

This Upanishad commences with a mantra in adoration of Lord Ganesha as the Remover of Obstacles (see chapter A3 of this book). Lord Shiva is referred to as the exclusive destroyer of all in the character of Rudra. Further, Rudra is confirmed to bring about the dissolution of the phenomenal world (as one perceives it) to be re-awakened in the same form again. This Upanishad contains multiple mantras on devotion to the deities and is linked in many locations to the Atharva Veda (see chapter B3 above). The Upanishad confirms the four aspects of human existence:

- Dharma (moral duty)
- Artha (purpose)
- Kama (love)
- Moksha (liberation)

Author's note: The different aspects of life are not to be confused with the four stages of life. The Brahmacharya student, the Grihastha householder, the Vanaprastha retiree, the Sannyasa aesthetic all tread the path of dharma, artha, kama and eventually moksha but there may be a different mix of priorities depending on the different stages of life one is at. As one progresses through the stages, one becomes a student, then a proponent , then an embodiment, and then a teacher of dharma. The same is true of artha and kama and one's understanding of these aspects may help us achieve moksha (liberation) of the Self.

Figure 26: Manasarovar – The Birthplace of Hindu Scripture

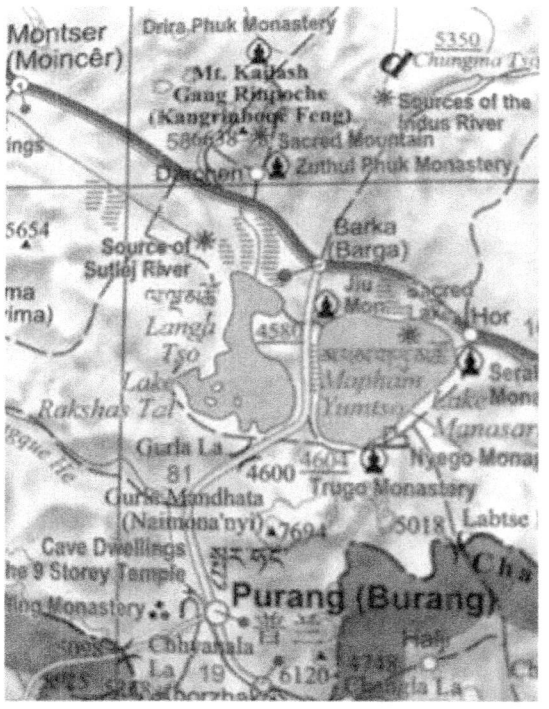

It is believed that the Vedas were first written down on the shores of Lake Manasarovar – the Lake of the Mind. Whilst the Hindu scriptures are believed to have been written down as far back as 1800 B.C., like many religious texts they have been passed down through generations in verbal form and are likely to have been conceived of in advance the date of recording.

PART C: *VANAPRASTHA*
LORD SHIVA TEMPLES

Introduction to PART C

Part C of this book is for the Vanaprastha (retired or approaching retirement and freeing oneself from material desires). Part C looks at fifteen religious/historical sites across the Indian Sub-continent and beyond it that are famed for their sculptures and carvings dedicated to Lord Shiva. The Vanaprastha may have the time and resources to undertake pilgrimages to these locations and there is much to be imbued from the impressive artwork and sculpture. There are thousands of Shiva Temples in existence; however, these fifteen locations have been selected for the detail and devotion that has gone into the depictions of Lord Shiva that are found on external walls, roofs and within the Temples. The Amarnath cave, the Unakoti stone carvings, and the Mohenjo-Daro excavation site are the exceptions which have been added due to the natural ice formation of a Shivalingam structure at the five thousand year-old Amarnath cave, the unique Lord Shiva stone idols at Unakoti, and the potential depiction of Lord Shiva in a fascinating four thousand year-old archaeological site in the Indus Valley.

The other Temples featured in this section were built many years ago; however, some have been rebuilt again and again after damage and destruction. By way of example, the Kedarnath Temple survived for four hundred years under snow and can now be visited once again. Each of the Temples has a vivid historical background and origin that will be explored in alignment with the tales and depictions of Lord Shiva. The carvings and idols reflect many hours of skilled craft and precision. These tell the stories of Lord Shiva in a visual manner which, when combined with the poetry of the scriptures, bring the deity to the front of mind. This is a crucial section as the synergy between the written word and

PART C: *VANAPRASTHA* – Lord Shiva Temples

artistic expression can assist us with one's comprehension of the features contained within them. A good analogy would be the combination of The Bible with Renaissance Artists' depictions of the holy text; the scriptures are complete as they are; however, the visual renditions help devotees with their analysis and understanding.

Temples/Sites covered in Part C

	Temple/Sites	Location	Cited in the Shiva Purana	Date constructed or rebuilt
1	Amarnath	Kashmir, India	N	Five thousand years old
2	Chidambaram	Tamil Nadu, India	N	900 C.E.
3	The Elephanta Caves	Maharashtra, India	N	500- 600 C.E.
4	Kailasnath	Maharashtra, India	N	500-800 C.E.
5	Kedarnath	Uttarakhand, India	Y	800 C.E.
6	Koneswaram	Sri Lanka	N	Original 200 B.C.
7	Mohenjo-Daro	Pakistan	N	2500 B.C.
8	Murudesawara	Karnataka, India	N	800 C.E.
9	Pasupatinath	Nepal	N	500 C.E.
10	Prambanan	Indonesia	N	850 C.E.
11	Rameswaram	Tamil Nadu, India	Y	1100-1700 C.E.
12	Somnath	Gujarat, India	Y	rebuilt in 800 C.E.
13	Unakoti	Tripura, India	N	1100 C.E.
14	Vadakunnathan	Kerala, India	N	500 C.E.
15	Viswanath	Uttar Pradesh, India	Y	1490 C.E. (rebuilt)

Char Dham Temples

There are four fabled "Char Dham" (four abodes) temples for Lord Shiva devotees where a yatra (pilgrimage) is believed in folklore to provide instant moksha (liberation) or at least help one along the way... These are:

- Kedarnath (chapter C5)
- Lingaraja (not covered in this book)
- Rameswaram (chapter C11)
- Somnath (chapter C12)

Pashupatinath (chapter C9) in Nepal is one of the four Nepalese Char Dhams. Other Char Dham's not associated with Lord Shiva, but Lord Vishnu include the holy sites of Badrinath, Dwaraka, and Puri. Kurukshetra, the holy city in Indian State of Haryana, is also an important site for devotees of Lord Vishnu as this is believed to be the location where the Bhagavad Gita was recited to Arjuna on the eve of the Mahabharata War.

Padal Petra Thalam Temples

The Padal Petra Thalam (or Shivasthalam) Temples are two hundred and seventy five temples that are referred to as sacred sites in the writings (the Tevaram hymns) of the Lord Shiva Nayanars. These were a group of around sixty sages living in South India in 600-800 C.E. who were devoted to Lord Shiva. They wrote a number of scriptures in the language of Tamil and set out the list of these important Lord Shiva Temples. The following Temples covered in Part C are all listed as Padal Petra Thalam Temples:

- Koneswaram (chapter C6)
- Pashupatinath (chapter C9)
- Rameswaram (chapter C11)

Only ten of these temples are outside of the state of Tamil Nadu.

PART C: *VANAPRASTHA* – Lord Shiva Temples

The Jyotirlinga Temples

The Shiva Purana and the Shiva Agamas both set out the saga of a battle fought between Lord Brahma and Lord Vishnu. The other deities were concerned about this encounter and appealed to Lord Shiva who went with Goddess Parvati and his army of one hundred Ganas to pacify his fellow members of the Hindu Trinity. When Lord Shiva reached the location of combat, he saw that Lord Brahma and Lord Vishnu and were on the verge of deploying their deadly weapons (called Maheshwar and Pashupat respectively). Fearing the destruction which these deadly weapons might have caused, Lord Shiva manifested himself between them in the form of "Analstamba" (a pillar of fire).

The celestial weapons were unleashed; however, both fell into the pillar of fire and were destroyed. Lord Brahma and Lord Vishnu were surprised to see this pillar of fire which was so enormous in scale that it reached above the sky and penetrated down into the earth. They forgot their battle and Lord Vishnu transformed himself into a boar and burrowed to the Patala (the underworld) to find the base, but he was unsuccessful in his attempt and came back. Similarly, Lord Brahma transformed himself into a swan and flew up in the sky to find the pinnacle but was also unsuccessful.

The Temples mentioned in the Shiva Purana (termed the Jyotirlinga) are believed to be locations where Lord Shiva has appeared as a column of fire on the Earth. Four of the original twelve Jyotirlinga Temples mentioned in the Shiva Purana are covered in the main chapters of this section: Viswanath, Rameswaram, Somnath and Kedarnath[cxxxi]. The renderings of Lord Shiva in the Temple shrines, idols, walls, artwork, caves, pillars, and interiors set out in the following chapters provide us with an additional level of clarity and consistency with respect to the stories already featured in this book and they help to build out *The Lord Shiva Narrative*. One would hope that the Vanaprastha retiree would find an opportunity to visit them.

Chapter C1 - Amarnath, Kashmir

The Amarnath (or "King of Gods") mountain peak is in the Himalayas in Jammu and Kashmir at the end of the Lidder Valley. This is a sacred cave that may Hindu devotees flock to each year despite the thirty-mile trek required to reach this natural shrine to Lord Shiva. However, the ongoing territorial dispute between India and Pakistan over Kashmir has complicated the situation for those wishing to undertake a pilgrimage. There have been terrorist attacks on travelers in recent years which has resulted in the annual journeys to Amarnath in the summer being cancelled.

The cave is at an altitude of just under four thousand metres but is accessible in the Hindu month of Shravan (July/August) notwithstanding the attacks referred to. The Amarnath cave is buried in the snow for most of the rest of the year. The cave is surrounded with mysticism and is believed to be one of the celestial retreats of Lord Shiva and Goddess Parvati in which Lord Shiva unveiled the secrets of Creation and immortality. A pair of doves can normally be seen in and around the cave and they are believed to be immortal creatures who heard Lord Shiva detail the divine secrets to Goddess Parvati. The cave is over five thousand years old which makes this an important place for the worship of Lord Shiva.

There is also a sacred lake (Sheshnag) on the pilgrimage route to Amarnath Cave from the town of Pahalgam (which itself is considered a sacred town for Nandi, the bull vahana (animal chariot) and Gana (soldier/attendant) of Lord Shiva). The folklore legend is that this lake was created by Vasuki, Lord of Serpents who adorns Lord Shiva's neck. The lake is abundant with large fish and Vasuki is believed by many locals to still reside in this lake in the Kashmir Valley to this day.

Key Idols and depictions

The Amarnath cave has a six-foot, naturally formed, ice Shivalinga which is believed to increase and reduce in size with lunar phases of the moon. The waxing and waning of the moon is associated with Lord Shiva as set out in the Introduction chapter of the book, and Lord Shiva is oft depicted with a crescent moon in his hair. There are two smaller naturally occurring ice linga either side of the main Shivalinga in the Amarnath cave. The ice formations are stalagmites that have formed over time, but they have an extremely smooth texture that creates the other-worldly appearance of this naturally occurring aniconic depiction of Lord Shiva.

The ice linga was once twenty feet high; however, the maximum height it reaches each year has been falling due to global warming. Given the age of the cave, Amarnath is one of the oldest locations for the worship of Lord Shiva that are in existence today. Natural formations of this ilk are a welcome focal point for devotees as they represent divine architecture as opposed to man-made constructions (which are nevertheless still impressive as Part C of this book sets out). In addition to the ice linga at Amarnath cave, the Himalayan peaks of Mount Kailas, Mount Trishul, and Mount Shivling are also worshiped as natural formations that link to Lord Shiva. Mount Kailas is the celestial home of Lord Shiva and Mount Shivling is a six thousand five hundred metre peak which has a naturally formed linga as the peak. Mount Trishul has three peaks in close succession which convey the impression that Lord Shiva's trident lays there dormant in the earth until called upon for him to snatch it up to battle Demons once again.

There are many examples of sacred natural sites around the world in other religions which include Uluru-Kata (Ayers Rock) in Australia, and Mount Sinai in Egypt. Beyond religion, there are also natural formations associated with mythology in many

Figure 27: Amarnath Ice Linga

Amarnath is a five thousand year-old cave with a natural ice linga formation that increases and decreases with the seasons. The cave is buried under snow for most of the year but accessible in the summer months. Given the location of the caves in Kashmir, many annual pilgrimages have been abandoned due to terrorist attacks on devotees. This natural shrine to Lord Shiva is believed to be one of the mountain retreats of Lord Shiva and Goddess Parvati. There are two doves that are often seen in and around the cave that are believed to be immortal having overhead Lord Shiva unveil divine secrets to Goddess Parvati in the cave. The ice linga increases and decreases in size due to the seasons; however, ardent devotees believe that this is achieved only through the divine power of Lord Shiva. The largest natural Shivalinga that ds devotees pray to is Mount Shivling in the Himalayas which stands at 6500 metres...

PART C: *VANAPRASTHA* – Lord Shiva Temples

jurisdictions including Mount Olympus, Table Mountain, and the Atlas Mountain range.

Chapter C2 - Chidambaram, Tamil Nadu

The South India Chidambaram Temple is associated with two legends[cxxxii] related to Lord Shiva as a dancer. The principal deity here is Nataraja, King of the Dance, and this cosmic performance to rid the world of the evils of ignorance and arrogance is believed by local devotees to have taken place here whilst Lord Vishnu and the other deities spectated. The second legend relates to a dance contest between Lord Shiva against Goddess Kali who the Shiva Purana confirms is an incarnation of Goddess Parvati in terrible warlike form. The Markandeya Purana also sets out the emergence of Goddess Kali from the forehead of Goddess Parvati to defeat a demon army who were threatening the three worlds:

"Out from the surface of her forehead, fierce with frown, issued suddenly Kali of terrible countenance, armed with a sword and noose. Bearing the strange skull-topped staff, decorated with a garland of skulls, clad in a tiger's skin, very appalling owing to her emaciated flesh, with gaping mouth, fearful with her tongue lolling out, having deep-sunk reddish eyes, and filling the regions of the sky with her roars, and falling upon impetuously and slaughtering the great asuras in that army, she devoured those hosts of the foes of the devas."

In the legend, once Goddess Kali had subdued the demon army, none but Lord Shiva could stop her terrible wrath by lying on the ground pretending to be one of the many slain on the battlefield. Once Goddess Kali's foot touch Lord Shiva, her wrath disappeared. There is a rich history of religious dance performances at Chidambaram in honour of the above legends.

Key idols and depictions

There are five main shrines dedicated to Lord Shiva; however, the Temple also reveres Lord Vishnu with a separate shrine and Goddess Parvati. There is a shrine to the Sun God (Aditya or Surya) portrayed on a great chariot in honour of the many battles he has fought on behalf of the deities. There are shrines for Lord Ganesha and Lord Kartikeya, the sons of Lord Shiva and there is a sacred pool for Goddess Ganga. The main shrine has a statue of Lord Shiva performing the cosmic Tandava dance and the legend of Lord Shiva and Goddess Kali is portrayed in artwork in one of the halls within the Chidambaram temple.

PART C: *VANAPRASTHA* – Lord Shiva Temples

Figure 28: Sacred Temple Pool at Chidambaram

Chidambaram Temple is an iconic work of devotional architecture in Southern India with impressive gopurams[cxxxiii], multi-pillared mandapas (halls), idols, and carvings in addition to a rich history for religious dance (Bharatanatyam). The above picture shows the sacred temple pool in honour of Lord Shiva as Gangadhara (Lord of the Rover Ganges).

Figure 29: Chidambaram Temple Gopuram

PART C: *VANAPRASTHA* – Lord Shiva Temples

Chapter C3 - The Elephanta Caves, Maharashtra

The glorious megalithic Elephanta caves are located on Gharapuri Island, also called Elephant Island, in the Indian State of Maharashtra. The Island and the caves were named after a large stone elephant that was once at the port of entry of the Island. In 1864, a crane was being used to lift the statue and take it to the British Museum. However, the crane broke, and the statue shattered into pieces. The pieces were lovingly restored[cxxxiii], and the elephant is now residing at the Jijamata Udyan zoo in Mumbai. Numerous Lord Shiva episodes from Hindu scripture are portrayed through rock carvings undertaken in 500 C.E. The Elephanta caves of rock-cut architecture include majestic pillars, courtyards, and stupas which have stories depicted upon them through intricate chiseling and stonework. Some of the archaeological remains at Elephanta are dated as early as 200 B.C. (the caves are much older of course) and this site has been added to the World Heritage List for UNESCO[cxxxiv] protection which describes the caves as having outstanding universal value.

The site is accessible from mainland India by ferry and is not far from the bustling city of Mumbai (Bombay). Despite the proximity to one of India's main cities, the Elephanta caves are a time machine to a forgone era of religious history. The stone depictions of Lord Shiva's adventures are equivalent to thousands of pages of detail in the scriptures. Despite the damage sustained by invaders using statues for shooting practice and erosion, the caves are remarkably well preserved.

Key Idols and depictions

There is a towering sculpture at Elephanta called Sadashiva (or perpetual Shiva) which includes renderings of Lord Shiva in several forms including Rudra (The Destroyer), Adiyogi (The First Teacher), Nataraja (King of the Dance) and Gangadhara (Lord of the River Ganges). The Nataraja fable is recounted in chapter A7 of this book and the Gangadhara fable features in the Introduction chapter on Lord Shiva. This twenty-foot masterpiece of masonry also includes carvings depicting the tales of Ravana's and Andhaka's interactions with Lord Shiva which can be found in chapter A6 and chapter A10 of this book, respectively. Multiple tales are displayed in one single piece of artistic devotion.

The alignment and execution of the stone representations are spectacular, and they have stood the test of time as mentioned above. The features of the idols present a great deal of emotion from serenity to violence depending on the aspect of Lord Shiva being described. They help one to visualize the tales of Lord Shiva as set out in the Puranas. In addition to the Sadashiva sculpture described above, there is an interesting sculpture of a Lord Shiva with five faces (Panchamukha). The Shiva Purana confirms that these five faces correspond to the combined Shiva-Shakti powers of (i) blessing, (ii) concealment, (iii) dissolution, (iv) sustenance, (v) creation.

There is a huge statue of the Hindu Trinity as represented by Lord Shiva, Lord Vishnu, and Lord Brahma. The sculpture portrays the important Advaita Vedic principle that the Hindu Trinity are one Supreme God (Brahman). The Elephanta caves also feature a sculpture of the androgynous Shiva-Parvati combined form of Ardhanarishwar. This is a statue split down the middle with Lord Shiva on the right side, and Goddess Parvati on the left side. The Ardhanarishwar form, as set out in the Brihadaranyaka Upanishad and the Linga Purana, represents the perfect synthesis of the Prakriti (body and mind) and the Purusha (spirit). The Ardhanarishwar form also denotes the feminine and masculine energies that created the universe (see chapter A14 of

PART C: *VANAPRASTHA* – Lord Shiva Temples

this book). Throughout artwork and scripture, Goddess Parvati is portrayed as an equal and inseparable part of Lord Shiva. This is a progressive view for the Indian Sub-Continent.

Figure 30: Lord Shiva as Nataraja at the Elephanta Caves

The high-quality temple carvings at Elephanta attract many Lord Shiva devotees and tourists each year. Many of the stories of Lord Shiva can be seen within the rock faces, pillars, and walls. The sculptures share similarities in terms of style and precision with Kailasnath Temple and the Ellora Caves, also in Maharashtra. The caves sustained some damage over the years but are at the same time well preserved and visitors can get close to the impressive feats of sculpture. They are works of great precision and devotion that help one to visualize the aspects of Lord Shiva. The caves are on Gharapuri Island (aka Elephant Island) and are close to the Indian capital of Bombay. There are five main caves that can be explored, each with their own impressive display of stonework. By way of example, the story of Andhaka is depicted on one work of art with Lord Shiva depicted in the terrible form of The Destroyer.

Figure 31: Lord Shiva and Goddess Parvati

Lord Shiva and Goddess Parvati are pictured together in happiness as the Deities and celestial beings all rejoice around them. The artwork portrayal of Lord Shiva as a loving husband is distinct from his other forms such as Rudra the Destroyer, Nataraja, King of the Dance, or the Adiyogi Aesthetic.

PART C: *VANAPRASTHA* – Lord Shiva Temples

Chapter C4 - Kailasnath, Maharashtra

Kailasnath, or "The Lord of Kailas" is in the Indian State of Maharashtra. Despite the name, the Temple is not in the region of Mount Kailas in Tibet; however, it is a tribute to Lord Shiva and his celestial Himalayan abode. Mount Kailas is mentioned throughout the Hindu scriptures as the location of Lord Shiva's residence.

Kailasnath is part of the impressive Ellora caves which contain many lucid depictions of Lord Shiva and exquisite shrines. The Ellora caves, which include over thirty temples and monasteries spread over a two kilometre area, are a UNESCO World Heritage Site and the sculptures are often compared in quality and style to the Elephanta caves from the above section. The Ellora caves were constructed during the same period of history (from 500 C.E.-800 C.E.) as Elephanta. There is an incredible richness of artistry and philosophy within the thousands of sculptures, drawings, and inscriptions in Kailasnath and the surrounding Ellora caves. In March each year, there is a Ellora festival of classical dance and music which is performed with Ellora caves as a backdrop. According to folklore, the King of the ruling dynasty became unwell and the queen prayed for a cure, promising to fast until the magnificent temple was built in honour of Lord Shiva and that she would be able to see the top. To ensure that the queen did not have to fast for an indefinite period, the temple was carved from the top downwards.

Key Idols and depictions

As mentioned above, Kailasnath is a large rendering of Mount Kailash, the abode of Lord Shiva and Goddess Parvati. The Temple is carved out of a single piece of rock and it is a free-standing structure with many stories of Lord Shiva told in the walls, pillars, and idols. It is the largest monolithic human built structure in the world at over one hundred feet high in places and over one hundred and fifty feet long. There is a huge four-storey stone courtyard with high columned galleries and a twenty-foot shrine dedicated to Nandi The Temple includes a large pillared mandapa (pavilion for the conducting of rituals) with life size stone elephants carved with detail. The Lord Shiva temple connects to the mandapa. The Temple is like a pyramid in appearance, resembling the architecture of South Indian temples. In addition to the depictions of Lord Shiva as the Lord of Kailas, there is a cave dedicated to Neelkanth with intricate carvings telling the story of Lord Shiva drinking poison to save all living creatures. One of the caves is dedicated to Lord Shiva's interactions with Rama, Avatar of Lord Vishnu. The UNESCO website offers the following description:

"Cave 16 (Kailasnath) is an excellent example of structural innovation and marks the culmination of rock-cut architecture in India featuring elaborate workmanship and striking proportions. The temple is decorated with some of the boldest and finest sculptural compositions to be found in India. The sculpture depicting Ravana attempting to lift Mount Kailas, the abode of Lord Shiva is especially noteworthy. The remains of beautiful paintings belonging to different periods are preserved on the ceilings of the front mandapa (pillared hall) of this temple...not only is the Ellora complex a unique artistic creation and a technological exploit but, with its sanctuaries devoted to Buddhism, Hinduism, and Jainism, it illustrates the spirit of tolerance that was characteristic of ancient India".

Devotees of Lord Shiva can witness the characteristics and tales of Lord Shiva in this location through the many artistic works on display. The caves are further afield from Mumbai than Elephanta but well worth the visit.

PART C: *VANAPRASTHA* – Lord Shiva Temples

Figure 32: Kailasnath Temple

Kailasnath (Lord of Kailas) Temple is in Maharashtra, India and is a remarkable homage to Mount Kailas, the abode of Lord Shiva that features in multiple locations in the Hindu scriptures. The monolithic wonder of architecture is carved from a single rock. The site is part of the world famed Ellora Caves which include many carvings dedicated to Lord Shiva. The Temple includes a large stone pavilion for conducting rituals linked to the Lord Shiva Temple. There are caves with intricate carvings within the rock faces that detail the many tales of Lord Shiva. The sculptures at Ellora are linked with the Elephanta caves in terms of style and quality and they are believed to have been created at the same time (circa 500 B.C.). The Kailasnath Temple is a long way from Mount Kailas which is in the Himalayas in Tibet close to the source of the Rivers Indus, Sutlej, Brahmaputra and Karnali (a tributary of the River Ganges).

Figure 33: Lord Shiva Depicted in The Ellora Caves

PART C: *VANAPRASTHA* – Lord Shiva Temples

Chapter C5 - Kedarnath, Uttarakhand

Kedarnath (or "Lord of the Field") is mentioned in the Shiva Purana as one of the twelve sacred Jyotirlinga Temples. It is also believed to be one of the four Lord Shiva char dham Temples that will provide instant moksha if one makes a pilgrimage there. It is in the snow-capped Himalayan mountains in Uttarakhand at a height of three thousand six hundred metres. The Temple is not accessible by road and involves a fifteen-mile hike to reach it but on arrival, the isolation and calm of the Temple is worth the journey. It is on the River Mandakini which is a tributary flowing into the River Ganges. The Skanda Purana mentions that this is the location where Lord Shiva received Goddess Ganga on his head.

The Temple is believed to have been constructed by the five Pandava brothers who paid homage to Lord Shiva after The Mahabharata War. Readers may recall from chapter A12 that this is also mentioned in the Puranas as the site where the wicked Demon Vrika performed penance and secured his terrible boon from Lord Shiva. The Kedarnath valley, was impacted by flash floods in 2013 and there was a landslide near the Temple. Water and rock cascaded with a thunderous sound down to the River Mandakini destroying everything in its path. A huge piece of rock became wedged behind Kedarnath Temple and protected it from the flood; waters gushed in two huge streams destroying everything to the sides of the temple. The Temple remained protected and mostly undamaged by this rock. The Temple was believed to have survived despite being under snow throughout the "Little Ice Age" period (1300 C.E. to 1850 C.E.).

Key Idols and depictions

The Temple is over a thousand years old and made from huge stone slabs. There are inscriptions on the steps and carvings on the walls depicting the tales of Lord Shiva. The great idol of Lord Shiva is moved each year to a neighboring location as Kedarnath becomes engulfed in snow and closed off to devotees. There is a religious ceremony undertaken as part of the relocation of the idol. In addition to the statue of Lord Shiva, there are depictions of Goddess Parvati (see chapter A2 of this book); Nandi, Lord Shiva's trusted vahana; the Demon Virabhadra created from a lock of Lord Shiva's hair (see Introduction Primer on Lord Shiva); and the five Pandava brothers (see chapter B1 of this book).

Figure 34: Kedarnath Temple with the Himalayan Backdrop

PART C: *VANAPRASTHA* – Lord Shiva Temples

Figure 35: Kedarnath Temple

Kedarnath Temple, in the Rudra Range in the Himalayas becomes covered in snow every year and the Idol of Lord Shiva is moved to a neighboring Temple with a religious ceremony. The Temple is on the River Mandakini which is a tributary that flows into the sacred River Ganges. Some believe it to be the location where Arjuna encountered Lord Shiva (see chapter A4) and the Kedarnath Temple is also believed to have been built by the Pandava brothers after the Mahabharata War when they were wandering in the Himalayas awaiting the final judgment of their lives. The Temple spent four hundred years under snow during the "Little Ice Age" period of 1300 C.E. to 1850 C.E. In 2013, the area was beset with a destructive flood which streamed down like a tidal wave of water and rock. A huge rock became wedged behind the Temple diverting the onslaught to the sides of the Temple and leaving the sacred place and the devotees inside unharmed.

Chapter C6 – Koneswaram, Sri Lanka

Koneswaram temple in Trincomalee is one of the five sacred "Pancha Ishwaram" temples of Sri Lanka. The temple is on the East Coast of Sri Lanka and connected to the mouth of the Mahavilli Ganga River. This is believed to represent the feet of Lord Shiva with Mount Kailas being his head; the temple lies on the same longitude as Mount Kailas. Whilst the temple origins date back to the second century B.C., it was destroyed in the seventeenth century. The underwater and land ruins were later discovered in the twentieth century and restoration has been undertaken. The main shrine is mentioned in a number of the Puranas, the Hindu Epics, and the Tevaram hymns making this one of the two hundred and fifty Padal Petra Temples. Koneswaram is steeped in history and the underwater ruins were famously re-discovered by science fiction writer Arthur C. Clarke when he was scuba diving in Sri Lanka.

Key Idols and Depictions

The architecture includes a one thousand pillared hall (mandapam), bas relief carvings, and a black granite megalith. There is a large ravine in the serenely named Swami Rock upon which the temple is built; this ravine is referred to as Ravana's cleft in homage to the Demon King of Lanka who in folklore dropped his divine sword here to construct the temple. The bas reliefs are constructed with skillful artistry to portray the many aspects of Lord Shiva, Lord Vishnu, and the other deities. There is a fifteen foot statue of Lord Shiva in meditation outside the main shrine which houses an ancient linga. There are ancient stone idols around the main shrines which depict many of the forms of Lord Shiva. There is also a naturally occurring stone cave with an ancient stone sculpture of Lord Shiva.

PART C: *VANAPRASTHA* – Lord Shiva Temples

Figure 36: Ravana's cleft

Local folklore says that the Demon King Ravana dropped his sword here to construct the Koneswaram Lord Shiva Temple.

Chapter C7 - Mohenjo-Daro, Pakistan

Mohenjo-Daro (or "Mountain of Dead") is an archaeological site in Pakistan that was built in 2500 B.C. It was a city from the great Indus Valley civilization (or Harappan[cxxxv]). This civilization from northern Asia spanning Afghanistan, India, and Pakistan lasted from 3000 B.C. to 1000 B.C., a time when many of the Hindu Scriptures were being recorded. The site was discovered in the 1920s and excavations have revealed that the mounds contain the remains of what was once the largest city of the Indus civilization. Because of the city's size (circa three miles) and the richness of its monuments and their contents, Mohenjo-Daro is believed to be a capital city. Whilst this excavation is not a Temple of Lord Shiva, the discovery of a potential Lord Shiva artefact is worth noting in helping to complete *the Lord Shiva Narrative*.

Key Idols and Depictions

The "Pashupati Seal" was found during the excavation and it is believed by historians to be a depiction of Lord Shiva as Lord of the Animals (hence the name Pashupati given to the seal). It is a small seal that would have been used to stamp goods or documents. The seal has several of the characteristics of Lord Shiva which include being seated in meditation (Adiyogi form of Lord Shiva); and the depiction of bull horns and animals provide a possible link to Lord Shiva as Pashupati as mentioned above. There is a ten thousand year-old cave drawing at the Bhimbetka rock shelters in Central India that is believed by many historians to be an early prehistoric painting of Lord Shiva dancing, Lord Shiva with a trident, and Lord Shiva atop his vahana (animal chariot) Nandi. These mark an interesting discovery for potential Lord Shiva worship from the Mesolithic[cxxxvi] period.

PART C: *VANAPRASTHA* – Lord Shiva Temples

Figure 37: The Pashupati Seal

The Pashupati Seal found in the Mohenjo-Daro Indus Valley archaeological site is believed by historians to be Lord Shiva in meditation (hence the name Pashupati – Lord of Animals). The Seal portrays a figure seated in mediation with animals to the sides and below. It is difficult to make out the salient characteristics of Lord Shiva such as the third eye and there is no trident. The circular horns certainly resemble crescent moons from Lord Shiva's Somnath depictions. The excavation site is over four thousand years old and is one of the largest Indus Valley cities that has been discovered.

Chapter C8 - Murudeshawara, Karnataka

Murudeshawara Temple is in the state of Karnataka in India. It is surrounded by the Arabian Sea and was built in 800 C.E. The Shiva Purana tells of a story involving the Demon King Ravana which forms the basis for the origin story for the Temple. After being blessed with invincible strength by Lord Shiva, Ravana requested for him to come along with him to Lanka. Lord Shiva gave Ravana a Shivalinga but warned him against keeping it on the earth, as once it is set down, there is no power on the earth could lift it once again. Ravana proceeded with the Shivalinga but needed a break, and he gave the Shivalinga to a cowherd boy for a moment so he could rest. The boy held the Shivalinga, but it became too heavy, and he placed it on the ground. When Ravana returned he tried to lift it but could not so established a Temple there.

The Temple is referred to in the Shiva Purana as Baidyanath; however, folklore stories state that Murudeshawara is the site of the above story. In the folklore tale, Lord Ganesha dupes Ravana into placing the Shivalinga on the ground.

Key Idols and depictions

The statue of Lord Shiva at Murudeshawara is a huge monument to this deity and portrays him in meditation with the many characteristics explored in this book from Hindu scripture:

1. Blue appearance (Neelkanth),
2. Crescent Moon in his hair (Somnath),
3. Cobra worn as a necklace,
4. Trident and drum,
5. Tiger skin,
6. Third eye.

PART C: *VANAPRASTHA* – Lord Shiva Temples

The rays of the sun fall upon the statue of Lord Shiva at dawn creating a captivating vision of this deity in his magnificence.

Figure 38: Murudeshawara Temple

The great statue of Lord Shiva at Murudeshawara portrays many of the familiar characteristics of Lord Shiva including the cobra and rudraksha beads around his neck. Nandi looks on from the foreground with the Arabian Sea to his back as he sits in meditation but with the deadly trident ready to strike if called upon. The devotees in the picture give one a sense of the proportions of this huge monument.

Chapter C9 - Pashupatinath, Nepal

Pashupatinath (or "Lord of the Animals") is in Nepal on the southern slopes of the Himalayan mountains by the River Bagmati. It is believed to be one of the four Nepalese Char Dham Temples that will provide instant moksha if one makes a pilgrimage there. Nepal is rich with spirituality and contains many ancient Temples dedicated to Lord Shiva. There are over five hundred Temples located in the region of Pashupatinath. UNESCO refers to Pasupatinath as a nexus of Hindu religion, art, and culture.

Each year, Hindu pilgrims from various parts of the world visit the temple during Mahashivaratri (The Great Night of Shiva discussed in the Introduction chapter to this book). The Temple is one of the two hundred and seventy-five Padal Petra Thalam Temples dedicated to Lord Shiva; it is one of only ten of these Temples located outside of the State of Tamil Nadu in India. These Temples are documented in Hindu Scriptures and poetry of South India written in the Tamil language in circa 600 C.E.

Key Idols and Depictions

The Temple displays a variety of artwork and is an important destination for art historians. The sculptures are made from wood, stone, and metal. The main idol is a one-metre-high stone linga bound with the silver serpent. The linga has faces in all four directions which represent various aspects of Shiva. The faces point due North, East, South, and West, and with the Zenith they represent the five primary elements of earth, water, air, fire, and ether. The main temple is a masterpiece of Hindu architecture; it is a cubic construction with four doors. There has been some earthquake damage over the years, but the Temple remains an

PART C: *VANAPRASTHA* – Lord Shiva Temples

important place among Shiva devotees to observe the tales of this deity represented in the stone walls.

Figure 39: Pashupatinath (Lord of the Animals) Temple

Pashupatinath Temple in Nepal has many idols portraying Lord Shiva as Pasupathi (Lord of the Animals). The Temple is one of the two hundred and seventy-five Padal Petra Thalam Lord Shiva Temples (one of only ten located outside of the State of Tamil Nadu). Monkeys of the type depicted at Pashupatinath above can be found throughout temples in the Indian Sub-Continent.

Chapter C10 – Prambanan Temple, Indonesia

Prambanan Temple is a wonderful work of architecture dedicated to Lord Shiva in Yogyakarta[cxxxvii], Indonesia. The name is believed to be a derivative of Parabrahman (the Supreme). It was built in the ninth century C.E. In addition to the central Lord Shiva shrine, the Temple features Lord Vishnu and Lord Brahma and is also home to a number of intricate carvings of The Ramayana. Prambanan is a UNESCO World Heritage Site, and the central Lord Shiva Temple is one hundred and fifty feet high with architecture resembling South Indian temples deploying a steeple mandala structure. The Shivagrha inscription, currently on display at the National Museum of Indonesia in Jakarta, confirms that Prambanan was built in 850 C.E and is dedicated to Lord Shiva. This is an authentic stone inscription that sets out the particulars of the temple and its construction.

Unfortunately, the Prambanan site sustained some damage in the 2006 Yogyakarta earthquake; however, it has since been restored with the reconstruction of many of the temples. Prior to the earthquake there were over two hundred temples within the Prambanan complex. Included in this is a temple dedicated to Nandi, Lord Shiva's vahana (animal chariot). The nearby Trimurti open air stage is home to a unique ballet production of The Ramayana (see chapter B2 of this book) that attracts many tourists each year to witness this spectacular performance. The dance takes place with the impressive Prambanan temple in the backdrop and there can be few more emphatic examples of artistic talent, architecture, and spirituality coming together.

Key Idols and Depictions

The main Lord Shiva shrine contains five separate chambers, four small chambers in each major direction (North, East, South, and

PART C: *VANAPRASTHA* – Lord Shiva Temples

West) and there is one larger chamber in the central part of the temple. There is a three metre high statue of Lord Shiva which bears a skull and sickle on the crown. Lord Shiva's third eye is portrayed on his forehead and the statue has four hands holding the rudraksha beads and trident. The statue is based on a stone lotus pad with engravings of serpents. The main inner section is a central compound and a square elevated platform surrounded by stone walls and stone gates on each of the four faces. In addition to the main Lord Shiva statue, there are two other shrines dedicated to the Hindu Trinity gods of Lord Vishnu and Lord Brahma. The Lord Shiva Temple is encircled with balustrades with carvings and galleries that depict the story of The Ramayana. If one enters from the East gate and moves clockwise then the story of this Hindu Epic will unfold with the correct sequence of events.

The large Lord Shiva Temple is flanked by two smaller shrines, dedicated to guardian gods, Mahakala (protector) and Nandhisvara (Lord of Nandi).

Figure 40: Prambanan Courtyard and Guardians

Figure 41: Prambanan Temple

The magnificent Prambanan Temple in Indonesia represents an important Lord Shiva Temple beyond the Indian Sub-Continent that is visited by devotees each year.

PART C: *VANAPRASTHA* – Lord Shiva Temples

Chapter C11 - Rameswaram, Tamil Nadu

Rameswaram (or "Lord of Ram") is mentioned in the Shiva Purana as one of the twelve sacred Jyotirlinga Temples. It is also believed to be one of the four Lord Shiva Char Dham Temples that will provide instant moksha if one makes a pilgrimage there. In addition to the above, it is one of the two hundred and seventy-five sacred Padal Petra Thalam Temples dedicated to Lord Shiva and documented in Hindu Scriptures and poetry of South India written in the Tamil language in circa 600 C.E. This religious site is on Pamban Island in Tamil Nadu and is one of the closest points to Sri Lanka from India. The Temple is known for ancient religious history and the sunrises and sunsets there are breathtaking. Rama is believed to have rested here to obtain blessings from Lord Shiva before his incursion into Lanka. The interactions of Lord Shiva with Rama and Ravana are in chapters A5, A6, and B2 of this book.

Key Idols and depictions

The Ramanathaswamy Temple has a one thousand pillared hallway with spectacular sandstone carvings telling the stories of Lord Shiva and the other deities. The architecture is common to South Indian Temples with huge colonnades, walls, and towers (or gopurams) and many intricate carvings. Much of the stone used in construction of the Temple was shipped from Northern Sri Lanka. The Temple is surrounded by sixty-four holy wells (tirthas). In addition, the Shivalinga was believed to have been built by Rama. The beaches at Pamban Island have serene sunrises and sunsets. When one sits on the sand and looks upon this beauty of nature, it is easy to be transported back to the time of Rama, Hanuman, and the army of Varanas who invaded Lanka and defeated the evil Demon King Ravana.

Figure 42: Ramanathaswamy Temple

Ramanathaswamy Temple at Rameswaram has many pathways and columns with stone carvings dedicated to Lord Shiva. It is a labyrinth of Hindu architecture and artwork and surrounded by sixty-four holy wells (tirthas). Twenty-four of the tirthas (mainly the wells inside the Temple) are mentioned in the Skanda Purana as being extremely sacred. Bathing in the waters from these wells is considered a powerful austerity of devotion. The Temple is believed to have been built on the location of Rama's blessing by Lord Shiva before the incursion into Lanka in The Ramayana Epic. Rama rested his armies here before they began their campaign. The Temple is one of the twelve sacred Jyotirlinga mentioned in the Shiva Purana where Lord Shiva is believed to have appeared as a column of fire. It is one of the sacred Char Dham locations and one of the two hundred and seventy-five sacred Padal Petra Thalam Temples dedicated to Lord Shiva and documented in Hindu Scriptures written in the Tamil language in circa 600 C.E. Ramanathaswamy has much to offer the Lord Shiva devotee. The sunsets at this Temple are serendipitous.

PART C: *VANAPRASTHA* – Lord Shiva Temples

Chapter C12 - Somnath, Gujarat

Somnath (or "Lord of the Moon") is mentioned in the Shiva Purana and is one of the twelve sacred Jyotirlinga Temples. It is also believed to be one of the four Lord Shiva Char Dham Temples that will provide instant moksha if one makes a pilgrimage there. The Temple is in the State of Gujarat and overlooks the Arabian Sea at the intersection of the River Kapila, River Hiran, and River Sarasvati with the waves of the Arabian Sea. The sunset during the evening aarti (ceremony) is a highlight of the visit to this sacred location. However, the proximity of the Temple to the sea is one of the reasons it has been attacked and destroyed multiple times over the years with many tens of thousands being killed at this site in defence of the Temple. In folklore, the Temple is believed to have been built by Chandra (or Soma), the Moon God.

Key Idols and depictions

Somnath temple has many intricate carvings dedicated to Lord Shiva and the temple has a honey hue due to the brilliant sandstone applied in its construction. There is a Shivalinga located on the west side of the Temple where Lord Shiva is believed to have appeared as a fiery column of light. There are idols and carvings that tell the story of Chandra, God of the Moon praying to Lord Shiva to free him from a curse that he would lose his power and potency (see Introduction chapter to this book). Lord Shiva's blessings countered the curse, and therefore the moon waxes and wanes to this day in the lunar cycle.

Colourful depictions of the tales of Lord Shiva line the north side of the Temple garden and there is a folktale at Somnath in relation to a magical floating Shivalinga that has been observed within the Temple.

Figure 43: Somnath Temple

The Somnath Temple possesses an unmistakable honey hue and provides a serene sacred location for devotees. Somnath is one of the four Lord Shiva Char Dham Temples and one of the twelve Jyotirlinga Temples.

PART C: *VANAPRASTHA* – Lord Shiva Temples

Figure 44: Somnath – Lord of the Moon

As set out in the Introduction chapter to this book, Lord Shiva is Somnath, Lord of the Moon. Lord Shiva is oft depicted with the crescent moon in his matted hair after countering Daksha's curse to ensure that the moon would wax as well as wane. The Temple at Somnath is an important pilgrimage sight for Lord Shiva devotees who flock there each year. The evening aarti (religious ceremony) with the sun setting over the intersection of the rivers with the sea is a highlight. The moon is an important aspect of Hinduism and in particular the religious calendar for important events, festivals, and rituals. There are twenty-seven constellations and twelve lunar months in the Hindu calendar: Chaitra, Vaisakha, Jyaistha, Asadha, Shravana, Bhadra, Asvina, Kartika, Agrahayana, Pausa, Magha, Phalguna. The Moon God (Chandra or Soma) is referred to at many points in the Vedas and Upanishads as an important deity from this era. Chandra also features as a warrior in the Puranic tales of Lord Shiva and the battles with demons.

Chapter C13 – Unakoti, Tripura

The unique Unakoti depictions of Lord Shiva and other deities have been carved into the rocky hillside in Tripura[cxxxviii], the State in India. These are large renditions of Lord Shiva that are unlike anything seen in other parts of the Indian Sub-Continent. Folklore legend describes the story of Lord Shiva on a journey with ten million other deities. When Lord Shiva awoke in the morning after resting at Unakoti, he became enraged that the others were still asleep and so he turned them all to stone. He then continued without them: Unakoti means ten million less one.

Figure 45: Lord Shiva as Gangadhara

Key Idols and depictions

One of the rock faces displays the matted locks of Lord Shiva with the River Ganges flowing down. Another displays the third eye of Lord Shiva. Both of these huge stone carvings depict the face of

PART C: *VANAPRASTHA* – Lord Shiva Temples

Lord Shiva. The carvings are thirty feet high and remarkably well preserved despite being thousands of years old and exposed to the elements. There has been some degradation through the passage of time; however, there are environmental efforts underway to preserve the existing structures whilst still permitting devotees to see the depictions. In addition to Lord Shiva, there are statues of Lord Ganesha and Nandi, Lord Shiva's vahana (animal chariot).

Figure 46: Stone Deities

According to the legends, Lord Shiva, accompanied by many deities stopped at Unakoti to rest for the night. Lord Shiva, famed for his great wrath, turned the ten million (less one) deities into stone when he awoke and realized that they had all overslept...to this day, Unakoti contains many stone deities awaiting the day when Lord Shiva will lift his curse and breathe life into them once again.

Chapter C14 - Vadakunnathan, Kerala

The Vadakunnathan Temple dedicated to Lord Shiva in the South Indian State of Kerala is believed to have been built by the legendary Parasurama, avatar of Lord Vishnu. The legend states that this warrior sage built one hundred and eight temples in Kerala and Vadakunnathan is believed to have been the very first of these. The folklore surrounding Vadakunnathan is that Parasurama hurled his mighty axe into the ocean causing the Sea God to retreat and thus Kerala was formed. He then undertook the journey to Mount Kailas to pray to Lord Shiva to accompany him to Kerala to bestow blessings upon the region. Lord Shiva duly set off to Kerala with Goddess Parvati, Lord Ganesha, and Lord Kartikeya. Lord Shiva is believed to have stopped at the Keralan city of Thrissur whereupon he disappeared with his family and in his place was a divine linga. The Vadakunnathan Temple was constructed around this linga on a hill overlooking the main town and surrounded by a large forest area.

Key idols and depictions

The temple has a number of murals, wood carvings, and paintings that are worshipped by devotees. These include a depiction of Lord Shiva as Nataraja. There is also an idol of the Goddess Parvati. The linga referred to in the above legend is now covered with a multitude of ghee that has been applied over many years and is believed to have medicinal healing properties having been exposed to intense prayer and devotion around it. There are animated celebrations each year during Mahashivaratri which includes a procession of many elephants that are decorated with sacred ash and garlands. Like many Keralan Temples, there is a theatre (or koothamalam) and there are also four large gopuram walls with intricate carvings and idols dedicated to Lord Shiva. The theatre is used for staging dramatic dances of devotion. There are many wood carvings when compared to stone carvings in other parts of India.

PART C: *VANAPRASTHA* – Lord Shiva Temples

Figure 47: Vadakunnathan Temple Festival in Kerala

Temple elephants can be seen throughout the Indian Sub-Continent and are deployed in grand ceremonies – this is particularly so in Kerala and Vadakunnathan where there is a procession during Mahashivaratri involving many bejeweled elephants carrying the temple deities in a colourful display. The ceremonies have come under intense scrutiny in recent years to ensure that the elephants are being well cared for and not mistreated by their mahouts, particularly during the "domestication" process in which they are sometimes hit with sticks while chained. The organization Save the Asian Elephants (STAE) is working with the governments across India and Asia to ensure that there is transparency and humanity in the handling of these temple animals. Their work includes the training of local mahouts and the improvement of facilities for the sacred elephants.

Chapter C15 - Viswanath, Uttar Pradesh

Kashi Viswanath Temple is mentioned in the Shiva Purana as one of the twelve sacred Jyotirlinga Temples. Viswanath means "Lord of the Universe" and the Temple is in Uttar Pradesh in India on the banks of the River Ganges. Like many ancient religious sites, the Temple has been destroyed and rebuilt over the years due to invasions and religious wars. The holy city of Varanasi in which the Temple is located is referred to in the Introduction chapter of the book with respect to the story of Goddess Ganga and Lord Shiva. Religious ceremonies are conducted at the Temple in praise of Mother Goddess Ganga. It is believed by devotees that after the rituals are complete, the Goddess showers her blessing onto all present at the ceremony as the River becomes filled with a colourful and serene display of lamps and aromatic flowers.

Kashi Vishwanath temple is recognized by devotees as one of the most important places for worship in the Hindu religion. A visit to the temple and a bath in the sacred River Ganges is believed to be one of many routes to moksha (liberation). There is a tradition that devotees should give up at least one desire after a pilgrimage to the Temple. Part D of the book sets out the philosophy of the Shiva Sutras for attaining moksha through deep meditation. However, there are a number of beliefs in folklore that can provide a different potential route to enlightenment such as the legend of Kashi Vishwanath. By way of example, it is said that circumambulating Mount Kailas in Tibet one hundred and eight times will provide instant enlightenment. As will passing away of the first day of Maha Sankranti (also referred to as Pongal or Uttarayan in different parts of India and representing the first day of the summer solstice). There is also a belief in relation to the Char Dham temples that provide instant

PART C: *VANAPRASTHA* – Lord Shiva Temples

moksha through a pilgrimage to these sacred sites (see chapters C5, C9, C11 and C12).

Figure 48: Dawn at Varanasi

Key Idols and depictions

Hundreds of temples across the Indian Sub-Continent have been built in the same architectural style as Kashi Viswanath which is a great tribute to the design and building of the structure. There is a colonnade of 40 stone pillars with intricate carvings and a seven-foot statue of Nandi which was a gift from the King of Nepal. There is a sacred well located inside the Temple where it is believed that a brave priest jumped in whilst holding the sacred Shivalinga to protect this when the Temple was being ransacked by enemy armies. The Temple has now been rebuilt with much splendour including domes of silver and gold[cxxxix]. Despite the violent history, there is an air of tranquility broken only by spiritual chanting.

Figure 49: Lord Shiva Temples/Sites[cxl] from Part C

**PART D: *SANNYASA*
THE Sivasutra**

Introduction to Part D

A Sutra is a law or aphorism; the Shiva Sutra (or Sivasutra) was revealed to and written down by Vasgupta in 900 C.E. It is considered to be of divine origin and has three routes to moksha (liberation) and attainment of Parabrahma[cxl] (the highest state of enlightenment). The objective is to free oneself from ongoing reincarnation (samsara) and to achieve self-realization of one's position in the universe. The different routes for this are (i) The Way of Shiva, (ii) The Way of the Competent One, and (iii) The Fine Way.

The "Way" a person adopts depends upon where they are at present on the road to liberation. Those who already reside in their own enlightenment and knowledge of the self need no additional effort or "Way" to achieve liberation. For all others, chapters D1-D3 below set out each Sutra in Sanskrit and in English[cxli], followed by the author's alternative translations as a guide for readers with their journey. Liberation is a personal concept. For example, on the way to this journey one may find that one is controlled less by external factors, persons, and events. Pain and desire are no longer experienced in the same manner. Freed from ego and ignorance, the person becomes more self-realized. There may also be an increased clarity of thought process, increased energy, and a more balanced and serene view of the universe and one's place in it. There may be a feeling of peace and calm despite the chaos of the external world.

Thus far, *The Lord Shiva Narrative* has explored the teachings about kama (love), dharma (moral duty), and artha (purpose), from the Puranic tales of Lord Shiva and the core Hindu scriptures. Part D explores the states of mind and some of the techniques and concepts that may be deployed in attaining self-

PART D: *SANNYASA* – The Sivasutra

realization and self-knowledge. Many of the concepts will be familiar to those who already practice Yoga and meditation techniques.

The following concepts may be helpful to readers:

- *Anatma* – Non-self (body, heart, and mind)
- *Antaratma* – Inner self
- *Atma* – True self
- *Cittam* – Mind and/or heart
- *Jagrat* – Conscious state
- *Jnana* – Knowledge
- *Karma* – Action
- *Maya* – Illusion
- *Moksha* – Liberation or enlightenment
- *Jagrat* – Conscious state
- *Parabrahma* – Highest Supreme state or Self
- *Paramatman* – as above, the Supreme Self
- *Prajna* – Wisdom
- *Prana* – Life breath
- *Samsara* – Reincarnation
- *Sariram* – physical body
- *Saushupta* – Unconscious state
- *Shakti* – Feminine creative force/Divine Mother
- *Svapna* – Sub-conscious state

Chapter D1 – *Sambhavopaya*. The Way of Shiva

The first part of the Shiva Sutras relates to the Way of Shiva and comprise twenty-two Sutras set out below. These Sutras relate to the state of Consciousness (being awake).

1.1 *Caitanyam atma.* Consciousness - Self.

Consciousness should be contrasted with awareness in assessing this Sutra. To be aware is to know that something is transpiring; however, to be conscious of something implies wisdom or morality to that awareness. Consciousness is a heightened sense of awareness and one of the four Vedic states of being awake, asleep, dreaming, and the *Parabrahman* or absolute higher consciousness (see Sutra 1.7 below). The above Sutra states that this heightened sense of awareness should *be* through one's true self/soul (*atma*) and not just through the mind, heart, and body (*anatma*). In Hindu scriptures, one is instructed to see through the maya (illusion) of life and free oneself from ego and physical attachments to reach *moksha* (liberation), freedom from *samsara* (reincarnation), and realization of the true self.

The Sutra implies that one can achieve this through the conscious state. The Vedas and the Bhagavad Gita address the three states of material nature and instruct that one must rise above the three to a fourth state of pure spiritual consciousness: "freeing oneself from dualities, eternally fixed in truth, and without concern for material gain and safety, be situated in the self". Caitanyam could be defined as intelligence instead of consciousness; however, to do so for the above Sutra would lose the link to the four states of being discussed above. Sutras 1.7-1.10 below explore the four states in more detail and help to provide additional instruction to this opening Sutra for the path to *moksha* being through the awake state with knowledge of the other states.

1.2 *Jnanam bandhah*. Knowledge - bondage.

This Sutra may initially confuse as devotion to study is a key tenet of the Vedas. However, within this context, the Sutra may be warning us that much of the knowledge one possesses can inhibit from following the correct path. *Bandhah* can be defined as attachment to this world, as in the phenomenal or tangible world as one perceives it as opposed to the true nature of the universe. Readers will note the distinction between knowledge and *prajna* (wisdom) in this regard: simply knowing things is not enough without the wisdom to apply that knowledge in *dharma*. The Tripurasura (see chapter A8 of this book) who study *adharmic* scriptures are examples of the dangers in the application of knowledge to an incorrect path with disastrous results. The Sutra could also be interpreted to warn against a dogmatic approach to facts and figures, and a mind closed off to spiritual concepts and teachings that will prevent the attainment of *moksha* (liberation).

1.3 *Yonivargah kalasariram*. The multitude of similar origins - the body of parts of the whole.

This is a Sutra which may have lost something in the translation into English. This Sutra could be informing us that many persons from a similar background (familial, spiritual, or ethical) can function as a collective, in the same way that different limbs and organs combine to make up one's physical body. However, *Kala* could also refer to time and death which provides attachment to the physical form. *Kalasariram* could therefore read as death of the body. The word *Yoni* could be translated as: spring or womb instead of origin, and *vargah* could be family. This renders a quite different meaning to the Sutra whereby death of the body stems from birth of the body and vice versa via samsara (reincarnation) of the soul/self.

1.4 *Jnanadhisthanam matrka*. The basis of knowledge - an alphabet.

At first, this appears to be clear in that one requires a system of letters to learn and pass on knowledge. This is consistent with Vedic teachings to free ourselves from ignorance. The Saiva Upanishads discussed in chapter B4 of this book also set out the use of fifty rudraksha beads along with the fifty letters of the Sanskrit alphabet as a form of mediation.

However, one possible translation of *matrka* is to interpose "alphabet" for "mother" or "that which comes from the mother" rendering a vastly different potential meaning. This alternative translation is consistent with devotion in Hinduism to the mother before the father as the person who first instructs us in life.

The passage could be translated as: the power of knowledge is the divine mother. Therefore, meditation upon Shakti may assist in the journey to spiritual enlightenment.

1.5 *Udyamo bhairavah*. Zeal - Bhairava[cxlii].

Udyamo as Zeal could be interposed for: diligence, perseverance, striving, elevating, undertaking, beginning. However, the term *bhairavah* is less subjective: The Lord Shiva form of *Bhairava* relates to the formidable, frightful, terrible attributes of this deity. In the Shiva Purana, *Bhairava* was created from Lord Shiva's third eye out of anger and proceeded to sever one of the five heads of Lord Brahma. One positive interpretation of this Sutra is that zeal or perseverance is required to achieve the characteristics of Lord Shiva. Therefore, only through diligence and striving can one attain liberation of the Self. Although less likely given the positive tone of the Shiva Sutras, the above Sutra may be warning us that if one is (over)zealous then the results may be catastrophic and bring forth Lord Shiva in his fury as *Bhairava*.

1.6 *Sakticakrasamdhane visva samharah*. In union of multitude of powers - destruction of the universe.

The above Sutra may be echoing the story of Nataraja (see chapter A7 of this book) where the dark sages applied their power for destructive purposes. Alternatively, the Sutra may be warning that overcomplicated devotion and practices may have negative consequences.

Samhara could be read as the periodical destruction of the universe that occurs at the end of each *kalpa* (cycle) as set out in chapter A14 of this book in the Hindu theory of Creation. Therefore, this is not a negative concept, but it is the natural order of the universe to be destroyed and created once again by the Hindu Trinity when there is equilibrium (or union) of the forces of Shiva and Shakti, the characterized (tangible) and the non-characterized (intangible). The Hindu scriptures state that the universe is formed when there is disequilibrium and destroyed when there is equilibrium.

1.7 *Jagratsvapna susuptabhede turyabhoga sambhavah*. In the distinction of deep sleep, dreaming and waking - the source of fullness of the Fourth.

The Fourth refers to the Vedic principle of the four states of the self: (i) Unconscious (asleep); (ii) Sub-conscious (dreaming); (iii) Conscious (awake); and (iv) the Absolute Higher Consciousness or Parabrahma.

The Sutra is informing us that the fourth state that one strives for can be achieved through distinction (or recognition) of the other states.

This Sutra should be read and interpreted with the following three Sutras (1.8, 1.9 and 1.10) which explore the Unconscious, Sub-conscious, and Conscious states in more detail.

1.8 *Jnanam jagrat*. Knowledge - waking.

There are few other ways to translate this Sutra and one can explore the definition of the first state of consciousness in which the phenomenal world is observed as one's mind conceives it. *Jagrat* is the term for this first state and taken in conjunction with Sutra 1.1, one is reminded in this Sutra once again that only through realizing maya (illusion) from the phenomenal world can liberation of the self be achieved.

1.9 *Svapno vikalpah*. Dreaming - in imaginations.

In contrast to the *jagrat* state explored above, the *svapna* (dream or sub-conscious) state occurs when the mind is not awake and creates objects using memories and ideas recalled from the awake or conscious state. These objects do not exist in the phenomenal world as one's mind perceives it and will disappear from view when one awakes. *Vikalpa* can be defined as "false notions, fancies, indecisions, doubts, hesitations" and these all can contribute to the illusion that stops us from attaining enlightenment.

1.10 *Aviveko maya sausuptam*. Non-distinction - deep sleep, which is Maya.

The above Sutra explores the third state of deep sleep (unconscious or profound sleep) and tells us that there is the absence of judgment or ability to discriminate in this state which leads to the illusion that there is nothing beyond the phenomenal world as one's minds conceives it. There is a thread here from deep sleep, to a lack of judgment; and then a lack of judgment to create the illusion of a physical life. The above states of *Jagrat*, *Svapna* and *Saushupta* must be understood and mastered to provide the possibility of attaining the final state of *Parabrahman*.

1.11 *Tritayabhokta viresah*. The Eater of the triad – Lord Shiva.

Viresah refers to Lord Shiva as the master of senses. *Tritaya* could refer to the three Vedic states discussed in Sutras 1.7-1.10 above. *Bhokta* could be interpreted as the characterized *anatma* (mind, heart, and body) enjoying and experiencing tangible physical attachments. *Tritaya* could therefore refer to the third state of deep sleep and as such Lord Shiva is the means to discriminate even in this state.

However, the word *bhokta* could be translated as any of the following:

- Eater,
- Enjoyer/Experiencer,
- Sufferer, or
- Possessor.

Bhokta is therefore a complex word with many potentially different meanings. Lord Shiva is often referred to in Hindu scriptures as the devourer of egos and so the translation as the "eater of the triad" may be consistent with this.

As an alternative consideration, Tritaya could refer to the Hindu Trinity of Lord Brahma, Lord Vishnu, and Lord Shiva (although *trimurti* is the more common Sanskrit word for this).

Sufferer of the triad is consistent with Lord Shiva's destructive form and Possessor of the triad consistent with the Advaita concept that the Hindu Trinity are one Supreme collective. Note that the wording "of the triad" most likely indicates Lord Shiva's position within the triad (as eater or destroyer or enjoyer or possessor) as opposed to the fact that he eats the triad.

1.12 *Vismayo yogabhumikah*. The stages of yoga - a wonder.

This Sutra is informing readers that the stages or steps of yoga (breathing, meditation, and posture) provide wonder or amazement. *Bhumikah* could be translated as perplexity or bewilderment which would change the meaning of the Sutra quite dramatically. However, given the Vedic principles and importance placed on yoga one can postulate that the Sutra conveys the former meaning.

The Yoga Sutras (distinct from the Shiva Sutras) set out seven different stages:

- I. Realization that knowledge comes from within and meditation will lead to truth,
- II. Recognition of the cause of suffering to free oneself from pain,
- III. Attain full knowledge of meditative consciousness of the atma (Self),
- IV. No longer a requirement for duties,
- V. Obtain compete control over all mental processes,
- VI. Become free of influences of external natural processes,
- VII. Parabrahman state of absolute freedom.

1.13 *Iccha saktir uma kumari*. Desire, power - Uma, the Virgin.

Uma is Goddess Parvati and often associated with Shakti the Divine power or force of Creation; the Sutra may be confirming this link between the Goddess and the feminine power that assisted in creating the universe. *Iccha* can be translated as desire, wish or inclination. *Kumari* can be translated as virgin, young girl, daughter, or maiden and so an alternative interpretation may be that Shakti is the mother of Goddess Parvati.

PART D: *SANNYASA* – The Sivasutra

1.14 *Drsyam sariram*. Any visible object - a body.

The above Sutra may be referring to the phenomenal or tangible world contextualized through what one sees. *Sariram* refers to the physical body as opposed to the ethereal atma self. However, the use of the word *sariram* instead of *anatma* is deliberate. *Anatma* relates to everything that is not the self or soul and would include the mind, heart, and body whilst *sariram* is just the physical body. The word has been adopted in Buddhist culture to refer to cremated remains of the body.

1.15 *Hrdaye cittasanghattad drsyasvapadarsanam*. From the union of the mind in the heart - the appearance of dreams of any visible object.

The above Sutra contains some important themes to include (i) the union of the mind with the heart, and (ii) the ability to see dream objects and tangible objects. The former aspect speaks to the importance of emotion alongside thought and the latter is consistent with Sutra 1.7 above which teaches that one must embrace all the Vedic states to achieve *Parabrahman*. In the same way that dreams arise from emotion and thought, so does the path to *Parabrahman* and liberation of the self. When the mind becomes united with the heart, one sees everything as a form of consciousness and are freed from maya (illusion).

The phenomenal world as one perceives it is from the mind, the inner world is from the heart. If one only applies the mind, then ignorance is a limitation. When one applies the heart in conjunction with the mind then one is able to see past this ignorance. The Sutra has some synergy with 1.2 above instructing us that an approach which focuses on the mind and knowledge may cause us to become attached to the world.

1.16 *Suddhatattvasamdhanad vapasusaktih.* Or from the union with the Pure Principle without the power of animals.

Suddhatattva could refer to being freed from the real state (or pure state). This is consistent with above Sutras that require us to move beyond the physical, tangible, phenomenal world as one's mind conceives it. Shakti refers to the Divine force of Creation and pasu often refers to animals (Lord Shiva's form of Pasupathi is the Lord of Animals). However, in the philosophy of Shiva-Siddhanta[cxliii], *pasu* refers to the soul (with *pati* referring to god and *pasc* to the world). This is a vexing Sutra and could be interpreted that: by contemplation of the true state of the Supreme reality can one attain freedom from attachment.

1.17 *Vitarkah atmanjnanam.* Reflection - knowledge of the Self.

Atman and *jnanam* are now familiar concepts to readers for the true self or soul and for knowledge. *Jnana* is sometimes interpreted as limited knowledge when compared to *prajna* (wisdom). *Vitarka* is a new concept which can be translated as follows:

- Conjecture/Supposition
- Reflection
- Imagination

The above definitions may appear to be different at first look; however, they share one thread in that they all require subjective judgment. Therefore, one can attempt to guess, imagine, or reflect in the three different Vedic states of being to then achieve knowledge of the self and *moksha*.

PART D: *SANNYASA* – The Sivasutra

1.18 *Lokanandah samadhisukham.* Pure happiness of the world - joy of contemplation.

Loka refers to the world or mankind and *ananda* means pure happiness. *Samadhi* is intense contemplation of an object (or intense concentration of the mind).

Sukham means happiness also; however, ananda is one of the three tenets of reality (*sat-chit-ananda*) of truth, consciousness, and pure happiness.

Taking these together, the Sutra may be informing us that the pure happiness of the world comes from intense concentration on a fixed focus point (the essence of meditation).

1.19 *Saktisamdhane sariropattih.* In the union of power - the origin of bodies.

The concepts of Shakti, Divine power of Creation and *sariram*, the physical body have already been encountered above. *Samdhana* is the union or joining together and *utpatti* is birth or origin. The Sutra may be instructing us that Shakti created the universe through union with the physical (characteristic) and this is consistent with the Hindu version of Creation set out in chapter A14 of this book.

1.20 *Bhutasamdhana bhutaprthakt vavisvanghattah.* Union of elements, separateness of elements, and all-pervading union.

Bhuta can refer to an element, spirit, or demon. *Samdhana* is a concept considered above meaning the union or joining together of two concepts and *prthaktva* means separating or being widely apart. *Sanghattah* could be translated as clashing together or conflict. There is synergy and poetry here for elements combined and elements apart all being contained by the all-pervading (Lord Vishnu) and the conflict (Lord Shiva).

1.21 *Suddhavidyodayac cakresatvasiddhih*. Fulfilment of being the lord of the world - from rising of pure knowledge.

There are some familiar words above including *vidya* (philosophy or science), *udaya* (coming from Creation), *cakra* (wheel), *Isa* (Lord). *Suddha* and *siddhi* can be translated as pure and fulfillment, respectively. Pure knowledge could be interposed for knowledge from creation. Note that Sutras 1.19-1.21 may relate to the creation of the universe as opposed to individual attainment of liberation and enlightenment. However, an understanding of the macro philosophy (of Creation) may help us with the individual path.

1.22 *Mahahradanusamdhananan mantraviryanubhavah*. From investigation of great deep water - the experience of the energy of mantras.

Mahahrada means great deep water (or lake). *Anusamdhanana* means arising from an investigation. *Virya* relates to energy or vigour and *anubhavah* is knowledge from personal experience. Therefore, by conducting mantras one can explore the depths of the mind to achieve liberation. The Vedas and Upanishads explored in Part B of this book confirm the importance of mantras to help with focus and concentration. What starts out as a simple devotional prayer can become a strong mind technique for meditation and self-realization. This is explored more in chapter D2.

PART D: *SANNYASA* – The Sivasutra

Chapter D2 – *Saktopaya*. The Way of the Competent One

The second part of the Shiva Sutras relates to the Way of the Competent One and comprises ten Sutras set out below. These Sutras relate to one who restrains one's thoughts maintaining a constant awareness of Lord Shiva.

2.1 *Cittam mantrah*. Mind - a mantra.

The Sutra is informing readers of the importance of clarity and control of the mind through an ordered and structured thought process. If one is able to govern one's thoughts in this manner, then every thought becomes a prayer of devotion or meditation upon Lord Shiva. *Cittam* can be translated as the mind, heart, thinking, reflecting, imagining, thought; however, this does not change the message of the Sutra. Control of all senses should be maintained in a similar manner. *Mantrah* (or mantra) is a concept readers will be familiar with referring to a prayer, hymn, sacred formula, or mystical verse of incantation. Mantras are deployed in devotion and also to focus the mind upon a core point such as Lord Shiva.

The comments attributed to Yama, Lord of Dharma, in the Upanishads are relevant here in that a person with no understanding and no sensory control in life is as a chariot where the charioteer does not hold the reins firmly. The horses can then become vicious if there is no control and so can the mind. Conversely, one who is able to channel their thoughts in this manner will retain a constant awareness of Lord Shiva in every aspect of their life. In doing so the individual is able to achieve moksha (liberation), not through extensive meditation and prayer, but through the practice of their everyday activities and thoughts.

2.2 *Prayatnah sadhakah.* Persevering effort - fulfilling.

Chapters B3 and B4 of this book explored the Vedas and Upanishads mentions of Lord Shiva and readers will recall that there are multiple references through the use of mantras, beads, rituals as an aid to concentrating the mind. The message of this Sutra is consistent with this concept, that through perseverance we are able to achieve our goal of liberation. The Sutra has application in all aspects of life in that we will achieve through effort. *Prayatnah* can be translated as endeavour or continued exertion and these are synonyms for perseverance. *Sadhakah* can be translated as effective, accomplishing, finishing, or even an efficient or skillful person (so the act of persevering will form the efficient person). One will attain the positivity associated with reaching one's destination after keeping focused and committed to the journey.

2.3 *Vidyasarirasatta mantrarahasyam.* The being of the body of knowledge - the secret of a mantra.

The Sutra may be informing readers that success through the use of a mantra will come from knowledge of the meaning behind the words as opposed to empty chanting of the words themselves. Sariram is a concept that has been encountered multiple times in the above Sutras to mean the physical body, or parts of the body (as opposed to the anatman which refers to the body and the mind). *Satta* refers to existence or being. Therefore, physical aspects of the mantra may be of importance here which may include yoga positions and may also include the use of beads as instructed in the Shiva Upanishads from chapter B4. *Vidya* could be translated as acquiring knowledge, scholarship, or learning and is distinct from jnana (knowledge). The distinction may relate to a priori and a posteriori knowledge acquired from reasoning or from evidence. *Rahasyam* refers to a secret doctrine or mystical teaching hence one acquires knowledge through the deployment of mantras.

2.4 *Garbhe cittavikaso visistavidyasvapnah*. Development of the mind in the womb - a dream of indistinct knowledge.

There are many religions and philosophies that consider the concept of the internal breath, which seeks to explore primordial or umbilical breathing. This is an interesting concept for attempting to recreate, through meditation, the breathing system deployed before one has been born into the physical world. The Sutra is instructing that if one manages this it will be a path to indistinct knowledge (i.e., not separable from one's view of the phenomenal world). *Vikasa* can mean opening instead of development; however, these both imply enlightenment of the mind. *Visista* could refer to something undefined as with the recollection of the facts of a dream on awaking. *Svapna* is the dream or sub-conscious state explored in the Sutras above and one of the three core states that must be mastered before achieving the *Parahbrhman* (Supreme state).

2.5 *Vidyasamutthane svabhavike khecari sivavaastha*. Flying the state of Shiva - the rising of knowledge arising from one's own nature.

There are complex themes within this Sutra. *Vidya* is a term one has encountered before meaning the acquisition of knowledge or learning. *Samutthane* means rising from the performance of work or effort. *Svabhavike* means belonging to one's nature or arising from one's inherent nature. *Khecari* refers to flying or moving in the air and *sivavaastha* refers to the state of Lord Shiva (the *Parabrahman* state that is the goal of meditation). Taken together this second part of the Sutra may be referring to flying through the void, space or supreme consciousness and this state is achieved from our own nature. One has everything needed to achieve this state, i.e., no external assistance is needed, and all may succeed in this quest.

2.6 *Gurur upayah*. The guru - the means.

Readers will be familiar with the word *guru* referring to one who dispels darkness, a venerable person, spiritual parent, or preceptor. *Upayah* means that by which one reaches one's aim (i.e., an expedient or solution). It is common for a particular Sutra to relate to the prior or post Sutra and in this regard 2.6 should be contrasted with 2.5 above which instructs that one does not need any outside assistance to achieve one's goal – one's own nature provides all that is necessary. However, before one is able to progress in this manner, a spiritual teacher may remain an important means to achieve moksha (liberation) by assisting with guidance and support. Alternatively, this Sutra could be clarifying that in Sutra 2.5, one has what one needs but a teacher will provide the means to bring this out. Guru could also be referring to Lord Shiva as the means instead of a physical teacher and the knowledge imparted by Lord Shiva in the Sutras, Vedas, Upanishads, and other scriptures will be the means with which one can achieve enlightenment.

2.7 *Matrkacakra somboodhah*. Perfect knowledge of the multitude of letters.

The Sutra could be referring to the application of meditation through the use of fifty rudraksha beads and the recitation of each letter with each bead as set out in chapter B4 of this book. Equally, this practice detailed in the Shiva Upanishads upon which each of the beads meditated on represents the Sanskrit alphabet may have been adopted following the instruction in this Sutra. *Matrka*, as set out in Sutra 1.4 above, could also be translated as the mother or divine mother providing a different overall message that perfect knowledge is attained through meditation on the Goddess Parvati/Shakti.

2.8 *Sariram havih*. The body - an oblation.

An oblation is something offered to god and this Sutra confirms that the body is such an offering. Recognizing the immanent form of worship, such an oblation could be made by fasting or not sleeping. The Bhagavad Gita confirms that "some people perform stern austerities that are not enjoined by the scriptures, but rather motivated by hypocrisy and egotism. Impelled by desire and attachment, they torment not only the elements of their body, but also, I who dwell within them as the Supreme Soul. Know these senseless people to be of demoniacal resolves". This is an emphatic reminder that the purpose of the oblation is not to hurt oneself but to concentrate one's devotion using the body and mind.

Readers will recall that *sariram* refers to the physical body and not the mind and therefore one is reminded that the body is an important element of worship and meditation through yoga. In the transcendent form of worship, one should not fear nor should one lament death as sacrifice of the body as this is consistent with the Vedic principles that the *atman* (self or soul) is immortal. Readers will recall from Part A of this book that certain Demons took this too literally and caused themselves physical harm. This is not the way of Lord Shiva.

2.9 *Jnanam annam*. Knowledge - food.

The concept of *jnanam* (knowledge) has been seen in many of the above Sutras and *annam* can be translated as food, or food in the mystical sense in which the Supreme self is manifested. Lord Shiva is oft referred to as the Devourer who eats our ignorance and sins. However, taken in another context, the Sutra may be proving the simple instruction that knowledge satiates our minds as food satiates our bodies.

2.10 *Vidyasamhare tadutthasvapnadarsanam.* **In the destruction of knowledge is the appearance of dreaming of a coming forth of the That.**

This Sutra has multiple elements that require careful exploration. *Vidya* is the concept one has encountered above in the learning or acquisition of knowledge when compared to *jnanam* (knowledge or possessing knowledge). Samhare refers to destruction or periodic destruction of the universe at the end of each kalpa (see chapter A14 of this book). *Tatuttha* can be translated as this world coming forth and readers will be familiar by now with the concept of *svapna* the dream state (*svapnadarsanam* meaning the appearance of dreaming). Taking these different components together, the Sutra may be instructing that one's knowledge of the periodic destruction of the universe and the coming forth or Creation of the next world, can be seen through the appearance of the dream state. This is a complex Sutra to complete Chapter D2, The Way of the Competent One.

PART D: *SANNYASA* – The Sivasutra

Chapter D3 – *Anavopaya*. The Fine Way

The third part of the Shiva Sutras relates to the Fine[cxliv] Way and comprise forty-five Sutras set out below. These Sutras relate to yogic efforts that may be more familiar to readers.

3.1 *Atma cittam*. The Self - mind.

One can contrast this Sutra with Sutra 1.1 which instructs that the atma (self or soul) is the state of being awake or consciousness. *Cittam* can be translated as the mind, heart, imagining, or thought. Only the physical body (*sariram*) is absent in this Sutra which instructs that the self is reflection or thought to leave the physical body behind. This is a familiar concept for those who meditate where one is encouraged to free the mind from all physical attachments.

3.2 *Jnanam bandhah*[cxlv]. Knowledge - bondage.

This Sutra may initially confuse as devotion to study is a key tenet of the Vedas. However, within this context, the Sutra may be warning us that much of the knowledge one possesses can inhibit from following the correct path. *Bandhah* can be defined as "attachment to this world" as in the phenomenal world as one perceives it as opposed to the true nature of the universe.

Readers will note the distinction between knowledge and *prajna* (wisdom) in this regard: simply knowing things is not enough without the wisdom to apply that knowledge in *dharma*. The Tripurasura (see chapter A8 of this book) who study *adharmic* scriptures are examples of the dangers in the application of knowledge to an incorrect path with disastrous results. The Sutra could be interpreted to warn against a dogmatic approach to facts and figures, and a mind closed off to spiritual concepts and teachings that will prevent the attainment of *moksha* (liberation).

3.3 *Kaladinam tattvanam aviveko maya.* Of the beginnings of any single part of the whole - non-distinction of realities, Maya.

Kaladinam could be translated as the beginning of time and *tattvanam* can mean realities or true principles. *Aviveko* can be translated as non-distinction or absence of judgment, and many readers will be familiar with *maya* as the concept of illusion that one must see through to achieve *moksha* (liberation). The Sutra could be defining *maya* as the absence of judgment (i.e., what one's mind perceives to be the case). An alternative view is that the Sutra could be informing one that *maya* creates the absence of judgment closing one off from the truth and we must focus to see through this so that we can obtain *moksha*.

3.4 *Sarire samharah kalanam.* The destroyer of parts - within the body.

Whilst Lord Shiva is not referred to in the Sutra, one identifies this deity with *samharah* as the destroyer or the periodical destruction of the universe at the end of each *kalpa* (cycle – see chapter A14). *Kala* could be a reference to death or time or *kalanam* could mean parts of the whole as in the original translation above. *Sarire* refers to the physical body, a term used throughout the Sutras explored above.

Cittam is mind and heart, *Sariram* is body and the anatman is mind, body, and heart. Therefore, when one of these words is mentioned in the Sutras in place of the other it is deliberate. *Samharah* could be referring to one's individual death and reincarnation as opposed to the destruction of the universe (this would be consistent with *kala* referring to death instead of time); thus, the physical body is destroyed, and the self or soul is reincarnated throughout time unless the cycle is broken by obtaining *moksha* (liberation).

3.5 *Nadisamhara bhutajaya bhutakaivalya bhutaprthaktvani.* The accumulation of channels, victory over the elements, detachment of the elements, and separateness of the elements.

At first sight, this Sutra appears to have instruction for meditative practices and everyday living. One must approach any undertaking by looking at the granular parts and mastering them. However, nadi refers to channels within the body that flow (breath, blood, energy) and *samhara* to the period destruction of the universe (or one's own reincarnation) as discussed in the above Sutras. *Nadisamhara* could be translated as reincarnation of one's life force; however, nadi is more related to the tube or channel as opposed to the item being carried. *Bhuta* refers to one of the five elements of ether, air, fire, water, earth and therefore the Sutra may be instructing that one must conquer tangible aspects in life by detaching these from the soul. *Jaya* can be translated as victory or conquest and *kaivalya* as detachment from the soul or perfect isolation. *Prthaktvani* means separateness.

3.6 *Mohavaranat siddhih.* Fulfilment - an act of concealing the delusion of mind.

Moha means delusion of darkness of the mind (even loss of consciousness). *Avaranat* means from the act of concealing and siddhih means fulfilment, prosperity, or the acquisition of supernatural powers. However, concealing one's delusion is distinct from seeing through one's delusion. Therefore, the Sutra may be warning us that this is false pride and sense of fulfiment if we are only concealing it and not uncovering the truth.

3.7 *Mohajayad anantabhogat sahajavidyajayah.* Through the conquest of the delusion of mind, through infinite enjoyment - the conquest of natural knowledge.

The Sutra is clear at first sight that one must conquer the delusions and ignorance we have to see the truth of the world.

Moha as per the previous Sutra refers to darkness of the mind as well as delusion. *Ananta* means infinite or eternal and *bhogat* is enjoyment or eating. Infinite enjoyment could be referring to the *Parabrahman*. *Vidya* as for previous Sutras is learning as opposed to *jnana* knowledge (already acquired). *Sahaja* could be translated as effortless or by nature (or birth). Effortless learning will be achieved by one who achieves the *Parabrahman* state through conquering the delusion of the mind. This is consistent with the belief that seeing through the *maya* (illusion) will result in *moksha* (liberation).

3.8 *Jagrad avitiyakarah.* Waking - the doer of forming the second part of anything.

Readers will be familiar with the concept of *jagrat*, the state of being awake as one of the three primary states (plus asleep and in dream) separate from the fourth *Parabrahman* state. *Dvitiya* can be translated as the second or second part/half and *karah* to make, cause, create, or produce. The second part of creating anything is to be awake in the conscious state. The first part is not alluded to in the Sutra. One awakens from either the dream or sleep state of consciousness and this Sutra has a consistent message to Sutra 1.7 which instructs on the importance of realization of all three states before the *Parabrahman* can be achieved.

3.9 *Nartaka atma.* The dancer - the self.

Sutras 3.9, 3.10, and 3.11 are interrelated and should be considered as a collective. The *atman* (self or soul) is the dancer i.e., the main performer. The *atman* is free from the mind and the body. Therefore, the Sutra is referring to a celestial or spiritual dance as opposed to the physical. *Nartaka* can be translated as performer or singer; however, the Sutra is consistent with Lord Shiva's role of Nataraja (King of the Dance) as explored in chapter A7 of this book.

3.10 *Rango antaratma*. The stage - the inner self.

Rangah refers to a stage and *antaratma* the inner self. Note that the *antaratma* has not been referred to in previous Sutras which have considered the *atma* (self or soul) and the *anatma* (mind, heart, and body). Inner self is sometimes used to refer to the *atman*. However, antar means within or amongst and the inner self in this sense may be referring to a deeper self that is reflected in both unconscious and sub-conscious states. The self or soul dances upon the inner self which is the platform.

3.11 *Preksakanindriyani*. The spectators - the organs of sense.

Preksakani refers to spectators or the audience and *indriyani* refers to the senses, organs of sense, or faculties of sense. These aspects should observe and not direct or control the dance or the stage. They should be led by the self and inner self. The above Sutras may be instructing that the sense can create the illusion of *maya* and so one must listen, observe one's internal dance as opposed to being influenced by what we see in the external phenomenal world as one perceives it.

3.12 *Dhivasat sattvasiddhih*. By means of wisdom - fulfilment of true essence.

The Sutra is clear. *Sattva* is a strong concept that relates to true essence, existence, disposition of the mind, strength of character, and goodness. Readers will have encountered siddhih in Sutras 1.21 and 3.6 above as fulfilment or acquisition of supernatural powers. *Dhivasat* refers to wisdom, understanding, or religious thought attained through force and is distinct from *jnanam* (knowledge) and *vidya* (learning or acquiring knowledge). *Dhivasat* is a stronger concept than both of these.

3.13 *Siddhah svatantrabhavah*. One who has attained the highest truth - a free being.

This Sutra is clear as for 3.12. *Siddhah* refers to one who has attained the highest object or truth, an inspired sage or seer. This could be a reference to the *Parabrahman* state and is a state that anyone in meditation will be trying to achieve. *Svatantra* refers to a free, self-willed, independent person and *bhava* means being or existing. *Svatantrabhavah* could be translated therefore as existing through self-will.

3.14 *Yatha tatra tathanyatra*. As there so elsewhere.

The Sutra requires careful examination. *Yatha* can be translated as the manner or way and *tatra* as so or in that place. *Tatha* refers to like in manner and *anyatra* elsewhere or in another place. The Sutra may be asserting the non-dualist concept that all places are one. Another interpretation may be that one should apply the same devotion to all undertakings.

3.15 *Bijavadhanam*. Attention of origin.

Avadhana means attention, intentness, or attentiveness, and *bija* refers to seed, origin, element, primary cause, or source. This is distinct from *yoni* seen in other Sutras and interpreted as origin in terms of birth. It is also distinct from *bhuta* which has been applied in the above Sutras to mean the five core elements. One requires focus and concentration of the primary causes or sources. This Sutra is therefore an instruction in meditation as to where to aim our central thoughts at the origin of all things. *Dhanam* could be translated as property or treasure; however, that would not be consistent with other Sutras we have encountered. *Avadhana* is more appropriate within the context of meditation. *Bija* is also referred to in meditation as the seeds planted in the mind that give rise to the fruit of knowledge.

3.16 *Asanasthahsukhum hrade nimajjati.* Practicing asana[cxlvi], he easily immerses in deep water.

The Upanishads discussed in Part B of this book oft refer to the mind as a deep lake. To immerse oneself in the deep water is to free oneself of the physical world and distractions by concentrating within. The practice of *asana* is a yoga position or posture. The Sutra is instructing that assuming these meditative positions which combine the mind and body will provide the enlightenment one seeks. *Sukha* means with ease, or joy instructing that once such positions are mastered the path is not complex. *Hrade nimajjati* as referenced above refers to plunging into a large deep body of water which is taken to refer to the mind.

3.17 *Svamatranirmanam apadayati.* One causes the creation of one's own measure.

The *Sutra* informs that one is in control of one's own journey to *moksha* (liberation). This is an empowering *Sutra*. Creation in this sense could refer to bringing about one's own measure. *Nirmana* could also refer to creation of the universe. *Apadayati* could be translated as bringing misfortune but that would not be in keeping with the tone of the Sutras.

3.18 Vidyavinase janmavinasah. Not in the destruction of knowledge - the destruction of birth.

Readers will recall *vidya* referring to the acquisition of knowledge or learning. *Vinasa* means destruction, utter loss, annihilation, decay, or death. *Avinasa* would refer to not in the destruction or loss of. The placement of a single "a" in front of *vinasa* would render the opposite meaning to the text. *Janma* refers to birth or production. One is familiar with the concept of destruction of ignorance and arrogance, plus the destruction of the universe at the end of each *kalpa* (see chapter A14).

3.19 *Kavargadisu mahesvaryadyah pasumatarah*. The Energy of Shiva in the beginnings of the class of guttural letters - the mothers of animals.

This Sutra has a number of concepts that need exploration. *Kavarga* refers to the class of letters that are spoken and as such one can infer that this is relating to the use of a mantra or chant. *Adisu* means beginning with and *mahesvari* can refer to the Energy of Lord Shiva or to Goddess Parvati. *Pasumatarah* refers to the divine mother of all creatures. Therefore, meditation on Goddess Parvati through the use of mantras.

3.20 *Trisu caturtham tailavad asecyam*. The Fourth should be poured like oil in the Three.

The "Fourth" state refers to the *Parabrahman* (Supreme) state of consciousness and the "Three" refers to the states of being awake (conscious), asleep (unconscious), and dreaming (sub-conscious). Readers may recall from chapter A4 that the Dakshinamurti Upanishad sets out the analogy for meditation where the innermost *atman* (self or soul) is referred to as a lamp of knowledge filled with the oil of detachment, furnished with the wick of devotion: and having the full receptacle (oil-can) as intense silence. This will irradicate the darkness of delusion.

3.21 *Magnah svacittena praviset*. One should enter with one's own mind immerged.

The Sutra is informing one that from the offset of our practices one must apply deep concentration (be fully immerged in the lake of the mind). *Magnah* can be translated as being totally engrossed in. *Cittam* is a concept we have seen in many of the above Sutras and refers to the mind and/or heart. *Praviset* is to enter into or devote oneself. Approaching any undertaking with concentration and purpose is the message in this Sutra and applicable for meditation and any everyday undertaking that one may enter into.

3.22 *Pranasamacare samadarsanam.* Within the practice of prana - a looking on all with indifferent eyes.

Prana refers to the breath of life and the practice of *prana* the spiritual and meditative practices that assist one to see beyond the phenomenal world as one's mind perceives it. *Samacare* refers to practice, procedure, or conduct. *Samadarsanam* refers to looking on all things and perosns with indifferent or equal eyes. This is an elegant Sutra that instructs on a non-prejudicial view of the universe.

3.23 *Madhye avaraprasavah.* Inferior generation in the space between.

Madhye can be translated as in the middle, between, or among (potentially the space or sky). *Avara* could be translated as inferior, younger, less important, and *prasavah* as generation, procreation, conception, birth, origin, offspring. The space in between could be referring to a lack of control or precision leading to inferior results. Such practices that occur without control are less important and one should attempt tasks with sensory and mind control to ensure success and fulfillment.

3.24 *Matrasvapratyaya samdhane nastasya punar utthanam.* In the act of uniting, one's own conception of measures - the act of rising again of the lost.

Matrasvapratyaya could be translated as measuring one's own conception (i.e., taking account of one's good deeds in life). *Samdhane* refers to the act of uniting or joining together and *nastasya* refers to the lost, perished or destroyed. Punarutthanam refers to rising or standing up again and may refer to reincarnation of the *atma* (self or soul). There is a cyclical element to this Sutra; however, the attainment of *moksha* (liberation) is to free oneself from this cycle. The measure of one's own contributions in life will determine this.

3.25 *Sivatulyo jayate*. He becomes like Shiva.

Tulyah means to be like, equal to, of the same kind, or comparable. *Sivatulyo* may therefore, be referring to the state of *Parabrahman* (or *Paramshiva* as it is sometimes referred to in relation to the Sutras). This is the goal of the Sutras. *Jayate* means becomes, generates, begets, produces, creates, causes, is born, produced, or comes into existence. This does not change the meaning of the Sutra that one must achieve *moksha* (liberation) and become like Lord Shiva.

3.26 *Sariravrttir vratam*. Maintenance of the body - a holy practice.

Readers familiar with the practice of yoga will appreciate that the body is as important as the mind in many contexts to practice and achieve the physical positions and forms that assist with breathing and control over the senses. *Sariram* is the word deployed in many of the Sutras analyzed above to refer to the physical body and not the mind and heart (*cittam*). *Vratam* refers to holy practice, religious vows, acts of devotion or austerity. *Vrtti* refers to maintenance, subsistence, behaviour, conduct. Thus, maintaining one's body is an important religious practice to achieve *moksha* (liberation).

3.27 *Katha japah*. Conversation - mantra recitation.

The Sutra is instructing that one's speech is a form of mantra, devotion, or prayer. Therefore, one must take care to ensure that one's spoken words embody the virtue, precision, and devotion of a mantra. Many of the Sutras encountered above suggest that how one conducts everyday activities is as important as the practice of yoga and meditation. *Katha* could be translated as story, or fable instead of conversation or speech. *Japah* means mantra recitation, muttering prayers, repeating scripture, chanting the names of deities – essentially the vocalization of the text.

3.28 *Danam atmajnanam.* The act of giving - self-knowledge.

There are some familiar words in the above Sutra. *Jnanam* is knowledge and *atma* the self or soul. Atmajnanam give us knowledge of the soul. *Danam* can be translated as the donation of a gift or charity. The Sutra could be read that to give charity to others is a way to achieve knowledge of the Self. The Katha Upanishad sets out Yama, Lord of Dharma's decree that charity, austerity, and the application of knowledge are three important aspects in one's life.

3.29 *Yo avipastho jnahetusca.* He who is engaged in guarding sheep and the cause of knowing.

The guarding of sheep may refer to one who looks after others in the life stage of Grihastha (householder). Such practice will lead to the cause for knowledge (to be able to teach others). The guardian of sheep could also be a reference to Lord Shiva in the form of Pasupathi, Lord of Animals. Thus, Lord Shiva is the cause for knowledge.

3.30 *Svasakti pracayo visvam.* The multitude of his own power - all-pervading.

Svasakti could be translated as one's own creative force or power. *Shakti* can also refer to the divine feminine power that created the universe. *Pracayo* refers to a multitude, quantity, or mass and visvam refers to all-pervading (from Lord Vishnu), the whole world or universe. The Sutra brings non-duality back into focus with the Hindu Trinity functioning as a collective. Thus, the quantity of divine creative power is the whole universe.

3.31 *Sthitilayau*. Maintenance of life and dissolution.

The Sutra may be referring to the cyclical nature of the universe (see chapter A14) with period *kalpa* (cycles) of creation and dissolution. On an individual level, the soul is reincarnated until one achieves *moksha* (liberation). *Sthiti* means maintenance, continued existence, remaining, and *layau* means dissolution, melting, extinction, destruction, death.

3.32 *Tatpravrttav apy anirasah samvettrbhavat*. Also, without exclusion, this world and acting - both from the character of one who has consciousness.

Samvettr refers to one who has consciousness, intellect, knowledge, understanding. *Bhavat* can be translated as from the character, nature, or manner. *Tatpravrtta* can be translated as acting or proceeding in or from this world. *Anirash* refers to without exclusion or casting out. Spiritual enlightenment can be obtained by one who has the state of *Parabrahman*.

3.33 *Sukhasukhayor bahir mananam*. Pleasure and pain - outwards thinking.

The Sutra may be instructing of the importance of internal reflection and aspects one can control as opposed to external influences that one cannot. The Hindu scriptures convey in multiple locations that a good life is to be preferred to a pleasurable one. One can control how much one suffers with respect to emotional pain more so than physical pain. However, it is also possible to exert control over the latter with concentration. If one is able to shut out external distractions, then *moksha* (liberation) can be achieved.

3.34 Tadvimuktas tu kevali. But freed from this world - one devoted to the doctrine of the absolute unity of spirit.

The Sutra informs one that devotion to the unity of spirit with mind and body will provide enlightenment and *moksha* (liberation). *Vimukta* means to be set free or liberated from. *Kevali* refers to a meditative aesthetic becoming one.

3.35 *Mohapratisamhatas tu karmatma.* But one whose character - action towards forming one mass of delusion.

Moha refers to delusion of the mind, or darkness and *prati* is a prefix meaning towards or near to. *Samhatah* means forming one mass or stuck together. The delusion (ignorance) one is under must be overcome. *Karmatma* is one embodied with *karma* (action). The Sutra may be warning against the approach one adopts in life that can add to the delusion and pursuit of *adharma* (immoral practices).

3.36 *Bhedatiraskare sargantarakarmatvam.* In the disappearance of the act of distinction - the state of action of another creation of the world.

At first sight, the Sutra is referring to Creation (see chapter A14 of this book). *Bheda* could be referring to breaking or cleaving instead of distinction and this is consistent with the periodical nature of the universe. However, applying this to the individual, one ceases to view aspects with distinction by viewing them as one collective. This leads to the *Parabrahman* state.

3.37 *Karanasaktih svato nubhavat.* The power of producing - from one's own experience.

Like many of the Sutras one has explored above, this is an empowering edict. The word *anubhavah* means through experience or knowledge derived from personal observation/experiment. Therefore, one is reminded that the benefits from meditation and any undertaking will depend upon the amount of time one devotes to this. *Karana* means to produce or make, and *Shakti* is power, or the divine feminine power represented by Goddess Parvati. The output of one's devotion will be related to the input.

3.38 *Tripadadyanu prananam.* Beginnings of the three parts - after the act of animating.

Three parts could be referring to the three states of being awake, asleep, and in the dream state. Concepts that have been explored throughout the Sutras. *Paranana* could be translated as animating or breathing (putting life into). This we begin with mastery over the three states and this gives life to the fourth state of the *Parabrahman*. The converse may also be true: we commence with life and control over breathing which then provides control over the three states of consciousness, sub-consciousness, and unconsciousness. The three parts could also be referring to the Hindu Trinity of deities of Lord Shiva, Lord Brahma, and Lord Vishnu.

3.39 *Cittasthitivac sarirakaranabahyesu.* In the outer of the organs of sense of the body - like being in a state of mind.

Readers will have encountered *cittam*, mind and heart. *Cittasthitivac* could be translated as remaining like the mind and heart. *Sariram* is the familiar concept of the physical body and *karanabahyesu* can be translated as an organ of sense, instrument of the outer exterior (or not belonging to the family). An alternative translation is therefore that the outer senses of the physical body remain like the mind and heart. This may be a reference to one's perception of the phenomenal world stemming from one's outer senses.

3.40 Abhilapad bahirgatih samvahyasya. From expression - the extroversion of the "to be carried."

Abhilapad refers to an expression or word and may be referring to mantras. *Bahrirgati* relates to the motion or path of the outer form or extroversion. *Samvahyasya* can be translated as being carried or borne.

3.41 Tadarudhapramites tatksayaj jvasamksayah. From the destruction of this world, of the manifestation brought to this world - the complete destruction of life.

The word *tat* can be translated as this or this world, and *arudha* means brought on or having reached. Whilst the above Sutra at first sight appears to convey a negative tone, one can apply the cyclical aspect of the Hindu universe of destruction and creation. One is reminded by the Sutra that the world equates to life and all living creatures. *Pramiteh* could be defined as knowledge obtained by proof, ksayat is destruction or loss, and *sanksayah* is the complete destruction of all things (or destruction of the world).

3.42 Bhutakancuki tada vimukto bhuyah patisamahparah. The snake of the world, which has recently cast its skin - then again like the supreme Lord.

Bhuta refers to that which exists, a living being, or a demon and *kancuki* refers to a garment or armour (or a snake). *Vimuktah* can be translated as having recently cast its skin, or freed/escaped. *Patisamahparah* can be translated as the supreme or highest lord or master. Whether one deploys the snake analogy or not, the message is the same in that liberation (from one's ignorance, arrogance, illusions) is the path to the *Parabhraman* state.

3.43 *Naisargikah pranasambandhah*. The connection with the breath of life - inherent.

The above Sutra provides a meditative instruction that concentration on breathing techniques is essential. Another way to read this is the positive message that life is permanent through the immortal *atman* (self or soul). *Naisargikah* means inherent or natural and prana is the concept of the breath of life that one has explored in previous Sutras. *Sambandhah* refers to close connection, union, or relationship.

3.44 Nasikantarmadhyasamyamat kim atra savyapasavyasausumnesu. From the control of the senses of the internal middle of the nose - what is in this respect in the susumna channels on the left and right?

Susumna[cxlvii] is a concept in yoga and meditation that readers may be familiar with. It is a central channel of the sacred River Saraswathi and also applied to breathing and energy channels within the body. The Sutra is informing one of the importance of breathing and sensory control.

3.45 *Bhuyah syat pratimilanama*. Again, one should be towards closing the eyes.

The opening of the Sutra with *bhuyah* implies that it is related to Sutra 3.44 (again, or moreover/further). *Syat* means that one should be and *prati* as a prefix denotes near to or like in comparison. *Milanam* refers to closing the eyes or the closing of a flower (certain flowers will close when deprived of light or as a proactive measure to conserve resources at night). Closing one's eyes may be referring to freeing oneself from distraction to focus all energy on the Parabrahman state, it may also refer to displaying temperance and control.

PART D: *SANNYASA* – The Sivasutra

Figure 50: Lord Shiva in Meditation

The Rig Veda states that "the vessels of truth will carry those of good deeds across the ocean of ignorance". And so, concludes the Lord Shiva Narrative with the Shiva Sutras and the metaphysical consideration of how one can achieve the Parabrahman state.

Epilogue – In Search of Lord Shiva

In 2018, I undertook a personal spiritual journey to Tibet and Mount Kailas, the celestial home of Lord Shiva. I did not know what I expected to find; however, as a child I had visualized Lord Shiva there in constant, quiet meditation atop the mountain. There are a multitude of fables that speak of devotees performing austerities in the wilderness to win the affections of the Hindu Lord of Destruction. My flights from the United Kingdom to the People's Republic of China[cxlviii] were beset with delays from the offset and when I finally arrived at the Tibet airport, after thirty-six hours of travel, it was conveyed to me that my luggage had been lost by the Airline. I did not have time to go shopping for replacement supplies and so I set off on an arduous voyage to pay homage to Lord Shiva with just the clothes on my back and minimal other possessions.

There was no phone reception, no radio, and there was no contact with the outside world. After a torrid internal flight on a single propeller aircraft and many hours of driving on dusty and uneven plains that seemed to be leading nowhere, I began to experience severe altitude sickness with fatigue and dizziness. However, it was at that exact moment of immense physical exhaustion that I beheld Mount Kailas: a solitary mountain fortress butting through the clouds, black as the night sky with a perfect white peak of snow like interspersed galaxies of stars. There is a brilliant light that seems to always shine upon the pyramid of snow. I was filled with a serenity that I had not experienced before plus renewed strength of body and mind. I sat in mediation for many hours with Lord Shiva within earshot.

Mount Kailas is a mystical place, believed by many religions[cxlix] to have strong spiritual energy and it is steeped in religious history

Epilogue

(some of those stories relating to Mount Kailas are featured in this book). I was fortunate to be able to bathe in the sacred Lake Manasarovar[cl] (Lake of the Mind) which is formed by glaciers from Mount Kailas. The Vedas are believed by many in folklore to have been written down on the shore of this placid lake. At the time of my journey to Tibet, I was looking for answers that could help me in my own life; Lord Shiva duly provided those answers but not in the manner nor at the time in which I expected.

I can say from experience that the journey into the ocean of Hindu scriptures that readers will undertake in this book is no less spiritual than the physical journey to Mount Kailas and the plunge into the cool, sacred waters of Lake Manasarovar.

Shiv Mahalingham, March 2021.

Figure 51: Mount Kailas – the Abode of Lord Shiva

Glossary of Key Characters and Key Concepts

Gods, Demi-Gods, Sages, and other Heroes

Aditya – the Sun God. Also referred to as Surya.

Agni – the Fire God.

Arihan – Created by Lord Vishnu to write adharmic scripts to fool the Tripurasura brothers into abandoning the Vedic principles.

Arjuna – the demi-god son of Indra, King of Gods.

Ashokasundari – the daughter of Lord Shiva and Goddess Parvati with unparalleled beauty who was created in the garden of the heavens.

Asvatthama – a central character in the Mahabharata War with the attributes of Lord Shiva who slaughters the majority of the Pandava armies in one single night.

Asvins – twin Gods of Dawn.

Bhageeratha – an Ancient King whose forbears were blessed when the River Goddess Ganga descended from the heavens.

Brahma – one of the Hindu Trinity, The Creator.

Chandra – the Moon God, cursed by Daksha due to his preferential treatment of his wife Rohini, blessed by Lord Shiva to remain near to him forever. Also referred to as *Soma*.

Daksha – the son of Lord Braham, father of Goddess Sati, and father-in-law of Lord Shiva.

Devas – the gods.

Ganas – the Tribe or Army (e.g., the Shivaganas were the loyal attendants and army of Lord Shiva).

Glossary of Key Characters and Key Concepts

Ganesha – the son of Lord Shiva and Goddess Parvati worshipped as the Remover of Obstacles.

Ganga – the River Goddess who descended to earth upon the head of Lord Shiva.

Himavat – the King of the Himalayas, Father of Goddess Parvati, and father-in-law to Lord Shiva.

Indra – the King of the Devas.

Isvara – the Supreme Soul, The Personal God.

Janaka – the noble King and father of Sita, father-in-law of Rama. King Janaka possessed the Bow of Lord Shiva used to test the worth of potential suitors for Sita.

Kamadeva – the God of Love and Lord of Pleasure.

Kartikeya – the son of Lord Shiva and Goddess Parvati worshipped as the Lord of War.

Kauravas – the cousins of the Pandava brothers who fight against them in the Mahabharata War.

Krishna – the Avatar of Lord Vishnu who orated the Bhagavad Gita to Arjuna on the eve of the Mahabharat War.

Laxmi – the Goddess of Wealth.

Markandeya – the devotee of Lord Shiva who attained immortality after being rescued from death.

Maruts – referred to also as Rudras in the Vedas this multitude of violent warriors may be the sons of Lord Shiva.

Nandi – the animal vehicle (vahana) of Lord Shiva and one of the main Ganas.

Shiva – One of the Hindu Trinity, The Destroyer.

Other names and forms of Lord Shiva include:

Adiyogi – The First Teacher
Bhairava – The Terrible
Dhakshinamurti – The Primeval Sage
Gangadhara – Lord of the River Ganga
Kalantaka – Ender of Death
Mahadeva – The Great God
Nataraja – King of the Dance
Neelkanth – One with the Blue Neck
Pasupathi – Lord of Animals
Rudra – The Destroyer
Sankara – Doer of Good Deeds
Somnath – Lord of the Moon

Pandavas – the five demi-god brothers who fight in the Mahabharata War.

Parvati – the Goddess of Beauty, Family, Harmony and Divine Strength. Also known as Goddess Sati or Uma.

Rama – the Avatar of Lord Vishnu who is born a man to destroy the evil Ravana, King of Demons.

Valmiki – a great sage and the scribe of The Ramayana

Varuna – the Sea God.

Vasuki – the Serpent King.

Vayu – the Wind God.

Vishnu – One of the Hindu Trinity, The Pervader.

Yama – the God of Death and Lord of Dharma.

Glossary of Key Characters and Key Concepts

Demons and villains

Andhaka – the Demon King created by Lord Shiva's sweat and defeated by Lord Shiva in battle. Andhaka later found redemption as the head of Lord Shiva's Ganas.

Apasmara – the Demon upon whose back Lord Shiva danced as Nataraja to save the universe from destruction by dark magic conjured by evil sages.

Asuras – a term for demons.

Jalandhara – the Demon King created by the force of Lord Shiva's wrath emerging from his third eye into the oceans.

Rakshasas – a term for demons.

Ravana – the Demon King of Lanka who was blessed that he could not be killed by a god or demon.

Shakuni – the dishonourable uncle of the Pandavas. Father of Vrika.

Shankachuda – the Invincible Demon King who conquered the three worlds before being killed by Lord Shiva.

Tarakasura – the powerful Demon King slain by Lord Kartikeya when the Lord of War was still a child.

Tripurasura – the Three Demon Brothers (Taraksha, Kamlaksha, Viddyunmrt) protected by impenetrable fortresses to the extent that Lord Shiva was compelled to use the destructive Pasupatastra to annihilate them.

Virabhadra – Demon created from a lock of Lord Shiva's hair who slayed Daksha, son of Lord Brahma.

Vrika – the Demon who had the power to kill anyone by placing his hand on their head and was tricked by Lord Vishnu into killing himself.

Key Concepts

Adharma – Immorality

Advaita – Everything is one

Anatma – Non-self (body and mind)

Antaratma – Inner self

Artha – Purpose

Atma – True self (soul)

Ashrama – Hindu stages of life

Brhamacharya – Stage one (student)

Cittam - Mind and/or heart

Dharma – Morality

Grihastha – Stage two (householder)

Jagrat – Awake state of consciousness

Jnana - Knowledge

Kama – Love

Karma – Action

Maya – Illusion

Moksha – Liberation

Parabrahma – Highest Supreme State or Self

Prajna – Wisdom

Prana – Life Force

Samsara – Reincarnation

Glossary of Key Characters and Key Concepts

Sannyasa – Stage four (Aesthetic)

Sariram – physical body

Saushupta – Deep sleep state of unconsciousness

Shakti – Feminine creative force/Divine Mother

Soma – Nectar, and another name for Chandra the Moon God

Svapna – Dream state of sub-consciousness

Vanaprastha – Stage three (retired)

Yoga - Physical, spiritual, and mental practices

Hindu Scriptures

Agamas – Hindu scriptures. Agama means "that which has been handed down".

Bhagavad Gita – Hindu scriptures. Bhagavad Gita means "Song of God".

Epics – Hindu scriptures comprising:

> The Ramayana (the scripture of Lord Vishnu's avatar as Rama), and

> The Mahabharata (the scripture of a war fought between the Pandavas and the Kauravas in which the Pandavas are assisted by Lord Vishnu's avatar Krishna).

Puranas – Hindu scriptures. Purana means "ancient".

Sutras – Hindu scriptures. Sutra means "thread".

Upanishads – Hindu scriptures. Upanishad means "secret teaching" or may also mean "sit close by" as one may sit close to a teacher.

Vedas – Hindu scriptures. Veda means "knowledge".

Bibliography and Suggested Further reading

The Bhagavad Gita – Translation by Swami Prabhupada

The Mahabharata – Translation by Kisari Mohan Ganguli

The Ramayana – Translation by Desiraju Hanumanta Rao & K. M. K. Murthy.

-

The Linga Purana – Translation by Motilal Banarsidass

The Padma Purana – Translation by Motilal Banarsidass

The Shiva Purana – Translation by Motilal Banarsidass

-

Shiva Sutra – Translation by Gerard D. C. Kuiken[cli]

The Principal Upanishads – Translation by Alan Jacobs

The Shiva (Saiva) Upanishads – Translation by G Srinivasa Murti

The Vedas – English Translation by Ralph Griffith

-

A Sanskrit Dictionary – John M Denton

Picture and Photo Credits

1. Lord Shiva in Meditation, Cornelia Kopp CC BY 2.0[clii].
2. Yamantaka God of Death, CC Public Domain[cliii].
3. Chronology of Hindu Texts by Shiv Mahalingham.
4. Lord Shiva Temple at Mahabalipuram. With permission of UNESCO©.
5. Lord Shiva Genealogy by Shiv Mahalingham.
6. Lord Shiva Statue, Scorius CC BY 2.0[cliv].
7. Lord Shiva in Meditation. Ninasarts.com, Shutterstock Licence.
8. Lord Shiva Challenges Lord Yama. Astroved.com, Shutterstock Licence.
9. Lord Shiva and Goddess Parvati. CC 1.0[clv].
10. Lord Shiva and Goddess Parvati with sons. CC 1.0[clvi].
11. Arjuna in penance to Lord Shiva. B Sheshadri CC BY 2.0[clvii].
12. Rama Breaks Lord Shiva's Bow, Arian Zweggers CC BY 2.0[clviii].
13. Lord Shiva imprisons Ravana, Arian Zweggers CC BY 2.0[clix].
14. Nataraja – King of the Dance. With permission of Louvre, A Dhabi ©.
15. Lord Shiva with Trident, Sunil Sonu art, Shutterstock Licence.
16. Lord Shiva Triumphant in Battle. Vectomart, Shutterstock Licence.
17. Lord Shiva, Warrior. Manju Mandavya, Shutterstock Licence.
18. Lord Shiva dances upon a demon. Richard Mortel CC VY 2.0[clx].
19. The Hindu Trinity at Elephanta. With permission of UNESCO©.
20. Horsehead Nebula, Hubble Images. CC BY 2.0[clxi].
21. Lake Manasarovar. Photo by Shiv Mahalingham.
22. The Mahabharata War Begins . CC BY 2.0[clxii].
23. Rameswaram – where Rama is blessed by Lord Shiva before the incursion into Lanka, Bing Maps.
24. Vedic manuscripts, Sarah Welch CC BY 4.0[clxiii].
25. Rudraksha bead. CC 1.0[clxiv].
26. Map Depicting Mount Kailas and Lake Manasarovar. Photo by Shiv Mahalingham.
27. Amarnath Ice Linga. CC BY 2.0[clxv].
28. Chidambaram Temple Pool, Sudhamshu CC BY 2.0[clxvi].
29. Chidambaram Temple gopuram, Arian Zweggers CC BY 2.0[clxvii].
30. Lord Shiva at Elephanta. With permission of UNESCO©
31. Shiva & Parvati at Elephanta. With permission of UNESCO©
32. Kailasnath Temple, Rajagopal. CC BY 2.0[clxviii]
33. Lord Shiva at Ellora, With permission of UNESCO©.
34. Kedarnath Temple. CC BV 2.0[clxix]
35. Kedarnath Temple, Govind Singh CC BV 2.0[clxx]

36. Ravana's cleft at Koneswaram. CC BV 2.0[clxxi]
37. The Pasupathi Seal. CC 1.0[clxxii].
38. Murudeshawara Statue of Lord Shiva. Arun Kumud CC BY 2.0[clxxiii].
39. Pasupatinath Temple Monkey. CC BY 2.0[clxxiv].
40. Prambanan Temple Guardians. With permission of UNESCO©.
41. Prambanan Temple. With permission of UNESCO©.
42. Ramanathaswamy Temple. CC BY 2.0[clxxv].
43. Somnath Temple. CC BY 2.0[clxxvi].
44. Photo of the moon. CC BY 2.0[clxxvii].
45. Unakoti Lord Shiva as Gangadhara. With permission of Unakoti District Website ©.
46. Unakoti Deities. With permission of Unakoti District Website ©.
47. Vadakunnathan Temple Festival in Kerala. CC BY 2.0[clxxviii].
48. Dawn at Varanasi. CC BY 2.0[clxxix].
49. Map of Temples locations for Part C by Shiv Mahalingham.
50. Lord Shiva in Meditation, Cornelia Kopp CC BY 2.0[clxxx].
51. Photo of Mount Kailash by Shiv Mahalingham.

Acknowledgements

This book is dedicated to the author's mother who told him the stories of Lord Shiva from an early age.

The author is also grateful to the support from his many uncles and aunts who suffered his many questions and challenges over the years.

A significant note of thanks is due to his father who introduced him to the intricacies and complexities of Hindu philosophy, his brother for a diligent proof reading of the text, and to an extremely patient wife for putting up with him over the past twenty years...

The book could not be a success without the valuable input from Dr. Thavasothy, Consultant Psychiatrist, advocate of the Hindu scriptures, and lifelong friend and counsellor to the author's parents.

Many thanks to all readers who have made it this far:

"May you see a hundred autumns, may you thrive a hundred autumns, and may you remain pure a hundred autumns".

Author Biography

Shiv Mahalingham is the author of *The Lord Shiva Narrative* and is at present working on a number of other books which will be published soon:

- *Glory to Hanuman*, A Novella of traditional stories interspersed with original stories about this legendary figure. See extract on the next page.
- *The Gautuma Buddha Narrative*, from the *Celestial Narratives* series following a similar format to *The Lord Shiva Narrative* and collating life lessons from the stories and philosophy of Buddhism.
- *Mindful of Children*, from the *Mindful Trilogy* setting out real life personal and professional examples of how the above philosophies can help with everyday life situations.

Shiv is a financial consultant with circa twenty five years' experience and has won multiple awards for authorship of business publications. He has also been featured on CNN. Shiv is the founder and guardian of The MAHA Foundation which makes charitable grants to fund projects supporting children and young adults in need. He is happily married with three children.

Acknowledgements

Excerpt from the Novella "Glory to Hanuman"

The three Elemental Gods commenced a coordinated tirade of expert marksmanship that began to push the demon armies into their fortresses in retreat. They hurled their Vayavastra, Agneyastra, and Varunastra weapons at the enemy battalions. These divine missiles flew in synchronization across the three worlds. The other generals rallied to them when they saw they were gaining ground. Yama, the God of Death rode his black bullock to the gates of the fortress being attacked by Vayu and the demon armies fled inside in panic. In this targeted onslaught, the enemies of the gods became entrapped within the three supposedly unassailable castles.

This provided Lord Shiva with the opportune moment that he had been waiting for. He unleashed his deadly weapon of destruction and in an instant he annihilated the three palaces, the three Demon brothers, and the entire demon army. The battle was won, and the three worlds celebrated their freedom from the evil oppressors. However, for the first time he could remember, Vayu felt weary from the campaign. He had sustained many injuries that he would not have noticed in his youth. As the other gods rejoiced, he gripped his shoulder and grimaced. The God of Fire smacked him hard on the back and let out a roar of laughter: "you are getting old my friend...". Vayu had witnessed Agni being aided by Lord Kartikeya on the battlefield. Agni was a surrogate father to Kartikeya, the God of War, as he had been instrumental in the birth of this young warrior. Vayu was happy for him and he knew that It was time to sire children of his own. Children who possessed the strength, skill, and virtuosity of young Lord Karitkeya. They would have their own destinies and adventures. They would be worshipped through the ages. And they could fight alongside him in the ongoing celestial wars against evil...

Published on 27th April 2021 to coincide with Hanuman Jayanthi.

End Notes

[i] licenced through Shutter stock.

[ii] as a young adult, the author was drawn into many a superficial debate about the Hindu Trinity as some are favoured above others in different parts of the Indian Sub-continent. The internet is awash with such analysis. It is very much like arguing about which side of an equilateral triangle is longer...

[iii] the epic verse composed in 1667 by English poet John Milton.

[iv] sacred Hindu scriptures composed from 1800 B.C. to 800 B.C. setting out principles of religion and philosophy.

[v] sacred Hindu scriptures composed from 200 C.E. to 1000 C.E. with significant accounts of the gods.

[vi] sacred Hindu scriptures composed from 900 B.C. to 300 B.C. setting out principles of religion and philosophy.

[vii] in Nataraja form, Lord Shiva dances on the Demon Apsarama; in other depictions, Lord Shiva dances on Lord Yama as Kalantaka (Ender of Death).

[viii] the Amar Chitra Katha comics depict the stories of Hindu gods and demons with illustrations and summarized content that are suitable for young children.

[ix] sacred Hindu scriptures composed in 900 C.E. setting out principles of philosophy.

[x] much of Hindu scripture was only written down after being transferred via word of mouth This is termed Shruti (heard) and Smrit (remembered).

[xi] set out in the Ashrama Upanishad.

[xii] the addition of "n" in Sanskrit converts the adjective to a noun.

[xiii] see Part D of this book.

[xiv] mukhya means prime or main.

[xv] the worship of Lord Shiva.

[xvi] Vedanta (or "end of the Vedas") is another name for the Upanishads. Vedanta philosophy explores themes relating to knowledge and liberation.

[xvii] Agni, Bhagavata, Brahma, Brahmanda, Brahmavaivarta, Garuda, Kurma, Linga, Matsya, Markandeya, Naradeeya, Padma, Shiva, Skanda, Vamana, Varaha, Vayu, Vishnu.

[xviii] the Song of God with philosophy relating to among other things the concepts of action and faith.

[xix] the Shiva Agamas contain a significant amount of information about the practice of rituals and building of temples. However, there are also philosophical themes within these scriptures. The Agamas are referred to in the instances where there is content relevant to the focus of this book, especially in the jnana (knowledge) sections of the Agamas.

[xx] Mahadeva is one of Lord Shiva's pseudonyms that means "Great God".

End Notes

[xxi] the concept that all things are one Supreme.

[xxii] Vasgupta is the author of the Shiva Sutras, there are multiple theories as to how he obtained this divine wisdom.

[xxiii] the author has used multiple sources for these stories as mentioned above which will assist in overcoming any subjectivity.

[xxiv] by way of comparison, Homer's Great Epic of The Iliad was composed in 800 B.C.

[xxv] these dates are based on forensic techniques deployed by recognized historians and linguists.

[xxvi] in the author's own life, he would have concentrated on Part A in childhood, progressed to Part B in young adulthood, and then in adulthood moved onto Parts C and D. However, there will be many readers that find all aspects of *The Lord Shiva Narrative* of interest.

[xxvii] one of the Puranas which form the basis for the stories in Part A.

[xxviii] developed by sixty sages and discussed in Part C of this book.

[xxix] see chapter C3 of this book.

[xxx] see chapter C4 of this book.

[xxxi] UNESCO World Heritage Site in Southern India.

[xxxii] unique pyramid style temple architecture deployed in South Indian temple design.

[xxxiii] there is a Mount Meru in Tanzania, and a Meru Peak in the Himalayas. Mount Meru in legend is sacred as the centre of the spiritual universe for many major religions.

[xxxiv] Rudra is the deity referred to in the Vedas with Lord Shiva being referred to in later Hindu Scriptures. Many of the characteristics of Rudra have been subsumed into Lord Shiva in the form of Lord Shiva the Destroyer.

[xxxv] this is based on the lunar calendar hence the date will vary each year in the Gregorian calendar.

[xxxvi] Phalgun is the twelfth month in the Hindu lunar calendar (coinciding with February or March each year).

[xxxvii] a priest, member of the Brahmin caste.

[xxxviii] as referenced in the Mahabharata, the Ramayana, and the Atharvashiras Upanishad

[xxxix] rudraksha beads are small circular brown beads with distinctive markings from the Rudraksha tree.

[xl] Lord Shiva is sometimes pictured in Hindu artwork and sculpture wearing the hide of a leopard, a tiger, or a snow leopard (which is native to the Himalayas).

[xli] often referred to as the Trisula. Note that there is mountain range of three peaks in the Himalayas called Mount Trishul and believed by many to be the dormant trident of Lord Shiva.

[xlii] the most destructive weapon described in Hindu scripture that can wipe out creation itself.

[xliii] 1984 adventure film set in India.

xliv giver of life, power f nature, source of creative energy – Shakti
xlv the God of Love or Lord of Pleasure. Conveyor of the Kama Sutra.
xlvi this is an interesting parallel with Greek Mythology were the gods also drink nectar of immortality.
xlvii adharma is unethical or immoral behaviour - the antonym for dharma.
xlviii yakshas often appear in Hindu texts as mischievous spirits of the forest.
xlix the Supreme existence
l King of the Himalayas
li referred to in Hindu scripture as halahala or kalakuta this is the black poison created when the oceans were being formed.
lii there is a volcanic mountain range in Africa called Mandara.
liii three demons
liv legendary King of ancient times – see glossary.
lv the subterranean realm of the universe, the netherworld, the underworld.
lvi city in the state of Uttar Pradesh in India.
lvii in many parts of the Indian Sub-Continent, the descent of the River Ganges (Ganga Dussehra or Gangavataran) is celebrated with a 10-day festival that coincides with Maha Sankranti on 14th January.
lviii there is an account in The Mahabharata telling of a time when Goddess Parvati placed her hands playfully over Lord Shiva's eyes and the third eye was created to stop the universe from being plunged into darkness.
lix the arrow of Kama, a similar concept to Cupid's arrows from Greek Mythology.
lx a caste in the Indian Sub-continent to which priests belong.
lxi Garuda is the vahana (animal chariot) of Lord Vishnu.
lxii the female Goddess
lxiii see Endnote xx.
lxiv Shakti is the feminine power of creation in Hindu scripture and believed to be Goddess Parvati.
lxv The Prakriti and Purusha denote the feminine and masculine divine energies that are referred to in Hindu scripture as giving birth to the universe.
lxvi Ibid.
lxvii sagun refers to the manifestation of god into a form (e.g., the Sun).
lxviii the three worlds in Hindu scripture are (i) the heavens, (ii) the earth, (iii) the underworld (Patala). Note that the Vedas refer to fourteen different Worlds (six above us and seven below us) with Patala as the lowest of the worlds.
lxix the Saptarishis are the seven great sages from Hindu scripture.
lxx the suffix "ji" in Sanskrit conveys a term of respect and affection.
lxxi the ninth lunar month in the Hindu calendar.
lxxii one of the Saptarishis.

End Notes

[lxxiii] Mount Kroncha or Krauncha is in the Indian State of Karnataka and possess a gap that is believed to be the spot where Lord Kartikeya pierced the mountain with his celestial weapon.

[lxxiv] a powerful club type weapon with the force of multiple thunderbolts wielded by Indra, King of the Gods.

[lxxv] see Endnote lvi.

[lxxvi] a darshan is a statue of a god to which religious ceremonies and offerings can be made.

[lxxvii] third among the twenty-seven lunar constellations in Hindu astrology.

[lxxviii] see glossary the Kauravas are the antagonists in The Mahabharata War.

[lxxix] see glossary – Shakuni is the evil uncle of the Kauravas.

[lxxx] as detailed in the Puranas, this mode of worship involves wearing rudraksha beads, ash on the forehead and praying to a Shivalinga.

[lxxxi] there is no existing mountain with this name save for a small peak in Indonesia.

[lxxxii] See glossary, Asvatthama is a critical character in The Mahabharata who possesses traits of Lord Shiva.

[lxxxiii] the Kirats are indigenous aboriginals of the Himalayas.

[lxxxiv] see Endnote xxvi.

[lxxxv] Valmiki is the original scribe of The Ramayana (circa 300-600 B.C.).

[lxxxvi] the island of Lanka is described in Valmiki's Ramayana to be a paradise of palm and plantain trees where many different nations had come together; however, were at present under the rule of the Demon Ravana and his kin.

[lxxxvii] Valmiki's Ramayana also mentions that King Devarata, ancestor of King Janaka was given the bow.

[lxxxviii] Hanuman is a powerful character from The Ramayana. He is the son of Vayu, the Wind God.

[lxxxix] this miraculous dance is said to have taken place at the Temple of Chidambaram in South India. The Temple is one of the most popularly visited places for devotees of Lord Shiva and each year Bharatanatyam dances are organized in praise of Lord Shiva. This dance originating in India is an artistic expression of devotion to Lord Shiva's cosmic dance that saved the universe from dark magic.

[xc] the concept of maya/illusion is referred to throughout this book. Readers who would like to explore the concept further are directed to Kant's Critique of Pure Reason, and Schopenhauer's Fourfold Root of the Principle of Sufficient Reason.

[xci] the one great personal God

[xcii] perpetual Shiva

[xciii] CERN is the European Organization for Nuclear Research. The dance of creation and destruction can be applied to the universe and also at the sub-atomic level.

[xciv] Pushkar features in the texts of different religions as a holy site. Regrettably, like many locations that are sacred to different faiths, this has led to the destruction of holy places of worship in the past .

[xcv] the Island of Gangasagar exists to this day where the River Ganges flows into the Bay of Bengal.

[xcvi] Mount Drongiri or Dunagiri is in the Himalayas. This is the fabled mountain with healing flowers that was lifted by Hanuman (see note lxiii above) in The Ramayana Epic.

[xcvii] the chakra (meaning wheel) is a spinning weapon from Hindu scripture that is thrown at assailants.

[xcviii] also referred to as Bhasmasura.

[xcix] Mount Kedarnath is in the Himalayas and the site of a Temple covered in Part C to the book.

[c] see Endnote ii.

[ci] this may relate to the twelve zodiac signs.

[cii] this may relate to the sixteen Lunar Phases.

[ciii] the unmanifest principle existed before creation. This book sets out the principles of atman (the self) , cittam (mind and heart), and sariram (body) – however, within the Upanishads there is mention of seven
principles: *Atman* (the self), *Buddhi* (the intellect), *Manas* (the mind), *Kama* (desire), *Prana* (life force), *Linga-sarira* (astral body), and *Sthula-sarira* (physical body)

[civ] powerful Goddess form of Shakti.

[cv] the Divine energy of Shakti giving rise to matter is consistent with Albert Einstein's special theory of relativity on equivalence between mass and energy and the ability for one to transform into the other.

[cvi] in 1927, Belgian priest and scientist George Lemaitre proposed that the Universe began as a large, pregnant, and primeval atom, exploding and sending out the smaller atoms that are in existence today. This is consistent with the Big Bang Theory and the Hindu account of Creation.

[cvii] scientists have recently put forward theories for "dark matter" which is distinct from "matter" and "anti-matter" and may provide an analogy for the Hindu Trinity.

[cviii] George Lemaitre (see note above) was the first scientist to put forward this theory in the modern-day era.

[cix] most notably Edwin Hubble who measure the acceleration of galaxies away from Earth and suggested the universe was expanding.

[cx] first put forward by Russ an scientist A Friedmann.

[cxi] there are 28 Shiva (or Saiva) Agamas.

[cxii] a great sage who is believed to have first recounted the story of The Mahabharata.

[cxiii] it is not specified in The Mahabharata where this Mountain is.

End Notes

[cxiv] Yama, Lord of Dharma; Vayu, God of Wind; Indra, King of Gods; and the Asvins, Twin Gods of Dawn.

[cxv] the five Pandavas were not present that night but their complete army was destroyed.

[cxvi] Drona was killed after becoming remorseful on hearing that his son Asvatthama was dead. However, he had been tricked as Lord Krishna had engineered the death of an elephant named Asvatthama.

[cxvii] the Hindu Epics unfold according to destiny and the Hindu Trinity play their part is assisting those events come to pass.

[cxviii] translation by Desiraju Hanumanta Rao & K. M. K. Murthy.

[cxix] there is no existing mountain by this name.

[cxx] Lanka is most likely Sri Lanka given the geography of The Ramayana. There is a wonderful extract from this Hindu Epic which talks about the armies of Lanka including the best warriors and most beautiful women from many different nations assembled by Ravana in his Kingdom.

[cxxi] Parasurama means Rama with an axe and is a separate incarnation of Lord Vishnu to the Rama from The Ramayana.

[cxxii] He also forged the great chariot of Lord Shiva (see chapter A13).

[cxxiii] the Book of the Dead is believed to have been written in 1500 B.C.

[cxxiv] also referred to as Surya in later Hindu scriptures.

[cxxv] the Maruts are storm deities or Rudras. They are violent and aggressive, described as armed with golden weapons and riding golden chariots.

[cxxvi] a hill in the Hindu Kush region.

[cxxvii] many of the older Upanishads refer to one hundred and eight Upanishads but over the centuries circa two hundred have been identified.

[cxxviii] Alan Jacobs (see Bibliography)

[cxxix] three marks of ash in parallel lines on the forehead

[cxxx] Parabrahman state of the Self.

[cxxxi] the Jyotirlinga temples mentioned in the Puranas not covered in Part C, are Mallikarjuna in Andhra Pradesh, Mahakaleswar in Madhya Pradesh, Omkareshwar in Madhya Pradesh, Bhimashankar in Maharashtra, Trimbakeshwar in Maharashtra, Baidyanath in Jharkhand, Nageshvara in Gujarat, and Grishnewshwar in Maharashtra.

[cxxxii] the Tevaram hymns composed by the Nayanar sages (see Introduction to Part D) are believed to have been discovered at Chidambaram.

[cxxxiii] by Sir George Birdwood of the V&A Museum.

[cxxxiv] United Nations Educational Scientific and Cultural Organization.

[cxxxv] Harappa and Mohenjo-Daro are the two main archaeological sites of the Indus Valley Civilization.

[cxxxvi] 10,000 B.C. to 8000 B.C.

[cxxxvii] on the Island of Java

[cxxxviii] not related to the Tripura Demons from chapter A8.

[cxxxix] Kashi Viswanath temple has been called the Golden Temple, but this is not to be confused with the temple in Amritsar.

[cxl] this state is sometimes referred to Paramshiva with respect to the Shiva Sutras.

[cxli] the initial translation is by Gerald Kuiken, and the author has provided alterative translations for readers to consider.

[cxlii] in one tale in the Shiva Purana not featured in the main body of this book, Lord Shiva created the terrible Bhairava Creature God, born from his third eye and the creature proceeds to sever one of Lord Brahma's five heads.

[cxliii] dualist philosophy of Shaivism not explored in this book.

[cxliv] fine as in minute, granular, or composed of many small parts as opposed to fine as in high quality.

[cxlv] equivalent to Sutra 1.2.

[cxlvi] yoga seated position

[cxlvii] readers may have seen the oft used visual of the human body with the channels moving throughout.

[cxlviii] it is possible to reach Mount Kailas from either Tibet or Nepal.

[cxlix] in particular: Buddhism and Hinduism.

[cl] located in Tibet about two miles from Mount Kailas.

[cli] the author has also set out different potential meanings of the Sanskrit into English.

[clii] Ibid.

[cliii] Creative Commons public domain, 2.0, or 4.0 attribution licenses with no changes made to the original photo: Creative Commons — Attribution 2.0 Generic — CC BY 2.0

[cliv] Ibid.
[clv] Ibid.
[clvi] Ibid.
[clvii] Ibid.
[clviii] Ibid.
[clix] Ibid.
[clx] Ibid.
[clxi] Ibid.
[clxii] Ibid.
[clxiii] Ibid.
[clxiv] Ibid.
[clxv] Ibid.
[clxvi] Ibid.
[clxvii] Ibid.
[clxviii] Ibid.
[clxix] Ibid.
[clxx] Ibid.

End Notes

[clxxi] Ibid.
[clxxii] Ibid.
[clxxiii] Ibid.
[clxxiv] Ibid.
[clxxv] Ibid.
[clxxvi] Ibid.
[clxxvii] Ibid.
[clxxviii] Ibid.
[clxxix] Ibid.
[clxxx] Ibid.

Printed in Great Britain
by Amazon